Handling Children's Aggression Constructively

Handling Children's Aggression Constructively

Toward Taming Human Destructiveness

Henri Parens, MD

JASON ARONSON
A division of
ROWMAN & LITTLEFIELD PUBLISHERS, INC.
Lanham • Boulder • New York • Toronto • Plymouth, UK

Published by Jason Aronson
A division of Rowman & Littlefield Publishers, Inc.
A wholly owned subsidiary of The Rowman & Littlefield Publishing Group, Inc.
4501 Forbes Boulevard, Suite 200, Lanham, Maryland 20706
www.rowmanandlittlefield.com

Estover Road
Plymouth PL6 7PY
United Kingdom

British Library Cataloguing in Publication Information Available

Library of Congress Cataloging-in-Publication Data

Parens, Henri, 1928-
Handling children's aggression constructively : toward taming human destructiveness / Henri Parens.
p. cm.
Includes bibliographical references and index.
ISBN 978-0-7657-0687-4 (cloth : alk. paper) — ISBN 978-0-7657-0689-8 (electronic)
1. Aggressiveness in children. 2. Aggressiveness in children—Prevention. I. Title.
BF723.A35P374 2011
155.4'18232—dc22

2010043841

Printed in the United States of America

™ The paper used in this publication meets the minimum requirements of American National Standard for Information Sciences—Permanence of Paper for Printed Library Materials, ANSI/NISO Z39.48-1992.

To the 40,000,000 children
In our world
Who are abused or neglected.

In the hope
That they will not become
The next generations
Of abusers.

***

"Consider UNICEF's report that 'An estimated 40 million children globally under the age of 15, [probably an underestimation,] suffer from violence, abuse, and neglect,' according to a UN-sponsored study led by Paulo S. Pinheiro, in what is deemed to be the first detailed look at how children experience violence all over the world, and what must be done to prevent and end the scourge."

—Henri Parens, "Malignant Prejudice
—Guidelines toward Its Prevention" (2007)

Contents

Preface

This is not a book about how to handle children who suffer from significant aggressive behavior disorders, such as teenagers who already have developed delinquent or even criminal behaviors. Fine books have been written in an effort to help parents and others deal constructively with such very challenging youth. This is a book about how to *prevent* the development of disturbed aggressive behaviors in kids. It can be very useful for the handling of problems in the making, to avoid them becoming difficult problems to deal with.

Indirectly this is also a book about how to prevent the development of problems that are secondary to the development of aggressive behavior problems. Many people are not aware of the fact that problems with aggression can lead to difficulty in learning in school, and in forming good relationships at home, in school, and in the neighborhood. Ultimately, these problems can turn out to be of greater consequence than the aggressive behavior problems themselves.

My experience working with parents and children has convinced me that handling children's aggression is one of the most difficult challenges for parents. In turn, children often encounter significant problems in dealing with their own aggression, and as adults many will continue to have difficulty. The constructive management of aggression greatly contributes to both the proper future emotional development of the child and the comfort of the parents.

In this book I talk to parents, mental health professionals who work with parents and children, pediatricians, teachers, daycare workers, and other child caregivers. In the course of my research on aggression in young children, I found a number of parent-child interactions in which aggression is especially activated. In these, aggression is generated or mobilized especially in the form of anger, hostility, hate, and rage—what I speak of as *hostile destruc-*

tiveness. My research and clinical work has convinced me that parental input and handling significantly influence the development of aggression, in both its *nondestructive* form—best represented by *assertiveness*—and in its *hostile destructive* form—best represented by *hostility*. The challenge for the parent is to promote what is constructive in aggression, that which is needed for adaptation, and to mitigate what is hostile, that which can undermine children's well-being, their relationships, and their life at home and in our society. I am convinced that informing parents about inherent features and dynamics of aggression and proposing strategies for their parenting interventions can help them in this enormous challenge.

I first present the reader with my model of aggression, which developed out of our research and my clinical work, which taught me to understand what aggression is and what causes it. This model provides us with the means for exploring, understanding, and developing strategies to deal constructively with a cluster of frequently occurring parent-child interactions in which the two basic forms of aggression—assertiveness and hostility—are at play. If this can help parents attain a clearer understanding of typical aggression interactions between them and their children, they will be able to apply this basic knowledge to the entire challenge of childrearing.

The issues I address are complex, and some may not be easily assimilated at first reading. There are, however, no unexpected rocks, whirlpools, or dragons. My aim is to help parents seize the rich opportunities inherent in these challenging interactions with their children. Keep in mind that the younger your child when you start to use these strategies the greater your chance of success. But, whatever the child's age, it is never too late to start.

Acknowledgments

I want to express anew, my gratitude to the parents and their children who not only participated in our original seven-year-long parent-infant research group with whom we worked since 1970 at the former Medical College of Pennsylvania (EPPI/MCP), now part of Drexel University, but also especially for their willingness to continue to participate with us in follow up studies through 37 years. Our old debt to the other early parent-child groups both in and outside of EPPI/MCP in whom we found results very similar to those we found in the original research group as well as to the parent-child groups we conducted over a nine-year period at the Germantown Friends School remains. What my colleagues and I learned by observing and working with all of them has been strongly supported and complemented by my many years of intensive psychotherapeutic clinical work.

I would like to express, again, personal gratitude to Peter G. Bennett, MD; Elaine Frank, M.S.W.; Estelle Harris, R.N.; Rogelio C. Hernit, MD; Betty Ives-Adams, M.Ed.; Leafy Pollock, Ph.D.; and Denise Rowe.

I will forever remain indebted to those in former the Department of Psychiatry at the Medical College of Pennsylvania who then supported my work for nearly two decades, from the late chairman of the department, Leo Madow, MD; to the late chief of child psychiatry at the Eastern Pennsylvania Psychiatric Institute, Robert C. Prall, MD; to the chairman of the department who followed Dr. Madow, Wagner Bridger, MD; the then director of training in child psychiatry, Joel B. Goldstein, MD; and the current chairman of the department of psychiatry, Susan V. McLeer, MD. I will forever feel special gratitude to the late Selma Kramer, MD, past chief of the division of child psychiatry at The Medical College of Pennsylvania, as a mentor, a collaborator, and a strong supporter of our work.

I want to now also thank Dr. Lotte Koehler of Munich, Germany, for her friendship and invaluable help in many matters professional and specifically here for her attention and the suggestions she made to strengthen chapters 7 and 8 of this book.

Lastly and foremost, I want to thank Rachel for always being there, encouraging my efforts and labors.

Part I

Can We Tame Human Destructiveness?

I dare raise the question of whether we can tame human destructiveness because I have learned that even while we are limited in our ability to tame unleashed human destructiveness, we can do much that may prevent its unleashing. I have found strong evidence for the fact that humans are not born bursting to be destructive, driven by an instinct to destroy as was once held. Instead, I have found and will talk about the fact that human destructiveness is generated by human experience, not by some absolute destructive instinct.

In part 1, I report on the 37-year-long project that has led to my conviction that we can do much toward taming human destructiveness.

Chapter 1

The EPPI/MCP Study of Aggression

The Research Project

In 1969, as director and principle investigator of the Early Child Development Program in the Department of Psychiatry at the Medical College of Pennsylvania (EPPI/MCP) in Philadelphia, I developed a prospective longitudinal research project to observe mothers with their newborn infants on a specified topic. In a call for volunteers from the neighboring community, some 48 mothers presented themselves. The number being much larger than our time and efforts could accommodate, given our research orientation and interests, we enlisted the seven mothers who at this time were pregnant. Three additional mothers joined the project during its first year.

In September 1970, the mothers and their infants, as well as their children who were not yet in school, started to meet twice a week for two-hour sessions, in a group, where we began our naturalistic, anthropological-style observational research. Mothers and children were free to act as they wished, no assignments were made, no tests were given or taken, and no formal challenges were presented. The mothers talked among themselves and, soon after our start, with the research staff while they tended to their infants and other children. Toys, milk and coffee, donuts, and the like were available, with comfortable enough couches and living room-type chairs, etc.

These mothers and their children who were not in school attended the group over a seven-year period. Of course, the children of age went to school; some of the mothers had two children while in the project, and one had three. The attitude and feeling in the group among the mothers, the children, and the research staff became increasingly friendly, mutually respectful, and fun.

While recording specified observations, I, the principal investigator, was teaching child development to trainees in child psychiatry who sat in on the research sessions, sitting outside of the circle of mothers and infants. As time passed, the mothers became interested in our observations and the comments I occasionally made to the professional trainees. Following several requests by the mothers that I tell them, too, what I was telling the child psychiatry students, I began to address the students and the mothers regarding the meaning of the children's behaviors, the developmental forces that elicited them, etc. The mothers began to ask how their infants' and children's behaviors could best be dealt with to make for their healthy emotional development.

Within months, the mothers' behaviors toward their children seemed to be positively influenced by our explanations and discussions. The mothers' questions seemed more and more open, and they showed genuine interest in and gave the impression that they appreciated our discussions. We came to realize that we were doing some unanticipated productive "parenting education."

In fact, my team and I became aware of this, when 18 months into the project, one of the group mothers told us that she was gathering some of her neighbors to share with them "some of the things she was learning at EPPI." We learned about this when she requested that we come to her house, "because some of the mothers were asking questions she couldn't be sure how to answer." She taught us that we had developed a productive method for parenting education.

Expressions like "I wish I had known this before I had my children" led us to consider developing formal materials for "Parenting Education" focused on the emotional development of children. The enthusiasm was high; the thought of being able to help parents optimize their children's development was exhilarating; and the rewards of seeing such optimizing of our project children's development were heart-warming. Driven by what we saw, in time, we developed three sets of materials.[1]

1. *Parenting for Emotional Growth: A Textbook;* then,
2. Parenting for Emotional Growth: A Curriculum for Students in Grades K thru 12;

And some time later, we added

3. Parenting for Emotional Growth: A Series of Workshops for Child Caregivers, Parents, Child Care Workers, Educators.

Over time, the benefits to the mothers, the children, and the research team were well beyond all expectations. These were documented in three follow-up studies: one at 19 years, one at 32 years, and the last at 37 years after our 1970 start.

THE FOLLOW-UP STUDIES

The 19-year follow-up study was published in 1993.[2] It showed that the 16 children of our small (in numbers only) project fared meaningfully better than the populations from which they had come (a city housing project and lower- and low-middle class surrounding communities in Philadelphia) in terms of general social behaviors (such as trouble with the law, use of alcohol and street drugs, and the continuation and success of their education). These children also showed significantly better aggression profiles. All in all, the children in our project fared much better than the population from which they came.

The positive effects were not restricted to the children, however. The mothers also benefited enormously from their participation in our study. They reported feeling that they understood their children much better than before and knew better now how to handle the challenges of their everyday childrearing; they became more effective parents, shifting dramatically in our measure from "growth-disturbing to growth-promoting"; and their self-esteem rose significantly and led to their completing unfinished education, such as earning GEDs and getting child services related jobs or going on to college.

The next follow-up occurred 32 years after the start of the project, in 2002.[3] This reunion was striking for its warmth and reciprocal pleasure in the mothers, the now-grown children, and the remaining research staff seeing each other. A videotape of that reunion was made. However, our efforts to gather follow-up data did not succeed due to short-handed staffing and our limited capacity to do so. The recorded video scanning the reunion of mothers and their children and the staff as well as of the individual interviews of the mothers and some of the children who were there, was entered into a documentary we developed in 2008.[4]

Thirty-seven years after the project start, our third follow-up gathering occurred and is now in the process of being further recorded and evaluated. One of our highly dedicated team members is in the process of interviewing each mother, each accessible grown child, and each remaining staff member to gather prescribed data as well as to record each person's experience of the project over time. This reviewer will also produce a book of these mothers' and children's personal narratives from the vantage point of the effect their parenting education experience had on them. The gathering and individual interviews done at this reunion have also contributed to our 2008 documentary. The testimonies of the mothers regarding the benefits to them and their children of the parenting education they experienced in our project are gratifying. They all strongly urge making parenting education a requirement in schools from the elementary school years on.

EFFECTS OF PARENTING FOR EMOTIONAL GROWTH ON AGGRESSION PROFILES

During the course of the seven-year project, while seeing the children and their mothers twice weekly in our group setting, we had the opportunity to watch again and again, in detail, the ways in which the mothers handled their children's aggressive behaviors. Handling these behaviors is challenging. To do so constructively optimizes the child's development. Aggressive behaviors are an unavoidable part of normal childhood development; they are part and parcel of the child's orientation to the world around him or her and his or her efforts to cope with life and the world.

We, the mothers and the research team, were in for an education. Observing the emergence of aggression in the children over time made it necessary for us, the researchers to abandon the then-existing theory of aggression that had become our way of understanding aggression. We had to start afresh to try to understand what brings aggression about and how to deal with the children's aggressive behaviors in such a way as to optimize each child's experience of them and help the child gain mastery over the aggression within him or her.

Yes, we were in for an education. We knew that children are not born with a ready-made program for how to deal with their aggression in socially acceptable ways. Discussion of how to handle the various aggressive behaviors we saw and help the children cope with them constructively may well have been the most common topic we addressed over the period of the project. We also knew that aggression develops. But how? From what? To what? I'll detail this in chapter 2. For now, I'll say that what we learned about aggression clarified significant problems we encounter when we mental health professionals who do psychotherapies treat people, most of whom have problems with aggression. Back to the project findings.

The changes in the mothers' handling of their children's aggressive behaviors began to be evident about 18 months into our seven-year project. Or to put it better, by 18 months into the project, the mothers' handling of their children's aggression was distinctly growth-promoting. And we saw evidence for the durability of the mothers' handling of their aggressive behaviors in our 19-year follow-up study. In this first follow-up study, we used a strategy to measure children's aggression profiles, the "Fitzgibbons Anger Inventory," which had been developed and tested by Richard Fitzgibbons,[5] who studied aggression in the same population as the families that participated in our project. The aggression profile developed by Fitzgibbons seemed to us, and still seems to me, to be a sound way of describing aggression in children. The profile consists of four parameters (see table 1.1). Note that while our study

Table 1.1. Fitzgibbons Anger Inventory

*Parameters**	*ECDP average to moderate*	*FAI average*	*Cut off mild*	(2-tailed T-test) Statistical significance
Anger	37.8	50.10	45	$p<0.05$
Trust/mistrust	6.1	6.07	6.0	NS
Passive aggression	8.8	10.11	9.0	NS
Violence potential	5.1	7.96	7.0	$p<0.05$

*n=12. Two permissions to interview not granted by one father, FAI not available; two lost to project; one not applicable.

sample is small (16 children), the two parameters critical to the children's outer-directed anger and hostility are significantly more favorable than the population from which they came. Also, the inventory is not an instrument that measures observed behaviors but rather, of teenagers' answers to an inventory of questions, which reveal hostile aggressive tendencies in them. Critical to note, the FAI measures only hostile aggression, not nondestructive aggression.

Just a comment on each of the four parameters (aspects or characteristics of aggression) in the FAI. First, the responses by the teenager respondent are catalogued in three intensity-levels of anger: mild, moderate, and high. The first parameter, anger, measures the collective inventory responses that outright give evidence of currently felt and experienced anger. The second, trust/mistrust, measures the degree to which the tested teens trust or mistrust those around them, especially adults. The third parameter, passive aggression, measures the tendency to express anger, hostility, or hate, in indirect, masked ways to protect the self against anxiety that direct expression of these feelings would arouse. For instance, being angry with his father, rather than expressing his anger directly, a teen (or younger or older person) might do something that would cause the father annoyance or even distress, but the father could not be certain that his son did what he did intentionally. The fourth parameter, violence potential, measures a tendency to violence in the teens' responses to the inventory inquiries.

Note that the two parameters that tell us most directly the state of the two most overt measures of the teen's hostile aggression profile—anger and violence potential—were significantly in the mild anger range in the teens from our study group. As I already said, it is critical to note that the FAI measures only hostile aggression, not nondestructive aggression. But then, we have found in the research and in our clinical work that nondestructive aggression tends to be more favorable; the less intense the level of the hostile aggression trend in the aggression profile of the individual.

Again, the number of children in the sample is small (for statistical research purposes), but the tendency demonstrated at 19 years after the start of our study is noteworthy. Equally noteworthy is the fact that at 32 years and 37 years, these aggression profile parameters as documented in these now adults' (the grown children's) histories and current state proved to have held up over the years. None got in trouble with the law, all graduated from high school, most went to college, and most had jobs and families.

SIGNIFICANCE OF THE INDIVIDUAL'S AGGRESSION PROFILE

I want to underline what I noted at the outset, which is that the child's aggression profile has large potentially life-long implications for his or her behavior, his or her adaptation and development (including education and work performance), for his or her relationships and interactions with others, and for his or her role in society.

For instance, later in this introduction, I will point out that many researchers have found that high accumulations of what I call *hostile destructiveness*[6]—which is the form of aggression best known to all of us that includes hostility, hate, and rage—tend to lead to rebellion against family and authority figures such as teachers; delinquency and crime; and a greater tendency toward intolerance of others and malignant prejudice and its social enactments.[7]

NOTES

1. H. Parens, E. Scattergood, A. Duff, & W. Singletary, *Parenting for Emotional Growth (PEG): The Textbook* and *PEG: A Curriculum for Students in Grades K Thru 12,* also H. Parens & C. Rose-Itkoff, *PEG: The Workshops Series.* All these Parenting for Emotional Growth (PEG) materials are available on one CD entitled *Parenting for Emotional Growth* (1997), which can be purchased at www.Amazon.com and at the Thomas Jefferson University Book Store in Philadelphia.

2. H. Parens. Toward preventing experience-derived emotional disorders: Education for parenting. Pp. 121–148 in *Prevention in Mental Health,* ed. H. Parens & S. Kramer (Northvale, NJ: Jason Aronson, Inc., 1993).

3. H. Parens, C. Rose-Itkoff, M. Pearlman, K. Reid, P. Turrini, T. Fallon, W. Singletary, & E. Scattergood. Into our 4th decade of prevention via parenting education: Where we have been—where we are going. *International Journal of Applied Psychoanalytic Studies* 3:17–38 (2005).

4. The documentary in question is entitled *The Urgent Need for Universal Parenting Education: A Documentary.* It was written and produced by H. Parens with media producer P. Gilligan of the Thomas Jefferson University, Medical School Media Division, Philadelphia, PA, 2008.

5. R. P. Fitzgibbons, MD, P.C. 1984, Anger Inventory. The Fitzgibbons Inventory (FAI) compared favorably with the Buss Durkee Hostility Inventory (BDHI), and is the product of a series of studies of comparative youth populations. Personal communication to members of our 19 years follow-up research team David Bockoven and Laura Goldberg, February 7, 1989.

6. In developing my model of aggression, I have made efforts to be as clear as I have found to be useful. In this, I distinguish between trends in aggression that are critically different and have distinguishable functions in human (and other animal) adaptation. I discuss the model of aggression more extensively in chapter 5. For now, I will say that there is a trend I label "hostile aggression," which for reasons I explain in chapter 5 also includes the sub-trend "hostile destructiveness," the specific form of hostile aggression that includes hostility, hate, and rage.

7. I have explained how this comes about in our book, *The Future of Prejudice,* ed. H. Parens, A. Mahfouz, S. Twemlow, & D. Scharff (Lanham, MD: Jason Aronson, 2007). In this volume, I detail what I have found in my studies on prejudice and detail the point I am making in the text above.

Chapter 2

The Critical Interaction between Human Attachment and Aggression

Our research and that of others has found that it is no longer tenable to assume, as has been and continues to be maintained by a large number of mental health professionals, that infants come into the world with inborn high levels of aggression (in the form of hostile destructiveness) and a tendency or need to destroy. These mental health professionals make this assumption following the theory that aggression is driven by a self-destructive instinctual force[1] that must be turned outwardly to protect the self against it. Aggression-research theorists of varying disciplines including psychoanalysis have not accepted this assumption.[2] My own research has led me to assert[3] that this assumption cannot be supported by observable or inferable evidence from healthy-enough normal infants and children and that, as I detail in chapter 2, observable evidence from normal infants rather points to a very different set of assumptions, and that the inborn-destructiveness theory is flawed and does not reflect or represent the inborn givens of the human child. Our findings amply documented that, rather than an inborn destructive tendency being the formative factor in a child's aggression profile, it is the child's experiences that over time are the largest factor that shapes each child's aggression profile.

There is a large consensus among neuroscientist and mental health researchers as well as clinicians that following the givens with which the infant is born, the development of the central nervous system of the child (the brain and its bodily extensions) and the child's personality formation are most shaped to adapt to the world into which the infant is born from just after birth and on.[4] The findings are that the largest development of adaptation-required brain functions occurs from after birth on and that the rate of this development essentially decreases as time passes. Thus, once born, the child's largest development in brain functions occurs in her or his first six years of life. This applies to the child's mental health and personality formation as well. The better the beginnings during the earliest years, the more likely, and the better will be the mental health of the child and his or her personality formation. These are large generalizations and like all generalizations there are exceptions; nonetheless, they are held in neurobiology, psychiatry, and psychology.

A large number of studies have documented that the earliest years of life are the most formative of the child's mental health and personality; this, however, does not diminish the fact that enormous developments in personality, in adaptive capability, and especially in intelligence and learning (education), and more, are still in front of the child as she or he develops into adulthood. The time and the opportunities for development in humans are awesome and never-ending. Even in the late years of life, creative individuals continue to grow. But it is critical to know that just because much development occurs after six years of age—people seem to more easily recognize development beyond six years of age than before—in those earliest six years, establishing basic bodily reactive systems including brain patterning and neural networks that shape the child's personality is of critical importance. And this is so for the child's aggression profile and for the play of aggression in his or her personality.

ATTACHMENT AND AGGRESSION

Considering the basic factors that go into the formation of the child's aggression profile, namely the child's genetic make-up and experiences (more on this in chapter 5), and that the child's baseline personality formation occurs in the first six years, home is where the child's aggression profile first gets formed. The largest determining factor of what "home" is includes the quality of the relationships between the child and his primary caregivers, most commonly, mother and father. This applies equally to very early life adoptive parents. Long-term substitute caregivers who emotionally value the child also play a part, a greater or lesser part in the young child's home-world-based aggression profile development. This can include long-term, favorable foster care.

The emotional investment the parents make in the child, with few exceptions, is most determining of the character of the child's developing an attachment to them. A large number of studies[5] have described, documented, and detailed the critical role of attachment in the child's emotional life and personality formation. Much has been found and written about the crucial role of the quality of the child's attachment to his or her primary caregivers. The child's emotional experience will significantly depend on whether that attachment is emotionally positive; that is, loving and respecting, as well as secure and predictable, or whether it is laden with stress, hostility, hate, uncertainty, and unpredictability.

While this next thought may stir some controversy, I have found from clinical work that the quality of the attachment to the mother (biologic or adoptive) is of utmost importance, commonly having a greater influence on the child's well-being than that of other family members, including the father.[6] In my more than four decades of clinical work I have not treated a person for whom the foremost and primary caregiver was the father. But this may change as in the past several decades more and more fathers have gotten involved in the direct care of their infants and young children in which case the attachment of the young to their father may well achieve equivalent emotional importance as to the mother. The trend of father direct-care-involvement has, I believe to the benefit of all, come so far as to include that fact that more and more, some fathers elect to be the stay-at-home dads, and care for children from infancy on, 24 hours a day, seven days a week. Findings in such cases, according to Kyle Pruett,[7] who has studied a group of such stay-at-home dads and their kids over time, are quite positive, and children are as equally well developed psychologically (and physically) as primarily mother-reared kids. In these cases, it seems that the fathers achieve the kind of utmost importance in the child's life that we find commonly in primarily mother-reared children.

We have furthermore found that not only are the early years of life so critical for personality formation, but that quite specifically regarding the development of aggression, while fathers are generally believed to be the prime disciplinarian in the home, it is in fact the primary caregiver, be it mother or much less commonly the father, who is the first to be in the position of needing to set limits with the child and is then the first to encounter and be the receiver of the child's hostility and even hate (I talk about the large challenge of setting limits in growth-promoting ways in chapter 5). In addition to the challenge of setting limits, by virtue of the mother's generally being the primary caregiver of the child and the child therewith, especially in the early years, most strongly attaching to her, the mother is the foremost caregiver to cause the child to experience anxiety due to the unavoidable normal reaction of separation anxiety, which invariably, brings with it anger toward her. We'll talk further about these matters in the body of the book. For now, the point I want to make is that the child's attachment to the primary caregiver is a critical determiner of the child's aggression profile.

As I found in my research on aggression and in my studies of the development of prejudice, there is "a stable positive correlation between the quality of the child's attachment to his/her mother and the child's aggression profile."[8] I noted in my work on prejudice, that the degree to which being hurt by one's own parents has a direct bearing on how hostile one becomes. I have even taken the position that when children are traumatized by their own parents, they suffer more and therefore become more hostile than when they are traumatized by any other individuals. And, as a Holocaust survivor, to the surprise of many colleagues, I have asserted that being traumatized by one's own mother or father is worse than being subjected even to genocide. Of course, degree of traumatizing plays its part. Nonetheless, to be traumatized by one's enemy is expectable; even kids know that. But to be traumatized by those who are supposed to love you, nourish you, and do the best they can to protect you against cold and evil, is the worst. Who then can you turn to? Kids know that too. I know some readers will be skeptical of what I am saying here. But I am not the only Holocaust survivor child psychiatrist who holds this view.

Pertinent to this, in their study of child survivors of the Holocaust, Judy Kestenberg and Ira Brenner[9] found that children who had had good family relationships prior to the Holocaust, in other words, whose attachments were loving and secure, endured the tribulations of the Holocaust better than those whose relationships had been troubled, laden with neglect and maltreatment. Furthermore, they found that those who had formed good attachments before the Holocaust were able to form good attachments after, re-create families, and achieve good lives. Those who had troubled attachments before the Holocaust were in general unable to rebuild their lives and families after.

Another related remarkable finding has also been seen repeatedly in a number of studies of resilience.[10] Those who had come from troubled families but who had learned to optimize their relationships with others outside of their families were highly advantaged in surviving well-enough. This came from the many human beings who despite a troubled childhood and even adolescence have been able to draw on their internal resource and, forming gratifying enough attachments outside of their families were able to make their life rewarding-enough. In these cases, good later attachments helped them tame the hostility and hate that had been generated in them by hurtful childhood family relationships. The better the child's attachments—and here, the better the early life relationships, the more likely he or she will make good attachments later—the less hostile their aggression profiles, and the better their ability to produce for themselves rewarding lives. Resilience studies, yet from another vantage point, point to the positive link between the quality of attachment and the quality of the aggression profile.

This has also been found again and again in many studies spanning the last century on the relation between early life attachment and delinquency and criminality. First among the pioneers to make this assertion was August Aichhorn,[11] who in 1925 published his thesis that the delinquent teenagers with whom he worked in his residential clinic had all come from families where they had been significantly neglected and maltreated.

John Bowlby[12] in 1946 published a volume on 44 teenage thieves who during their childhood also had been significantly neglected, even abandoned, or maltreated. Kurt Eissler (1949) in his volume on delinquency points to this correlation as well.

Emmy Werner[13] reports that in a population of kids reared in families with multiple problems, "homes . . . troubled with discord, desertion, or divorce or marred by parental alcoholism or mental illness" developed serious learning or behavior problems by age 10 or "had a record of delinquencies or mental health problems . . . by age 18" (p 2). She speaks of families where there are multiple risk factors that lead to the children developing a wide range of problems but one of the foremost factors responsible for the kids' behavior problems and delinquencies is their highly troubled attachments, their family relationships. Werner and Smith also hold that a number of other studies have shown that "psychological maturity in adulthood correlated strongly with childhood experiences that were conducive to the development of trust, autonomy, and initiative" (8). It is well established in the mental health field that Erik Erikson's[14] studies of "trust" (of others and of oneself), "autonomy" (the ability to feel a sense of being able to do things oneself), and "initiative" (the ability to make things happen, to undertake challenges), that the development of these highly valuable adaptive capabilities is directly linked to the quality and character of the child's attachment to his or her caregivers.

Sociologist Joan McCord spent decades, much of her work published in the 1980s, studying delinquency and criminology and reported extensively on the important protective factor of the positive quality of the mother-child relationship against the development of disorders of conduct, delinquency, and crime in the offspring.

James Gilligan (1997)[15] who studied inmates on death row reported in his book on violence that the inmates who had been subjected within their families, from early childhood on, to serious neglect and maltreatment led to their feeling humiliated, enraged, and depreciated. And as commonly happens, that rage is rarely directed at the parents who caused the growing child enormous emotional and physical pain; it is most often displaced onto others in acts of abuse and criminality, including malignant prejudice.[16]

Specifically addressing the intimate link between the quality of the child's attachment and that of his or her aggression profile, in one of his studies (Egeland et al, 2001), Byron Egeland remarked that "A very large number of studies have found an association between parental neglect or harsh treatment and later conduct problems [and names a cluster of additional references to the ones I have already here made reference to], as have we" (in Sroufe[17] et al. 2005, 256). And in this same volume, the lead author, Alan Sroufe writes that " . . . aggressiveness is highly predictable from early in life, but from patterns of organization in the infant-caregiver system, not from isomorphic behaviors of infants" (26). By this Sroufe is saying that aggressiveness from very early childhood on tends to arise not from inborn dispositions in the child but from the ways in which the caregiver tends to and interacts with the child. This fact is clearly visible in the work of researchers such as Brazelton[18] (1981) and Beebe[19] (2005) for instance who have recorded infants' reactions of irritability, distress, and turning away from the mother in adverse interactions. These experiences over time organize in angry or other negative reactions toward the primary caregiver on the part of the young child.

Fonagy and his colleagues[20] share this view as well (2002, 97), while they emphasize the dominance of the child's interpretation of his experiences over the actual reality of these experiences. Fonagy and his colleagues have identified a process they call "mentalization," wherein the child progressively acquires the psychological (cognitive) ability to recognize that what he perceives as real may not coincide realistically with his actual, factual experiences. The ability to "mentalize" is not achieved until about four to five years of age. As has long been held in psychodynamic thought, these authors are quite correct to hold that how the child experiences life events is, psychologically and emotionally, more real than actual reality. One should not construe, however, that how the young child interprets what he experiences is not determined by strong elements of what really happens to him. A young child who consistently feels that he is neglected or maltreated is most likely being neglected or maltreated.

Put simply, the positive correlation between the quality of attachment and the aggression profile of children has been found by researchers in sociology, psychology, attachment theory, psychiatry, and psychoanalysis. This consensus suggests that the quality of the child's attachments to his or her primary caregivers, foremost mother and father, correlates strongly with the quality, benign versus hostility-weighted, of the child's aggression profile.

NOTES

1.Sigmund Freud opened our eyes to the large role of unconscious forces and dynamics that govern our everyday life and developed the mental health discipline of psychoanalysis. Among the highly valued explanatory theories of human behavior that he proposed, several theories have created much controversy and have been duly challenged by mental health itself and allied disciplines. Among his most controversial theories, his theory of aggression stands out, side by side with his now much revised theory about some aspects of the development of women. Freud's aggression theory, based on the death instinct, holds the assumption that humans come into the world with an inborn tendency to "return to [our] inorganic state" (Freud, 1920, in *Beyond the Pleasure Principle*). "To return to [one's] inorganic state," means that there is a tendency in our body to break down in order to revert back to the individual atoms that combined to form our incredibly complex body. This biologic tendency to "self-destroy," as he saw it, is countered by the life instincts, which are in the service of maintaining life. In our mental life (our individual psychology), this tendency to self-destroy is countered to protect the living self by "turning the destructive tendency outward." This is what gives rise in each of us, the theory holds, of our individual aggression. Understandably then, those who have accepted this theory or derivative theories, thus believe that the infant comes into the world with an inborn tendency to destroy, some even believe, to destroy very harshly. I should also note that within five years of his proposing the death instinct basis of aggression, as Freud said "within his own circle" of colleagues, they rejected this explanation of aggression. On the other hand, some colleagues have held onto it and it has been continued even into the present among descendent-students of those teachers.

2. H. Parens, *The Development of Aggression in Early Childhood,* (Lanham, MD: Jason Aronson, 2008).

3. H. Parens, *The Development of Aggression in Early Childhood.*

4. Of course, the greatest degree and rate of development occurs before the infant is born. Imagine the miraculous degree and rate of development from the fertilized egg to the nine-month-old fetus. This is why, particularly given that the fetus' health and development is totally dependent on the environment the mother provides her fetus, her self-care is so vitally important.

5. Psychoanalytic studies starting with Sigmund Freud from the early 1920s, to Rene Spitz (*The First Year of Life* [New York: International Universities Press, 1965]), followed by Margaret Mahler (with F. Pine & A. Bergman, *The Psychological Birth of the Human Infant* [New York: Basic Books, 1975]), Daniel Stern (*The Interpersonal World of the Infant* [New York: Basic Books, 1985]) and quite a number worldwide who followed into the present. See also attachment theory studies started by John Bowlby (*Attachment* [New York: Basic Books, 1969]), with and followed by Mary Ainsworth (with M. C. Blehar, E. Waters, & S. Wall, *Patterns of Attachment: A Psychological Study of the Strange Situation* [Hillsdale, NJ: Lawrence Erlbaum, 1978]) to a long array of attachment theorists worldwide well into the present.

6. Referring especially to the work of D. P. Farrington from Cambridge, England, and his colleagues, E. Werner (Werner & Smith, 1992) notes that "The more successful men were likely to have [had] mothers [who] had high opinions of their sons" (p 9). I have heard from Holocaust survivors, as from Henry Krystal, Anna Ornstein, and know from my own Holocaust experiences, that we ascribed our sense of self value in the face of the humiliations and abuses to which we were subjected to: "I knew that my mother loved me." Sigmund Freud is known to have said as much. I have also

found the converse, which is that even in the face of being loved and thought well of by one's father, the pain of not having felt well-enough loved by one's mother may have life-long painful reverberations.

7. K. D. Pruett, *The Nurturing Father* (New York: Warner Books, 1987). Pruett also made this point in a lecture he delivered in Philadelphia on May 4, 2002, entitled, "Fathers and young children: Longitudinal lessons in autonomy, gatekeeping, overnights, etc." at the Annual Margaret S. Mahler Symposium.

8. In a lecture I gave in Munich, Germany, at an international conference held in November 2008, I spoke to this point. The lecture, entitled "Attachment, aggression, and the prevention of malignant prejudice" appears in German in *Bindung, Angst und Aggression,* KH Brisch & T Hellbruegge, Hrsg. (Stuttgart, Germany, 2010), pp. 12–46. It will appear in English in *The Psychoanalytic Inquiry* (in press).

9. J. Kestenberg & I. Brenner, *The Last Witness: The Child Survivor of the Holocaust* (New York: American Psychiatric Press, 1996).

10. Authors of such studies include among others, N. Garmezy, E. James Anthony, E. Werner, B. Cyrulnik—a prolific student of resilience—and S. Hauser.

11. A. Aichhorn, *Wayward Youth* (New York: Viking Press, 1944) (First German edition, 1925).

12. J. Bowlby, *Forty-Four Juvenile Thieves* (London: Balliere, Tindall & Cox, 1946).

13. E. E. Werner & R. S. Smith, *Overcoming the Odds: High Risk Children from Birth to Adulthood* (Ithica NY: Cornell University Press, 1992).

14. E. H. Erikson. Identity and the life cycle. *Psychological Issues* 1(1959):1–170.

15. J. Gilligan, *Violence: Reflections on a National Epidemic* (New York: Vintage Books, 1997).

16. *The Future of Prejudice,* ed. H. Parens, A. Mahfouz, S. Twemlow, & D. Scharff (Lanham, MD: Jason Aronson, 2007)

17. A. Sroufe, B. Egeland, E.A. Carlson, & W.A. Collins, *The Development of the Person* (New York: Guilford, 2005).

18. B. Brazelton, Affective reactivity in mother-child interaction. Presented at the 12th Annual M. S. Mahler Symposium on Child Development, May, Philadelphia, PA (1981).

19. B. Beebe. Infant research and implications for adult treatment. Video presentation to the Psychoanalytic Center of Philadelphia Scientific Meeting, March 4, 2005, Philadelphia.

20. P. Fonagy & M. Target. Playing with reality: I. The theory of mind and the normal development of psychic reality. *Int. J. Psycho-Anal.* 77(1996):217–233. As well as P. Fonagy, G. Gergely, E. Jurist, & M. Target, *Affect Regulation, Mentalization, and the Development of the Self* (New York: Other Press, 2002).

Chapter 3

The Impact on the Child of Internally Accumulated High Levels of Hostile Destructiveness

I said earlier that high levels of hostile destructiveness tend to lead to (1) rebellion against family and authority figures; (2) delinquency and crime; and (3) a greater tendency toward intolerance of others, and malignant prejudice and its social enactments. I want to briefly explain what I mean. Because I have not defined the concept of "hostile destructiveness" yet—I do so in chapter 4—and I am using it here, just a word is needed to understand its role in the three assertions I just made.

In chapter 4, I make the point that there are three major trends in aggression: nondestructive aggression, nonaffective destructiveness, and hostile aggression. I have now added[1] that the trend hostile aggression contains a subtrend hostile destructiveness, so labeled because not all aggression is both hostile and destructive. When a child pushes an obstacle to his goal out of the way or when he asserts himself in a conflict with a peer, he is standing his ground, protecting his right to strive for his goals, and is not being either hostile or destructive. This is nondestructive aggression. Such aggression is most evident in properly played sports. In a quieter way it is also what drives him or her to achieve in school in his or her studies. When a lion chases a gazelle, catches it, and destroys it, the lion is not being hostile; it's hungry and has to have food in order to survive. The lion is being destructive, but not hostile. This is nonaffective destructiveness, which means it is aggression that is not driven by emotional feelings but by hunger. Hostile destructiveness is that familiar range of aggressive feelings that increases in intensity from anger, to hostility, rage, and hate. These feeling are what I am pointing to here to explain the three assertions I made in the prior paragraph.

What our research has taught me is that the most critical factor that generates hostile destructiveness in humans is the experience of intense emotional pain.

In chapter 4, I explain the basis for this assumption. In the course of growing up, children experience much emotional pain. It is, to a greater or lesser degree, part of life. It is important to note that while physical pain may make us angry, it is emotional pain that makes us feel hostile and destructive. But how then does this have a bearing on the three assertions I have made? Here's how.

REBELLION AGAINST FAMILY AND AUTHORITY FIGURES

Much research and clinical work documents that the foremost accumulation of large loads of hostility and hate in kids and teenagers tends to be generated at home, especially by children who are being maltreated and emotionally and physically abused by their own parents during their growing years. Physical abuse is easily identified even if parents at times rationalize and give reasons that are not sound or sensible for their abuse, the most common being "I'm just doing this for your own good." Not as easily seen is that intentional physical pain at the hand of one's own parents, which is experienced also, perhaps even more, as emotional pain. Emotional abuse, which is often carried out without physical abuse, however, is often not recognized; it is often just a parent's blurting something out that the parent may feel at the moment, but does not really hold to. For instance: "Why don't you ever do anything right?" Or, "You'll never amount to anything!" Or, "Do you know how much I bled giving birth to you?" Remarks such as these—and there are a million—expressed in a moment of exasperation injure the child's or teenager's sense of self, his "healthy narcissism," we say, and wound emotionally deeply when said by one's mother or father. Narcissistic injury, that is, being insulted and humiliated, causes acute emotional pain and sharply generates hostile destructiveness in the child or teenager. And narcissistic injuries caused by one's own parents are the most painful.

Histories of such parental abuses of children often lead to the rejection of well-meaning authority figures such as teachers who unavoidably are perceived by the child as "just like my mom and dad." In many cases, all grown-ups are perceived as "like my mom and dad." And the resemblance does not need to be large. It has become the child's common experience that "grown-ups maltreat and hurt kids."

DELINQUENCY AND CRIME

A number of the studies I noted before document the fact that in the histories of delinquents and criminals one discovers that at home, growing up, they were neglected, physically and emotionally abused—sexual abuse has its own very troublesome consequences—and suffered no end of insults and humiliations. I believe that the hostile destructiveness that is generated[2] by neglect and maltreatment is a large motivating factor in these antisocial behaviors.

MALIGNANT PREJUDICE AND ITS ENACTMENTS

My studies on prejudice (as documented in *The Future of Prejudice*) have led me to propose that we all have prejudices. Prejudice, defined as a preconceived negative judgment about others, is experienced by all of us. Having become who we are, we tend to prefer to be with people like ourselves and to feel less at ease with people perceived to be more or less different than we are. How does it come about that we prefer to be with our own? And why does being with people "different than we are" tend to cause us some discomfort, even anxiety?

Two normal psychological developmental factors cause this. One is "stranger anxiety," and the other is "identification" (to be like someone we value). Let me explain.

Stranger Anxiety

A normal baby comes into the world equipped with instincts to attach to her or his caregivers. We can assume that this is fostered by Mother Nature's biological order that "you must preserve the species." It's simple: if we don't reproduce, our species, homo sapiens, will die out. Equipped to attach, the human infant must attach to humans in order to eventually reproduce. But then more demands are made on the young.

Given that humans like many other mammals are pack animals, they must attach to their own pack. Without that, stable packs—stable families and communities—would not form. How much this became inherited over time, I cannot answer. The fact remains that it is advantageous to society formation that stable families be formed. There are other types of packs than families, such as peer groups, or even communities organized around principles like communism or national socialism that attempt to minimize the role of the family; but it is questionable whether these are as stable as communities formed by clusters of families. Now, to form families, infants' attachments have to be particular. The infant, to be a member of a specific family, will have to attach to members of his particular family. So, the infant is prescribed, probably genetically, to attach to those caregivers that most care for the infant. The mother seems to be universally the chosen candidate for this role. Pretty good thinking too, because no one is likely to be as eager and devoted to fostering the baby's attaching to her than the baby's own mother.

So, the baby's brain is prewired to lead the baby to attach to his or her primary caregiver. But there's this other nice lady next door who smiles at him nicely and the baby smiles back at her. In fact, as Rene Spitz found,[3] at the very beginning, at about five or six weeks of age, the baby will smile at any face, even a drawing of a face. That won't do! If the baby is to become a member of his family, the baby can't just go on smiling at any face. It has got to be a family face. And lo and behold, as the weeks pass, the baby begins to sort out who is part of the family and who is not. And by five months or so, the baby knows that this is the one who cares for me most and seems to want to have me around the most. She's my mother! And then, there's that one with the loud voice who always seems to want to play; well, that's my dad. And that smaller one, who seems to sometimes be nice to me and at other times not, that's my brother or my sister. Of course, babies don't have these thoughts, but they seem to act as if they do.

And the next thing that happens is that the five-month-old begins to really rely on her or his mother. She just disappeared. Actually, she just went into the kitchen, but the baby can't see her right now so he believes she has disappeared. The reason the baby believes she has disappeared is that, as Jean Piaget taught us,[4] the six-month-old baby's memory development is such that she or he can't yet remember the image of her or his mother when she is not in the baby's field of vision, but can recognize her when the baby sees her, when she reappears. Now that she just disappeared, the six-month-old feels abandoned and that is in fact outright scary. The baby then experiences separation anxiety.

Side by side with this development and the emergence of separation anxiety, whereas the six-week-old baby used to just smile at almost everybody who looked at him or her, now the baby seems to get frightened when someone the baby doesn't know looks at him or her and smiles. This person may well be the child's grandfather whom the baby has not seen for three months. And much to the mother's shock the baby starts to cry when grandpa tries to pick her or him up. Now along with separation anxiety, the baby also experiences stranger anxiety. Why?

I have proposed[5] that stranger anxiety is in the service of funneling the prewired infant's attachment behavior toward a small number of people that are constantly in the infant's immediate world, his family world. If grandpa was a frequent visitor during these months, the baby would not have experienced stranger anxiety; he might not have been as warmly responsive as dad or one of the siblings, but it would not have triggered the "I don't want to be with you" reaction. So, while stranger anxiety has potential negative implications for the infant's future reactions to others, it secures the infant's becoming a member of his specific family. In other words, while protecting that infant's attachment to persons who constitute his immediate family, stranger anxiety also becomes the generator of the reaction "I don't want to be with you!" This is a key factor then in the child's fear of strangers; and this fear of strangers, while decreasing over time, may continue throughout life, especially so if his environment encourages him or her to "beware of strangers" as occurs in the education—religious, nationalistic, and ethnic—of the child.

Identification

Infants come into the world equipped with a pool of genes half of which come from her or his mother and the other half from her or his father. One may expect from this that the baby will eventually have features of one parent or the other or both. A parent with red hair is likely to have one or more children with red hair. A number of such features, physical and behavioral, will make it easy to assume that this baby may well be this mom's and dad's child.

Identification goes well beyond that. Infants imitate their caregivers. Even in infancy, when mother holds the baby and looks at it and opens her mouth, if she waits patiently enough the weeks-old baby will open his or her mouth. It's not fair to try this with a smile, because a smile will yield a smiling reaction; that's not imitation; that's reacting to mom's smile. In 1921, Freud described a three-year-old boy who put on his father's hat, picked up his briefcase, and said "good bye" to the family as he walked to the door. He was imitating his father going to work in the morning. In our documentary DVD,[6] we show a movie clip of a mother sitting on a couch holding her baby on her shoulder in order to burp or calm her; standing next to her, a less than two-year-old girl is leaning against the couch's back rest, turned toward the baby, smiling at the baby softly. As the comforting mother is gently patting the baby on the back, the little girl, too, begins to pat the baby on the back, much like the mother is doing. She is imitating the mother.

But she is doing more than imitating. She is grasping a complex scene: a mother comforting her baby. She wants to do it too. She is not just imitating, she is taking in the function of doing this; she is identifying with the comforting mother. Some day she will be a comforting mother. Step by step, taking in parents' reactions, ways of doing things, and views on all sorts of matters, and doing what her or his mother and father do, the child becomes like her or his parents. And the child will note over time that some other parents do not do what his or her parents do. The child will progressively find that many other people do things differently.

Thus, stranger anxiety and identification combine to make the child a member of his or her specific family. It will produce a child who, as I have said (borrowing on what Freud said), will bear the stamp "Made in the H

Family," where H = His or Her family. And with that comes "the distinction between my family and others." And similarities between the child's family and other families will bring a feeling of connection with these families. By contrast families that are seen by the child as different will bring a feeling of difference between them and us.

Given these developments, it is unavoidable that we all have prejudices. But these are not prejudices that of themselves bring with them the feeling that "others" are not as good as we are. They are different and I feel more at home with my own. And I have no wish to bring harm to those different people. This is why I have called these prejudices, "benign prejudices."[7] Given that family formation is central to community formation and that as pack animals this serves us well, it would not be desirable to try to eliminate this benign form of prejudice. But how do we get from benign prejudice to that other type of prejudice, the type where one person or group wants to cause harm or even destroy another person or group because they are Blacks, or Jews, or Muslims, or Armenians, or Tutsis, or . . . ?

This is where our concerns about aggression in our children come into view. Study of prejudice has led me to propose that two factors lead to the conversion of *benign prejudice* into *malignant prejudice*. These two factors are (1) the displacement and projection of a person's own accumulated hostility and hate onto innocent others, and (2) militant education.

THE DISPLACEMENT AND PROJECTION OF HOSTILITY AND HATE ONTO INNOCENT OTHERS

Hating those we love creates difficulty for all of us.[8] Even being very angry with someone we love causes us distress and anxiety. Unfortunately, it is impossible to rear kids well without causing them some distress and therewith they experience anger toward us. Having to leave a young child to go to work, setting limits (see chapter 9), demanding that the child eat, or go to bed, or do his or her homework, etc., all tend to make children angry with their parents.

Consider then how difficult it is for the young child whose ability to cope with his or her feelings is immature, his or her ability for instance to control very angry feelings is only in the process of becoming. In my research and clinical work I have often seen how the child's experience of hostile feelings toward those he loves creates in the child a large dilemma. After all, if a child is angry with his or her mother, the child will be very worried about the reaction he or she might get if he or she were to let loose on mom. It is also more or less worrisome if the child's very angry with dad. So the child will either swallow his or her anger and it will accumulate inside his or her psyche. But what often happens as well is that the child will find ways to get rid of the accumulating hostility and hate by using some strategies we call "defense mechanisms."

In our observational research, we saw a striking cluster of defenses young children erect when very angry with their mothers. For instance, by the time the children were 12 months of age, we already had seen much evidence of displacement (when angry with mother, Jane picked up a block and threw it not at her mother, but at the woman sitting next to her mother). By the time the children were 18 months of age, we saw clear evidence of projection (a strategy where the child projects her own hostility onto someone else: "I'm not angry at her, she's angry with me"), rationalization ("I'm angry with her because she was mean when she told me to brush my teeth"), and denial ("I didn't do that; it was an accident"). Then, especially organizing of prejudice, starting from five to six years on, we saw behaviors from which we could infer "reality-distorting defenses," including reductionism ("All Blacks want to do is rob you"), caricaturing ("All Jews have hooks for noses"), depreciation ("All Spics are lazy and don't deserve to be paid like Whites"), and vilification (All Jews are greedy and will cheat you"), defenses that play a key role in the organization of what I now call "malignant prejudice."

THE ROLE OF TRAUMA IN THE PREDISPOSITION TO MALIGNANT PREJUDICE

Given that even in normal-average homes, rearing children leads to their getting angry with their parents, consider the amount of hostility and hate children accumulate when they are neglected or abused at home, be it physically or emotionally.[9] We'll talk more about this in the course of the chapters. For now, I want to say that trauma is a major contributor to the generation of hostility and hate in humans. Of course, much hurtfulness happens to people; but people are vigorous so that not all intense pain is traumatizing. It is when one feels overwhelmed by a highly painful event of shocking meaning to the self that we experience it as traumatizing. Various factors determine the degree of psychic pain we experience: the nature of the traumatic event, the age and state of self at the time of occurrence, who is the perpetrator, whether it is episodic or chronic, what meaning do we give to the event, and highly critical, whether the event is perceived as intentional or accidental. All these combine to determine the degree to which we are traumatized. For example, abuse at the hands of one's own mother or father causes much more psychic pain than when the abuse is caused us by a stranger or an enemy. Neglect or abuse by those we count on for love, nurture, and protection multiplies the degree of psychic pain experienced and as we have said before, drives many an individual to delinquent and criminal behaviors.

I don't want to oversimplify how traumatized humans may behave. As has been amply documented, many cope with severe trauma with remarkable resilience, which brings out in them striking creativity and productivity. Nor do most who are traumatized become delinquents and criminals; many become depressed and self-punishing, and some become emotionally very disturbed. In addition, although many will erect the cluster of defenses I have noted, these defenses may not result in the development of malignant prejudice. They may not target a given group of "others" toward whom their hate is discharged, nor share their outrage with others; they act alone, sometimes with particular, sometimes with any random target victims. Regrettably, as James Gilligan[10] found, many who are heavily traumatized develop a pressing need to discharge their hate in the form of revenge, which creates in them, as Vamik Volkan[11] has proposed, the need to have enemies.

The children in our project, being quite well cared for, experienced only modest levels of accumulating hostility toward their caregivers. Consider though how the extremely painful experience of being traumatized (neglected and or abused) in your own family heightens the child's feelings of hate and rage toward his or her own caregivers. The more children are traumatized, the greater the load of accumulating hostility, the more the defenses set up to cope with heightened levels of hate and rage persist, the more they become patterned. For the past two decades, neurobiological findings have taught us that patterns of reactivity and behavior become structured in brain neural pathways[12] early in life and thus become part of personality formation.

But in addition then, there is the role education plays in our developing the tendency to feel malignant prejudice toward others.

THE ROLE OF EDUCATION IN OUR DEVELOPING MALIGNANT PREJUDICE

Yes, high loads of accumulated hostile destructiveness may transform our benign prejudice into malignant prejudice. But malignant prejudice can be greatly facilitated, even in individuals whose accumulating hostile destructiveness is moderate and is not sufficient to lead to the formation of malignant prejudice. As I have said,[13] that aspect of education that is programmed to socialize the child tends to mandate, to coerce the individual to be like the other members of the group. This can be a major contributor to transforming benign prejudice into malignant prejudice. A dear German friend, painfully distressed while and after reading my Holocaust memoirs,[14] wrote to me that when he was young, even though he did not even know one Jew, he had learned to hate Jews because he was taught that "the Jews had killed Christ."[15]

This teaching—to hate one's enemy—is driven in large part by the demand that the child identify with his or her parents and the society the parents represent. It is an "identification demanded by the universe into which the child is born." This teaching of dogma often carries with it malignant distortions brought about by those reality-distorting defenses that rationalize and justify malignant prejudice. Here education is put into service to compel malignant prejudice. This form of teaching dishonors education.

NOTES

1. In my original aggression model design (first published in 1979), I proposed that the trend I call *hostile aggression* be labeled *hostile destructiveness.* In a further effort to sharpen the clarity of the model, I am here limiting the subtrend hostile destructiveness specifically to aggression feelings we all commonly link with destructiveness, namely, hostility, hate, rage, and more complex feelings that include hostility and destructiveness, like revenge. I need to do this because as I define them (see chapter 5), more benign negative feelings like anger, and lesser intense negative feelings such as irritability do not bring with them the wish to harm, to inflict pain, and certainly not to destroy. Aggression is a complex phenomenon; it has defied scientists' efforts to fully understand it and explain it. See chapter 5 for the more fully laid out model.

2. I explain how this comes about in chapter 4.

3. R. Spitz. The smiling response: A contribution to the ontogenesis of social relations. *Genetic Psychology Monographs* 34(1946):57–125. R. Spitz. *The First Year of Life (*New York: International Universities Press, 1965).

4. J. Piaget, *La Construction du Réel Chez* l'Enfant (Neuchâtel: Delachaux et Niestle 1937). J. Piaget, *The Child's Conception of the World* (Paterson, N.J.: Littlefield, Adams, 1967).

5. I proposed this in chapters 2 and 16 in *The Future of Prejudice,* edited by H. Parens, A. Mahfouz, S. Twemlow, & D. Scharff (Lanham, MD: Jason Aronson, 2007).

6. The documentary in question is entitled *The Urgent Need for Universal Parenting Education: A Documentary.* It was written and produced by H. Parens with media producer P. Gilligan of the Thomas Jefferson University, Medical School Media Division, Philadelphia, PA., 2008.

7. H. Parens, *The Development of Aggression in Early Childhood* (Lanham, MD: Jason Aronson, 2008).

8. H. Parens, *The Development of Aggression in Early Childhood.*

9. H. Parens, *The Development of Aggression in Early Childhood.*

10. J. Gilligan, *Violence: Reflections on a National Epidemic* (New York: Vintage Books, 1997).

11. V. D. Volkan, *The Need to Have Enemies and Allies: From Clinical Practice to International Relationships* (Northvale, NJ: Jason Aronson, 1988).

12. E.R. Kandel, Psychotherapy and the single synapse, *The New England Journal of Medicine,* 301:19(1979):1028–1037. E.R. Kandel, J.H. Schwartz, & T.M. Jessell, *Principles of Neural Science,* 3rd ed. (New York: Elsevier, 1991).

13. H. Parens. *Renewal of Life: Healing from the Holocaust* (Rockville, MD: Schreiber Publishing, 2004).

14. This has, of course, been recanted since 1965 by the Second Vatican Council as was again reported in the *National Catholic Register, Nostra AEtate, 4.* From *US Catholic News,* the Internet, July 27, 2004, reprinted with permission from the *National Catholic Register,* March 7–13, 2004. Religious malignant fundamentalism relies heavily on misinterpretations of religious scriptures; for example, Legionary Father Thomas Williams, dean of the school of theology at Regina Apostolorum Pontifical University in Rome, refuted that the Second Vatican Council—that met yearly from 1962 to 1965—in November 1965 had reversed prior Passion teachings that the Jews killed Christ. Father Williams emphasized that the Second Vatican Council only "reaffirmed perennial Catholic teaching that all of humanity's sins and the sins of Christians in particular are responsible for the death of Christ. . . . The Second Vatican Council document states: 'Even though the Jewish authorities and those who followed their lead pressed for the death of Christ, neither all Jews indiscriminately at that time nor Jews today can be charged with the crimes committed during his passion' (Nostra AEtate, 4)." (*National Catholic Register,* 2004).

Part II

Handling Aggression in Our Children

Chapter 4

What Is Aggression?

There would be no point helping parents understand what aggression[1] is, where it comes from, or what causes its various manifestations, were it not for the fact that dealing with our children's hostility—toward us, others, and themselves—is among the most troublesome tasks of parenting. Difficult and unpleasant as it is for us to admit, it is unavoidable that our children—little ones, grade-school ones, and adolescents—will often be angry with us, even at times hate us, wish they could be rid of us, and then dread the thought ever after. Often we seem pressured to deny that they feel hate for us.

A 30-month-old, upset because mother reasonably prohibits his taking a toy from another child, half shouts at her, "I hate you!" Troubled, the mother—even though she knows that children are less able than adults to control the expression of their feelings—tells him, "I know you don't mean that." Unfortunately, this is not a helpful comeback. Why it is not helpful is what we will talk about.

A 15-year-old bright boy has been searching to buy a guitar. He's never had one before and is eager to try his hand at it. His father raises the question whether the one he is considering buying, one offered for sale by a friend, is as good a deal as he might get in a particular instrument store in town. Seemingly convinced by his friend that "it's a good deal," he blurts out as he's walking away from his father in sharp annoyance—possibly because he is uncertain about his friend's sales pitch—"You always mess things up!" Stunned and upset, his father backs off.

It is equally unavoidable that we, as parents, will at times be furious with our children and, because we love them, will feel terrible about it afterward. Few experiences produce more guilt and shame in good parents than those moments when we feel, "I'd like to be rid of that little . . ."

Ambivalence—being angry with, feeling hostile toward, and even hating a person we love—is experienced in all primary relationships. These are the relationships most meaningful to us: between parents and children, siblings, boyfriend and girlfriend, husband and wife. Being angry with or hating those we love is a large source of difficulty in our close relationships.

WHEN SHOULD PARENTS START TO DEAL WITH CHILDREN'S AGGRESSION?

People have asked me: when should I start to set limits with my child? I answer: when limits are needed. When a teething seven-month-old bites mother's breast while suckling, it's reasonable for the mother to react with "Ouch! Don't do that!" in a gentle, even loving scolding manner. This informs the baby that he or she hurt you and you want him or her to not do that. You are then gently setting limits that are quite appropriate for the baby at this time. Obviously, no harshness is needed to let the baby learn that biting mother—or anyone for that matter—is not acceptable behavior.

The child's aggression profile develops from the first days of life on. Parents often tell me that their young children won't understand; that it makes no sense to them to tell them to not do something. Children understand our communications much earlier than many parents believe. It is not that the seven-month-old already understands mother words. It is that when we communicate with them, children don't just listen to our words, they also hear the sounds we make in reaction to something they do; they hear our tone, see our gestures and our facial expressions that tell them much even if we say nothing. A mother's or father's look can cast sunshine into the child's life or terrify and even mortify the child. We all know the look of joy that opens the skies, and we know "the evil eye" and "the look that kills." This understanding begins very early, from the early weeks of life.

Most important and basic in child rearing is this. It surely makes sense that when growth-promoting[2] child-rearing efforts are made to optimize a child's aggression profile, the earlier in the child's life such growth-promoting strategies are put into play, the healthier will the development be of the foundation of the child's aggression profile. The healthier its foundation, the more likely that the child's further developing aggression profile will be healthy.

Equally expectable, the poorer the young child's foundation and developing aggression profile, the more difficult will it be to restructure the aggression profile into a healthy one as the years pass. It is a mistake to assume that "I can wait until my child is old enough," say five or six, or older, to institute child-rearing strategies regarding any aspect of the child's behaviors, especially so with respect to aggression and communication. Some parents make the gross mistake of thinking that they'll "talk to their kids when they are teenagers, because what good is it talking to young kids when you can't really talk to them. After all kids don't really understand and they don't remember." Many parents know that this is totally wrong; children understand and remember only too well.

Ii is well known now, that with an adolescent whose aggression profile has developed into one leading to antisocial behavior, delinquency, or criminality, it will be difficult to convert that teenager's aggression profile into a healthy one. It can be done. But it will require much work to undo established unhealthy trends in aggression leading to antisocial behaviors and to replace and modify these into healthy, constructive trends in aggression. Difficult as this may be to achieve, it will benefit the growing teenager; but it will require time, repeated efforts many of which will fail, and much patience. It is well to recognize, as we have learned over decades of research and clinical study that a poorly developed aggression profile always comes from the maltreatment if not outright abuse or dire neglect that a teenager experienced from early life as a child.

For this reason, the parent who picks up this book and books like it and tries to apply to a conduct-troubled teenager some of the principles I and others talk about is very likely to find it a struggle to undo the teenager's troubled beginnings and to change his or her established patterns of coping with life. Working with conduct-disturbed teenagers has taught us how difficult it is to change their view of others, adults, and peers, and of the society in which they live. The earlier in a child's life one institutes positive, growth-promoting child-rearing strategies, the greater the chance that the child will grow into a caring and socially responsible adult. And in this, the child's aggression profile is a key player.

UNDERSTANDING OUR CHILDREN'S BEHAVIORS HELPS US DEVISE GROWTH-PROMOTING STRATEGIES FOR CHILD REARING

When we understand a problem, we are more likely to know how to solve it. When we understand what our child's behavior is about, whether the child is a toddler or a teenager, we can parent more reasonably, more constructively, and with more confidence; our child-rearing strategies are more likely to work. There is much that parents understand, and much they do well, without recourse to the help of others or books. Much of what we do that is based on what we feel, understand, and believe is best will, most likely, be best for our children. However, we may at times not be as right about what to do as we believe. And, even the best of parents at times find themselves in a quandary about what to do, particularly with respect to their children's aggressive behavior.

As noted in the preface to this book, I have had the privilege and opportunity to study and work, clinically, and educationally,[3] for nearly four decades with parents and their children. From these decades of work and from our personal experiences as parents, my colleagues and I have gained much respect for parents, for their devotion, ingenuity, and all-consuming efforts to rear their children well. We have learned well what a taxing and challenging job parenting is.

Also, we have learned that there is much information available to mental health professionals and educators that can be of great use to all of us in our work of parenting. To a degree never available to us before, mental and physical health clinicians and researchers have enlarged our understanding of children's behaviors and what they require for mental and physical healthy development. The study of infants and children over the past century has given us information that, if made available to parents everywhere, can inform and help them enormously in their parenting work. Here, I focus on children's aggression, which my colleagues are convinced is a central factor in their mental health. Once parents understand several key interactions that are emotionally significant to their children and challenging to their parenting, then, with ingenuity, they can apply what they have learned about dealing with aggression to other areas of child rearing.

WHAT A CHILD'S AGGRESSION CAN DO

Many years before the project I started in 1970, Alex Weech and I, understanding aggression then as we did, knew that when children and adolescents (and many adults) are very angry with those around them it creates no end of problems for them. Frightened by their own intense hostile feelings—especially since during childhood these are mostly felt toward their own mother and father—without being aware of it, unconsciously, kids do all they can to not feel these intense hostile feelings. They do so by using psychic (mental) "defense mechanisms" such as denying they are angry and inhibiting any expression of the anger or hate they feel. To be intensely angry with one's mother or father is felt by children and teenagers as very threatening. We see this already very early in life. "Thirteen-month-old Mary was angry with her mother, beside herself, she raised her arm visibly intending to hit her, but stopped her motion, her arm upright, stopped in mid-air. She inhibited her motion to strike the mommy to whom she was already so well attached."[4]

We are all very clever at protecting ourselves against knowing what we feel when what we feel causes us much anxiety, fear, distress, and pain. Freud and many psychoanalysts who followed him have talked about this for a century now. But while these psychic defense mechanisms can protect us, they can also have maladaptive effects both at the time the defense is erected and, if these defense mechanisms become part of our customary coping strategies, even later. What mental health professionals have long known is that, when children and adolescents (and adults) do all they can to hold back their intense hostile and hate feelings they also tend to inhibit what we used to think of as neutralized aggression. This neutralized aggression we then believed was a large source of energy used for coping with the many challenges of life. In addition, we believed that such neutralized psychic energy is used in the service of learning in school and on the street. Alex Weech and I found[5] in the psychotherapeutic treatment of a cluster of elementary and high school kids that when we could help them understand what made them so angry and helped them tolerate these feelings and deal constructively with them, they began to do better in school, as well as at home and with their peers. We believed, thinking along these lines, that lessening their feelings of hostility and hate, they were then able to free up their hostility-bound energies and apply these to learning. While this explanation of aggression was helpful, was it in fact right? Our aggression project showed that this explanation did not adequately represent what seems to happen. In other words, the aggressive behaviors we saw from birth on in our project kids did not support this theory of aggression. In fact, observing infants from birth on, we saw behavior in the first six months of the infants' lives that could not be explained by this then most prominent theory of aggression in use in dynamic psychiatry and psychoanalysis. It is this finding that led us to the study of aggression I talked about in the introduction.

WHAT IS AGGRESSION?

Let's establish what we mean by aggression. Aggression is not uniformly defined. One reason for this is that behaviors of very different kinds can plausibly be catalogued under the heading of aggression. For example, *hostility* is a form of aggression we know to be very troublesome, both to ourselves and others. *Assertiveness,* on the other hand, is a form of aggression that can serve us well in achieving our goals; in fact, we cannot cope well without it. Most problematic is that we do not all mean the same thing when we call some behavior aggressive. Some scientists, for instance, do not consider assertiveness to be aggression. Like many others, I do.

Several available models could serve us nicely in talking about handling our children's aggression. Here is one that we developed out of our research and clinical findings. Over four decades of study, it has served us very well.

A WORKING MODEL FOR UNDERSTANDING AGGRESSION

Our own naturalistic studies of normal young children with their mothers—which I described in the introduction—have taught us that aggression shows itself in different forms that are evident in even very young children. All of these forms (or kinds) of aggressive behaviors have one common feature: *each is an attempt to control, act upon, and master oneself and one's environment, including the people within it.* These aggressive behaviors seem to be propelled by inborn adaptive mechanisms and by an inner force that motivates them.

I want to repeat for emphasis that this model of aggression was not developed while sitting in an armchair. Quite the contrary; I was pushed to study aggression when our research team found that young children's behaviors put into question some of our past theorizing[6] about aggression. As I said in the introduction, to resolve this problem, we set out to look afresh at children's aggressive behaviors. Early in the course of our observations of young children and their parents, we were faced with a confusing, bewildering array of behaviors, all of which we were compelled by their character to classify as aggressive. However, we found that certain types of aggressive behaviors seem vastly different from others. For example: an infant's seemingly obligatory exploratory behaviors, or a child's pressured efforts to make something happen, differ significantly from a hungry infant's rageful crying or a young child's teasing and taunting another. With much effort, we were able to distinguish several categories of aggressive behavior.[7]

Categories of Aggressive Behaviors

We were able to catalogue most of the aggressive behaviors we saw even within the first 15 months of life into four categories of aggressive behaviors:

1. Unpleasure-related destructiveness (rage reaction of infancy);
2. Nondestructive aggression (pressured sensori-motor activity);
3. Nonaffective destructiveness (feeding activity); and
4. Pleasure-related destructiveness (teasing and taunting activity).

Unpleasure-Related Destructiveness

The easiest behaviors to catalogue were those we all know so well, those that look like rage. Rage, of varying intensities, is a built-in reaction visible from birth on. It's like a reflex to intense pain. It may start in the infant with whining and then crying, but if the pain that triggers it is not tended to or does not spontaneously stop, the crying will become more intense and at some point will explode into a rage reaction. Since this is the clearest evidence of the type of aggression we all know, I used the rage reaction of infancy as the best example of what I called "unpleasure-related destructiveness," the technical term for pain-triggered behavior, which in an older individual might lead to destructive behavior. In quality, a rage reaction is clearly hostile, but we do not believe that it requires an idea associated with pain; it seems to be an automatic reaction, like a reflex to pain that is experienced as unbearable by the baby. I'll say more about that shortly.

Nondestructive Aggression

The behavior that pushed us to research aggression is what I eventually labeled nondestructive aggression. In 1973, I described in detail[8] how a 15-week-old baby demonstrated the type of pressured exploratory activity—"sensori-motor activity," according to Jean Piaget, which he proposed is the first stage of the development of intelligence[9]—which I believe, by virtue of the pressure on the child's face and in her entire body as well as the persistence of her 25 minute-long handling of the object she seemed to be exploring, suggests the remarkable aggressive activity intended by the term, *nondestructive aggression.* I am speaking of the energy in her persistence. Here is the example.

Jane was 15 weeks old when after a 25-minute nap she woke up and we recorded on film "excerpts from one continuous 30-minute period of activity," which I felt posed a serious challenge to the theory of aggression then held by most psychoanalysts.[10]

> Within minutes of waking, Jane begins to look at (people)—her mother and observers. She smiles broadly, already . . . focusing on her mother. She then looks around at articles on the floor, looking at several quite intently as she briefly fixes on these in passing. She now turns her attention to a set of plastic rings on a string, which she very busily explores. She begins by pulling them apart, mouthing them. The sensorimotor effort is visible on her face; one soon also hears vocal (sounds) of that effort. She moves the rings back and forth while she looks at them, a serious look on her face, and a good deal of pressure can be inferred from the way she seems to be "working." She waves her arms as she attempts to reach the rings, which she inadvertently just pushed out of reach. Her mother (cooperating with us) then advances the rings so that she can reach them again, and Jane does so promptly, her attention continuing to be focused on those rings.

> The affect (feeling tone), which bespeaks the effort she makes to bring the rings to her mouth, the effort with which she pushes and pulls them, suggests that this pressure is in the service of [discovering the nature of] the rings.[11] The activity is of course interrupted by physiological needs (i.e., pooping), as well as socialization. She looks around and smiles at her mother. She then returns to the rings. Notable is the intent, work-like affect, the constancy of the effort she invests in exploring the rings, the inner-drivenness of that activity. Much energy seems to be invested in the exploratory mouthing, pulling, and pushing of the rings. While she explores these rings, there is no thumbsucking activity. Repeatedly she mouths the rings, sometimes with simultaneous pulling movements of her arms and lifting of her torso; her legs are activated as well, and indeed her entire body is involved in her effort. Her facial expression and entire body posture indicate the tension of, and the large effort invested in, that protracted activity. After 18 minutes of nearly continuous effort, she pauses, lying down on the mat. One sees she is tiring. She pauses for about 15 seconds, looks up at her mother, smiles softly, and returns to the rings, at once very busy. Soon she pauses again, and one begins to see signs of unpleasure on her face. She cries as if annoyed and stops her exploratory activity, rings in hand; and now, for the first time in a 20-minute period, she puts her thumb in her mouth and lies quietly. (After a brief pause) she returns to the rings. . . . From here on she alternates between exploration of the rings and thumb-sucking . . . giving the impression that she is recovering from tiredness and unexplained frustration . . . she cries momentarily, and looks up at her mother. . . . She spits up a bit. Her mother picks her up to comfort her. Jane has now been awake for about 25 minutes and has been continually busy (Parens 2008, pp 35–36).
>
> This . . . type of pressured, driven, "exploratory" activity was observed in eight of our (then) nine infants from the ages of 8 to 16 weeks on, during periods of wakefulness and physiological and (emotional) comfort. . . . In Jane, the strong pressure and duration of this exploratory activity from the time she was nine weeks old was impressive. . . . The persistence of this . . . exploratory activity is compelling; Jane, like our other children, did not elect to look; she seemed driven from within to look, and at the risk of thinking (that everything we do is driven or caused by something), I would add, to gratify the push from within to assimilate, to control, to master her visual experience (37).

This aggressive activity is totally different from what we see in *hostile destructiveness;* I therefore, identified it simply as *nondestructive aggression.* More on this follows below.

Nonaffective Destructiveness

The third type of aggressive behavior category, nonaffective destructiveness, is widespread and evident day in and day out. And that is the fact that when we eat, we do so by destroying animal and vegetable life. In infancy, the feeding activity of the human young is principally one of taking in liquids. But it will not be long before solids are introduced. As I shall detail below, we must consider this form of aggression if we are to understand aggression in our universe. But this destruction is not driven by the wish to harm what we destroy and eventually chew to bits and enjoy. In fact, we need to do this or we will not survive. I therefore, labeled this activity, *nonaffective destructiveness;* nonaffective meaning without feelings, specifically feelings or hostility, hate or rage. I do not in this thinking consider hunger to be an emotional feeling, while we know that we all I say "I feel hungry," which is a physical feeling, not an emotional one—except where eating serves to lessen anxiety or some other emotionally distressing feeling. This fact distinguishes this type of aggression from the type where the destruction is driven by those negative feelings that lead to wanting to cause harm.

Pleasure-Related Destructiveness

The fourth category of aggressive behaviors, pleasure-related destructiveness, took us by surprise. We began to see it when the infants were just about turning one year of age. We did not see evidence of this type of aggression before that time. Two examples stand out. The first is of an event that took place between two 11-month-old kids. Jane seemed to be pleasantly busy exploring the environment in her usual way. She came to Tammy, also 11 months old, just standing about, pacifier in her mouth as was her wont at this time. Jane paused a moment standing in from of Tammy, both looking at each other, when Jane just reached for and plucked Tammy's pacifier from her mouth. Jane's mother reacted immediately, getting up and returning the pacifier to Tammy while telling Jane not to do that. Jane didn't seem particularly troubled by her mother's reaction. She walked away, looking around. But she circled back to Tammy and looking at her, reached for Tammy's pacifier and again pulled it from her mouth. Jane seemed to look a bit more intently now. Tammy got upset, turned to her mother for help, which she got as both her mother and Jane's mother reacted to the event; each mother tending to her own kid. Jane's mother's tone was more troubled and firm this time. Jane walked away seemingly not too dismayed about all this. In fact, she had a bit of a smirk on her face. After a few moments, there she was again in front of Tammy and again, pulled the pacifier from her mouth. This time Jane smiled as she did this; Tammy now started to cry. Both mothers were there in an instant. Jane's mother scolded her, which did not seem to surprise Jane.

What was this behavior about? Was it Jane's wish to hurt Tammy? Was it her experiencing pleasure at having an impact on her universe? Was it real pleasure at seeing someone react with distress and cry? Clearly it felt nasty to Tammy. Was this Jane's intention? It certainly was not an act of affection or friendliness. Was it aggressive? Yes, it was acting upon her universe and to have an effect on it. Where do we categorize this type of aggression? I could not be sure what category to put it in.

The second event was more complex, but helped us see and understand a well-known but extremely important dynamic of hostile aggression. When Candy was about 18 months old, she and her twin sister were playing among the other children and their mothers as we carried out our usual observations (during the project I described in the introduction). For no reason visible to us, 2 1/2-year-old Donnie approached Candy and thrust his arm around her neck and grabbed her head—in the wrestling move called "a half-Nelson." We were all startled—the mothers, the observers, and certainly, Candy. Candy did not retaliate against Donnie. She moped and she disrupted her sister's play with some toys. Her mother calmed her nicely and sympathetically.

At our next group session three days later, Candy, her sister, and her mother came as usual. Candy seemed subdued. Some 20 minutes later, I saw Candy's face come to attention as she focused across the unit's day room where we met. Donnie, his younger sister (one of our research subjects), and their mother had just walked in. Quite directly, Candy walked up to him and without a sound, raised her fist and struck him in the arm. With this she smiled softly, a bit like Mona Lisa. Donnie was startled, but interestingly did not strike back. Candy's mother readied to get up, but saw that the event was over. It made clear sense to me; it might have to Candy's mother as well. In fact, I commented to the mothers that it seemed as though Candy had been planning how to let Donnie know that she was very angry with him for what he had done to her three days before. I wondered if Donnie's reaction of doing nothing might have suggested that Donnie too understood that this was retribution for what he had then done to her.

And then here is another example. This time the hostile behavior is expressed with pleasure and the overt wish to cause emotional pain. This kind of behavior becomes evident in children from about one year of age on, in behavior we would identify as taunting.

Two-and-a-half-year-old Susan seemed rather restless one morning. As she went from one toy to another, she noted with interest a toy that 1 1/2-year-old Tommy was exploring. With a half smile on her face, she reached for that toy and pulled it from Tommy's hand. Her mother was looking elsewhere and did not see this. Within moments, Susan—again smiling—grabbed the next toy Tommy picked up. Again, she watched Tommy's reaction with pleasure and some satisfaction. Tommy fussed. He picked up yet another toy, and in a moment, Susan grabbed it. Her smile now conveyed a feeling of getting pleasure out of being nasty to Tommy. Now Tommy was heard, and Susan's mother, who tuned in to what was going on, intervened.

We felt that most of the aggressive behaviors we saw in the young children could be classified in these four categories. To be sure, some behaviors are more complex and fall between the cracks, such as a six-month-old tearing a page out of a book. It best falls under the category of exploring, that is, nondestructive aggression. But clearly, it is destructive although the infant is totally unaware that it is. From here, having these categories of behavior what could we say about aggression as a whole? Being researchers, we had to come up with some explanatory ideas, with hypotheses about aggression. Here's what we came up with.

Three Trends of Aggression

I proposed that these four categories of aggressive behaviors show us evidence of three trends of aggression, or basic types of aggression.

1. Hostile aggression (categories one and four),
2. Nondestructive aggression (category two), and
3. Nonaffective destructiveness (category three).

Hostile Aggression

The hostile aggression trend is acknowledged in all models of aggression as being just that: aggression. In the model of aggression I use, this trend of aggression, hostile aggression, is what we see in angry, nasty behaviors, and especially in hurtful behaviors that is driven by hostility itself, by hate and rage as we find in bullying, torturing, vengefulness, and the like. Although hostile aggression is self-protective, it often causes many individual and collective problems and much human suffering.

Note that we use different words—*anger, hostility, hate*—to express the different degrees of this type of aggression we feel. We know that the level of intensity of this aggression we feel gives the aggressive feelings we then have very different qualities. It's not the same to be angry with and to hate someone. So the trend hostile aggression, as I have conceptualized this type of aggression, represents a wide range of hostile feelings. So, when I use the concept hostile aggression, I mean this as an umbrella term, which includes that well-known range of hostile feelings that spans varying levels of intensity from irritability to anger, then, to hostility, hate, and rage and all the increasingly more destructive thoughts and behaviors these feelings give rise to.

And we all know that these various intensities of hostile aggression tend to lead to very different outcomes. I should define these terms, familiar as they are—although people often use them differently and it is difficult at times to know just which level of hostility a given person means—because there are important distinctions between them that can be guiding to caregivers.

Anger is a negative, that is, unpleasant and troubling feeling we have when someone causes us distress of any sort, but it is moderate distress. In anger, our negative feelings toward the source of the anger, that is the one person or thing that causes us distress, does not lead us to the point of wanting to cause that person or thing harm; we are satisfied by telling that person to stop causing us distress or stop the thing that does so, and if it stops, we can go about our way. In contrast to rage, which is more like a reflex reaction, anger as well as hostility and hate, are always associated with an idea. That is, true feelings of anger require the child's ability to think, to have thoughts, such as: "She is bothering me; she is annoying me; that makes me angry with her."

Hostility per se, the noun, is what we feel when the distress causes us to reach a level of emotional pain that leads us to want to inflict pain on that source, person or thing, in order to be rid of it, to make it stop doing what he or she is or what it is doing. Whereas in anger we don't want to inflict pain, in hostility we do. A critical step has taken place: hostility is experienced when one feels, "this pain is too much!" Or, "I can't take it!" The intensity of unpleasure or emotional pain has crossed a line of tolerance. This line of tolerance, how much emotional pain one can take at a given moment, is critical for what the emotional pain leads us to want to do. With *anger*, one just wants the pain to be stopped. With *hostility*, one wants to cause the person pain and then some more. With *rage*, one may want to tear them to bits. With *hate*, one may want to do a variety of hurtful things or never see that person again. Each word has an individualized meaning determined by the intensity of the emotional pain experienced.

In 1979, I said that there is a biological model, the "Roux experiment,"[12] which demonstrates this type of self-protective aggression. Since I cannot rely on the "Roux experiment" for this assumption, I defend my thesis by saying that, as a student of medicine, I assume that when an irritant gets into a one-cell organism, the protoplasm of that cell—which is the largest part of the cell, much like the white of a chicken egg—reacts forcefully to rid the cell of that irritant because it threatens the one-cell organism's survival. I assume that this a tendency of all living cells whether in a one-cell organism or a billion-cell organism. I assume that there are more detailed and probably more accurate explanations than mine to account for the effects of irritants on a living cell.

Despite this problem, having earlier found and proposed that *excessive unpleasure is what generates hostile destructiveness in humans*, I proposed then[13] and propose now, that "No doubt the (reaction to emotional pain) has a (physical, bodily) root: irritability of the protoplasm, (a fundamental principle in medicine). By virtue of the irritability of the protoplasm . . . the (toxic) accumulation of tension in the cell (organism/self) is experienced psychically as 'unpleasure.' This sensory reactivity of live matter serves to protect against the destruction of the cell (self) and acts primarily to rid the cell (self) of noxious tension. . . . The (biopsychological) force in this ridding activity is 'aggression.' This activity is (put into action by one's adaptive) functions under the aegis of primary narcissism.[14] Insured by this vital (biopsychological) protective mechanism, the aggressive-ridding impulse is brought about reactively to rid the self of the (toxic) agent, which instigates the excessively felt unpleasure (irritability)."

Note too, that physical pain caused us by something or someone may make us angry. But the degree of emotional pain that comes with it will be mostly determined by whether the pain experienced was caused accidently or intentionally. Intentionally caused physical pain carries with it a much larger load of emotional pain than if it occurs accidently.

In addition, both anger and hostility are associated with a given event and tend to be associated with that event and to not last long beyond it, especially so if the person causing us the emotional pain attempts to repair the hurt caused; commonly sincere apology can do the trick. Hostility too requires the ability to have thoughts; thoughts always giving explanation as to why "I feel hostile toward him."

Rage, is an intense reaction of hostile aggression caused by a painful event that brings with it unbearable emotional pain. A rage reaction is a physiologically driven reaction to pain that is unbearable. Even newborns have such reactions. A rage reaction is automatic, and may occur even before an infant thinks, can put into thought or understand what the source of the pain is, whether it is accidental or intentional. Rage is therefore the most primitive form of hostile aggression.

In contrast to rage, anger and clearly expressed hostility do not appear until about six months of age.[15] This is because as I noted before, both anger and hostility require a thought (an idea), of which we assume the newborn is not yet capable. The newborn has feelings, but we believe that thinking associated with feelings seems to be observable only by several months after birth; so we think that by six months there is much evidence that the baby thinks. Also, while anger and hostility are reactions to pain, they don't give the impression of being reflex-like as is rage.

Hate is the most developed of the hostile aggression feelings. Hate is complex. Among those I know who have studied it,[16] we hold the belief that hate is not possible until the child is about 18 months of age given hate's tendency to endure well beyond the events that give rise to it and that it tends to be difficult to reverse. An apology or even a series of apologies will not do it.

One more word here about hostile aggression. I have said that emotional pain (unpleasure or psychic pain) is what generates hostile aggression. I believe it will be of much value to caregivers to consider the fact that when the emotional pain one experiences crosses the line of tolerance I mentioned before, the line "I can't take this! It's too much!" *hostile aggression undergoes a qualitative change that has led me to speak of this aggression as hostile destructiveness.* I have done this to emphasize that in reaction to excessive emotional pain (excessive unpleasure), the aggression carries with it the wish to harm or even destroy. Milder levels of hostile aggression, as when we feel annoyance, irritation, or even anger do not lead to the wish to harm or destroy. This makes it important and highly valuable for the child, for caregivers to try to evaluate the level of emotional pain the child they care for is experiencing. I talk about this in chapter 6.

Humans are known to use aggression in ways that are not commonly found in other animals, such as in genocides. But it is not just humans who can run amuck with hostile aggression, indeed, with hostile destructiveness. For instance, in 2003, speaking of the way the attack on the World Trade Center in New York on September 11 is not unique in the history of civilization, Thompson wrote the following:

> In 1974, in Jane Goodall's preserve in Africa, one of the field workers watched as a group of male chimpanzees came together and with coordination, stealth, and surprise moved through a neighboring community, sought out a lone victim, and murdered him. Over the course of the next few weeks, they watched the same group repeatedly attack the neighboring community until they had destroyed all the males. Since then, this violent raiding has been observed repeatedly in chimpanzees.[17] Such complex behavior requires considerable cognitive sophistication. These animals have the ability to form a group, move with stealth to another area, wait, pick out a victim, and then murder him. In chimpanzees, there is no one-on-one killing: all murderous violence occurs in male bonded coalitions. This is (strong) evidence that . . . terrorism existed in our common ancestor and was retained in the two separate developmental trajectories over the following five to seven million years.[18]

So I have now talked about that type of hostile aggression that is clearly identifiable in the way it shows itself in behavior, such as the example of the rage reaction of infancy. But what do we make of Jane's behavior with Tammy? It was not clear what this behavior was about. Did Jane hurt Tammy? Did she get real pleasure at seeing Tammy react with distress and cry? Was this Jane's intention? It was aggressive behavior; at the very least, it was acting upon her universe; to have an effect on it. But I could not be sure what category of aggression to put it in. While Jane's intention may not have been to hurt Tammy—which I think is the case—Tammy was hurt. I felt that this example fell between categories. If it was Jane's intention to upset Tammy, then it had to be categorized as hurtful, as in teasing.

But I learned more, something critical from the example of Candy and Donnie, in what seemed to be a discharge of hostile feelings with a smile on Candy's face; that is, that it seemed to be a pleasurable discharge of hostility toward another. The event was clear. My interpretation of Candy's seemingly pleasurable "attack" on Donnie was not really driven by a primary pleasure if I can put it that way, but rather, by a quietly planned, perhaps unconscious, belated retribution for Donnie's startling her painfully and hurting her three days before. This, then was not driven in origin by pleasure, but by a prior experience of unpleasure (emotional pain) resulting from Donnie's intentional "attack" on her. So, when someone enjoys hurting another, while the attacker is experiencing pleasure, this hurtfulness of another probably owes its origin to experiences of excessive unpleasure (excessive emotional pain) that occurred before, even long before. I therefore put this type of aggression into the trend *hostile aggression*, assuming that this is the aggression that drives this kind of behavior. This would account for the hostility, even if only the little that is present in *teasing* and, always more than little in *taunting* behavior. So the *pleasure-related destructiveness* category of behaviors really belongs in the trend of *hostile aggression.*

Nondestructive Aggression

The trend nondestructive aggression is well represented in the activity I described in 15-week-old Jane. This example, which I use as example for nondestructive aggression, could be considered by some to be assertiveness. And in fact, I consider assertiveness to be driven by nondestructive aggression. So too, mobilized by what psychoanalysts call "primary narcissism,"[19] nondestructive aggression is the engine of autonomy. The child's sense of autonomy,[20] of "I want to do this or that; I can do this or that!" is a critical element in the development of a sense of self, of the mental construction we call one's "self."

I call it *nondestructive aggression* because this aggressive behavior is not used to destroy something, and it is aggressive because of the quality of its inherent pressure. It is the energy that drives us to pursue our goals, to gain control over things, including oneself and those around us. By "control" here I don't mean to make oneself into an automaton, but to have some influence on how we react to events, what we do with our feelings, how we drive ourselves. In so far as to control others, it is not to make them automatons either, nor to just make them do what we want, but to be able to accommodate ourselves to the others and have them act toward us in ways that we would like, in ways that do not harm us. When the need to control others becomes restrictive of others, in human interactions, it is driven by anxiety or it is in the service of achieving goals that may or may not be in the interest of others.

Several other psychoanalysts who have written about this type of aggression consider it to be a "life force,"[21] perhaps following on Henri Bergson's concept of "élan vital." Anthony Storr[22] especially, but a number of other analysts also proposed before I did, that we must account for a trend or type of aggression that is not inherently destructive. I learned about these writings after I had developed the theory of aggression I first reported on in 1973, which by 2000,[23] I formally called, *the multitrends theory of aggression.* In 1979,[24] I held that the aim of nondestructive aggression is "the exploration, asserting oneself upon, control, assimilation, and mastery of the self and environment" (101). This I then came to believe to be the primary aim of all aggression, including that of hostile destructiveness.

Nonaffective Destructiveness

I believe that it makes much sense to included the trend nonaffective destructiveness when we speak of a theory of aggression. Of course, in this book I am speaking of aggression in humans. But in our efforts to understand the nature of aggression I have long been puzzled by the fact that the many theories of aggression we scientists have come up with do not account for all aggression in the animal kingdom. Yes, our focus on what I call hostile aggression, and especially on its subcategory hostile destructiveness, is of central importance to us. But we have generally left out what most likely is to most frequently evident aggression. I am referring to that (third) category of aggression I have labeled *nonaffective destructiveness.* True, during wartime, hostile destructiveness preoccupies us from morning until night. But overall, the most common animal aggression is what ethnologists have called *prey aggression,* the aggression brought into play when an animal chases another for its dinner. The lioness chasing a gazelle will, once she catches it, destroy it and tear it to bits. The lioness uses sheer destructiveness to achieve her end, namely provide herself with the food she needs. The fact is that self-preservation requires us to destroy animate organisms, animal or plant, to meet the needs of our body. To do so we destroy, we break down magnificently formed tissues, meat or vegetable.

But clearly, we do not do so out of anger, hostility, or hate. True, if the gazelle gets away from the lioness, the lioness may get frustrated and, perhaps even angry—if lionesses have such feelings. To be sure animals other than humans can get enraged; if their life is threatened they will growl and attack viciously or try to get away or pretend they are lifeless. But the essential daily acts by all animals of tearing down animal or vegetable tissue is not driven by hostility or hate, but rather by hunger and the need for food to survive. I have therefore insisted that this trend in animal aggression, prey aggression, which we humans act out daily—since most of us do not ourselves chase or kill animals or vegetables for our food, but are satisfied to just tear down and chew what was not long before live tissue—be included in what we call aggression and I have specified that we consider it to be nonaffective destructiveness. As I said earlier, while this destructiveness is driven by feeling hungry, feeling hunger is generally a very different feeling than the emotional feelings of anger, hostility, and hate.

For our purposes in this book, which is how to help parents deal constructively with their children's aggression, we do not need to concern ourselves with helping parents deal with their children's nonaffective destructiveness. Our challenge is to help parents optimize the way they help their children cope with their hostile aggression and with their nondestructive aggression. I think it helps parents to understand just what activates these trends in aggression; what are they really? Let me first talk about nondestructive aggression.

What Is Nondestructive Aggression?

We see evidence of nondestructive aggression in assertive, nonhostile, self-protective, goal-achieving, and mastery behaviors.

Nondestructive aggression is essential for constructive adaptation. It seems to be generated in us as part of our development and survival system.

It is the clearest example of the inherent nature of aggression.

I believe the aim of nondestructive aggression is to assert oneself upon, control, and thrust oneself toward mastery of one's self and one's environment.

This type of aggression is a large motivational force inherent in the child's efforts to develop and become competent and self-reliant.

It also motivates self-fulfilling competitiveness without being hostile and destructive.

It serves to secure and protect our self, needs, property, and rights.

It propels and sustains our self-determination and drives us in the achievement of our personal wishes and aims, as well as in our capabilities to adapt. Indeed, a sufficient capacity to experience this type of aggression is essential for healthy adaptation.

Most important: the evidence suggests that nondestructive aggression is the product of an inborn system and that its primary function is to drive adaptation and therewith to serve survival. Some have spoken of it as a "life force."

This system is present and functioning at birth; in fact we find evidence of nondestructive aggression in the behavior of children as early as the first months of life.

What Are Hostile Aggression and Hostile Destructiveness?

Hostile aggression is evident in the range of feelings we consider to be "dysphoric," meaning that the feeling is unpleasant, unwanted, and leads us to a negative reaction. The reaction is in essence a "wanting to rid oneself of" reaction. We commonly describe these feelings as irritability, annoyance, anger, hostility, rage, or hate. These basic dysphoric feelings lead to all sorts of hostile and destructive behaviors as meanness, cruelty, revenge, etc.

Hostile aggression is *not* inborn. This is one of its most critical features. Oh yes, you say, so why does the newborn come out of the birth canal screaming at you? Just think of it. Sure, you're happy; most of us are, but. . . .

When the newborn comes out of the birth canal screaming, he or she has just gone through a being-squeezed-to-life experience. Just imagine being squeezed out like toothpaste, pushed through a very tight flesh-canal, out of that wonderful warm chamber where it might have been very pleasant (for you anyway) to stay for a while longer. Your head is squashed and squeezed—well documented by how it's misshapen at birth—your shoulders are squashed and squeezed, first one . . . then your trunk followed by the other . . . then you're grabbed by some rough, well maybe some gentle hands that tug at you to get the hell out, and you're lunged into a void, half gasping, half choking, suddenly in dire need of oxygen and you scream for air. It's a harrowing experience, for both the baby and the mother. And we all jump for joy; at least most of us. Nonetheless, for the totally uninformed and innocent newborn, it was a rough voyage . . . and it caused the infant much unpleasure, which is why the newborn is screaming—and not because the newborn is angry to begin with.

Hostile aggression is *not* spontaneously activated. It is not produced by some inner bodily or physiological need like the need for food or the need for sleep. We don't need hostility per se to survive like we need food or oxygen or sleep.

But, we have all been made to feel hostility, everyone of us. So, there must be a mechanism in our brain that can be activated to generate or produce in us hostile feelings. And I have proposed that this mechanism *is* inborn. And we learned from the behaviors of the babies and the mothers in our project (see introduction to the book) that this mechanism is activated by an experience of unpleasure, most commonly emotional pain or distress. It led me to postulate, following our observations that:

An experience of unpleasure is *required* for the generation in us of hostile aggression.

And it is unpleasure that gives to aggression the *emotional* quality characteristic of anger, hostility, hate, etc.

As I mentioned earlier, there is a critical additional assumption to be made: it is that hostile aggression changes into hostile destructiveness when the emotional pain or distress (unpleasure) experienced crosses one's emotional tolerance line "I can't take this; it's too much."

This emotional pain tolerance line, when the emotional pain gets too much, changes the quality of the hostile feelings from just wanting it to be stopped to wanting to harm or destroy that which is, or the person who is, causing the emotional pain. This critical fact brings with it a most powerful one, which is that

Most important: *the degree to which one experiences hostile destructiveness can be lessened or it can be heightened by the degree to which we experience emotional pain.* This fact, that the degree to which in our childrearing we are able to reduce or by what we do we heighten the degree to which they experience emotional pain, we will influence the degree to which our children become angry or hostile individuals. This, of course, is of great relevance to parenting. It should guide us in how we handle our children. It is critical for us as parents to know that our children are not born hostile, but that they can become that way. And there is much we parents can do to influence whether or not they become that way. This is what this book hopes to help you with.

IMPLICATIONS FOR PARENTING

The implications of this model of aggression for parenting are large. These are the trends in aggression that concern us most in child rearing because our entire emotional life is influenced by them. Both of these forms of aggression are shaped by the experiences our children have, especially the experiences we provide as parents.

To be sure, of course, the trends in aggression are determined by the interplay of the child's biological make-up (which can already be detected in the temperament of the few-weeks-old child) and his or her real life experiences from birth on.

On the side of their biological make-up for example, an infant born with a disturbance of any of her or his vital body systems such as the digestive system (as with colic), or the respiratory system (as with asthma), or the skin (as with eczema) commonly suffers much distress, which the infant experiences both physically and emotionally, in fact as "emotional pain." Also, infants born with immaturities of their central nervous system may find it difficult to tolerate the rhythms of daily life. For instance, an infant born with a tendency to react rapidly to any event—a "quick-reactor" we say—when beginning to feel hunger will quickly signal the need for feeding, but may feel much distress when mother cannot be there immediately to feed the baby. Or an infant with a low-threshold for irritability or physiological intolerance is likely to react intensely to any unpleasant experience he has, be it being too hot or too cold or too tired. Some infants react with distress to loud noises or to what they experience as unbearable sounds. Of course, infants with allergies are likely to react adversely to items to which they are allergic. All these kids and others with inborn biological vulnerabilities not here noted, experience various kinds of bodily pain that they also experience as emotional pain.

Fortunately, most babies are not burdened with such biological vulnerabilities. In fact, most are born with remarkable tolerances, even patience and resilience. They are able to wait reasonably to be fed, diapered, and tended to in the varied ways caregivers do 24 hours a day, seven days a week.

Experience is by far the largest factor that weighs in on the formation of the child's aggression profile. And this is why understanding what aggression is all about, what shapes its trends in the course of development is so critical. Decades of research and clinical work has led me to propose as I said before that "nondestructive aggression tends to be more favorable, the less intense the level of hostile aggression in the aggression profile of the individual." I also have found that the most determining of this balance is the level of hostile aggression. This is because the individual's efforts to handle his or her hostile aggression feelings, hostility, hate, or rage, interferes with the free expression of nondestructive aggression. What I mean is this: clinical work has shown that, quite commonly, when an individual struggles to contain a large accumulation of hostile aggression and tries to control the discharge of hostile or hate feelings, the adaptive system—the *ego* we say—of the individual tends to falter, the individual experiences intense anxiety, and unconsciously feeling helpless, this adaptive system blocks the discharge of all expressions of aggression, both hostile *and* nondestructive. While blocking the discharge of intense feelings of hostility and hate in human interaction is desirable, it is not desirable that nondestructive aggression, needed for adaptation, be blocked. It deserves emphasis that nondestructive aggression fuels constructive assertiveness, the persistence to pursue our goals, self-containment and regulation of action, and morally responsible compliance. Therefore, in child rearing, it is best for parents to try to see to it that the child's level of hostile aggression not be too high. In order to achieve this, it is highly facilitating to understand how hostile aggression gets generated in the first place.

For instance, looking at infants (even before they are capable of thoughts and wishes to destroy) has led us to propose that there is always a trigger for a rage reaction. Indeed, this is true for all acts of hostility. That trigger is the experience of excessive pain or distress. We have spoken of it as excessive unpleasure. We have found, over years of observing young children, that, as all parents know intuitively, whenever a child experiences a rage reaction, something is causing it.

It is only when parents have tried all they know to do, are at their wits' ends, and cannot identify the source of excessive pain or distress, that they resort to the explanation that children need to cry "to exercise their lungs." We believe this to be a false explanation for children's crying. One good thing about children's crying is that they are letting themselves express the pain (of whatever sort) they are feeling. That is generally desirable. But our point here is that whenever an infant experiences rage, it is because he has experienced excessive pain or distress in one form or another—some type of excessive unpleasure. This condition is a prerequisite for the experience of rage.[25]

Given the nature of the aggression trends, we cannot deal with all aggressive behaviors in the same way. In fact, it is highly undesirable to do so. To help our children learn to adapt to our world, it has to be possible for them to be aggressive at certain times in certain ways and not be aggressive at other times in other ways. "What should I do if my child hits another child?" is a question we have often heard. To know what to do, one has to know the characteristics of the given child, the context in which the child is hitting another child, and the history of the child's relationship to the other. Is he attacking the other child? Is he defending his own possession? Is he retaliating for a prior attack by the other child? In other words, is he being self-protective, or is he being hostile, displacing rage from elsewhere onto an innocent playmate or bystander?

Aggression, we emphasize, on the one hand, may be inherently nonhostile and serve adaptation, the protection of oneself and one's rights, the fulfillment of one's wishes and aims. Thus, appropriately expressed, aggression plays an important part in our capacity to learn and to succeed in our enterprises.

On the other hand, aggression can take the form of hostility and hate. It can lead to the wish—even to the need—to hurt others, and to the need to hurt oneself. It can lead to the production of bullies and to the production of children terrified to stand up for themselves. Both are products of hostile aggression. It can lead to pain and to the destruction of our own aims and wishes, as well as to the destruction of the environment. In extreme forms, it can lead to the destruction of those around us, even those we love and oneself.

Looking at it from the vantage point of the parent with regard to his or her own child, we want to help our children learn to become self-confident: to be able to assert themselves where desirable, to sustain their efforts in mastering a task, and to mobilize their energies toward achieving their aims and goals. On the other hand, we do not want our children to be hostile to themselves or unnecessarily hostile to others, nor do we want them to do things that are damaging to themselves or society.

We do not want them to be riddled with internal conflicts, guilt, and shame. We want our children to respect themselves, to respect others, and to be socially responsible, as well as able to form good love relationships, work effectively, and enjoy their lives sufficiently.

Having an appreciation of the fact that aggression can be nondestructive and fuel autonomy and assertiveness, and that it can be hostile and destructive can make clearer the answer to the question, "What should I do if my child hits another child?"

The degree of hostility generated in the child influences the quality of the child's well being. We all recognize the havoc that excessive hostility produces in our world: crimes in the home and on the street, preparations for and the carrying out of wars, and the unprecedented and highly threatening nuclear arms race. Although as parents we are highly concerned about these issues, it is not our intention here to address issues at that level of social concern, but simply to underline that unresolved problems of hostile destructiveness could have widespread consequences.

Here we want to talk about the implications of hostility for the well being of our individual children. To inflict pain or harm and to destroy that, which causes us pain and distress, is quite understandable. This is what hostility, hate, and rage are all about. Difficult as it is to accept, we have to recognize that some degree of hostility is unavoidable in our children. Even in the best of worlds and families, normal disappointments and restrictions on the gratification of wishes are often needed to rear a child in a growth-promoting way. In other words, good parents will unavoidably elicit hostility in their children, even in the course of loving and growth-promoting rearing. Modest levels of hostility may create modest degrees of difficulty within the child. This cannot be avoided. However, to a substantial degree, we can modulate both the frequency and intensity of hostility generation and mobilization. Therefore, we can protect our children against experiencing excessive levels of hostility. In this way, we can be of particular help to them.

Fortunately, in most instances with most children, we are capable of preventing the development of excessive hostility. Since hostility is mobilized by experiences of excessive pain and distress, if we can find ways to prevent or lessen the impact of their experiencing excessive unpleasure, we will prevent or lessen the generation of hostility in them. There is a way of preventing the generation of excessive hostility in our children while recognizing that hostility in moderate degrees cannot and does not need to be prevented. A number of years ago,[26] we made several recommendations to those concerned with children.

We can help parents, caregivers, teachers, and other child tenders learn and recognize that excessive unpleasure experiences generate or mobilize hostility in the child. The key phrase is excessive unpleasure. The caution is twofold: First, experiences of unpleasure are unavoidable; second, benign experiences of unpleasure lead to adaptation, learning, and growth. Benign experiences of unpleasure lead to efforts to master and improve our life situation. For instance, even infants have built-in adaptive mechanisms that become activated when they experience discomfort. Infants adapt to benign levels of unpleasure by putting their thumbs or pacifiers in their mouths. In doing so they are adapting, they are learning to soothe themselves. In fact, they are learning to be independent. It is when unpleasure is felt as excessive that it may wreak havoc in the individual.

Children ought to be protected against too frequent and too prolonged excessive unpleasure experiences. It is important for parents and other child tenders to know that children vary widely in the way they tolerate unpleasure. We all have different thresholds of irritability and pain tolerance. During the child's earliest years, parents should study their child's ways of expressing the experience of excessive unpleasure. Each child has his or her own unique combination of behavioral and vocal ways of expressing feelings of excessive unpleasure. We are calling for parents to further develop their innate ability to feel what their child is experiencing and to look for those expressions that signal the experience of excessive unpleasure.

Parents need to know that there are ways of enhancing a child's capability to modify the hostility generated within the child. This capability, in large part, depends on the child's having a good relationship with his or her parents. Each child has the capability to lessen the amount and mitigate the intensity of hostility that life circumstances generate within him or her. A sufficiently positive attachment to his or her mother or father is necessary for the development of that potential capability. A loving, generally positive emotional relationship will help the child cope better with his or her hostility. Thus, the child can be spared a great deal of pain and can better secure for himself or herself a greater degree of well being. A good emotional relationship with our children has far-reaching implications, not only in the area of aggression, but in all dimensions of emotional life.

We are convinced, from our work with parents and children, that parents can be helped to intervene constructively in their children's lives and lessen the production and mobilization of hostility, as well as help them cope in growth-promoting ways with the unavoidable experiences of excessive unpleasure and hostility. In the course of our studies in aggression and in education for parenting, we have identified specific areas of parent-child interaction and experience where hostility most commonly becomes generated or mobilized. These are also the areas of interaction where nondestructive aggression can be protected and enhanced. These are:

1. Dealing constructively with the child's experiencing excessive unpleasure.
2. Recognizing the need for—and allowing children—sufficient and reasonable autonomy and exploratory/learning/practicing activity.
3. Setting limits constructively.
4. Teaching the child how to express and discharge anger and hostility in reasonable and acceptable ways.
5. Handling the child's rage reactions and temper tantrums in growth-promoting ways.
6. Helping the child cope with painful emotional feelings such as anxiety and depression.
7. Optimizing the parent-child relationship.

In following chapters we will discuss dealing with aggression in each of these areas of parent-child interaction. We will do so from the vantage point of providing a rationale for parenting intervention, and we will propose general steps that can be taken to achieve growth-promoting parenting. We will not address all aspects of aggressive behavior in children; this is neither feasible nor necessary. In the process of exploring these seven types of parent-child interactions, parents will learn much that can also be applied in other circumstances.

Our prime aim is to help parents gain a better understanding of their children's behavior and aggression. Based on such understanding, they will be able to develop helpful strategies for intervening with their children. We feel that if parents do this, they will be able to deal more constructively with the hostility that life experiences often unavoidably mobilize in the child and in themselves.

NOTES

1. "Aggression" is defined so variably that, among professionals and in the vernacular, one often cannot be sure what the user of the term means. I have addressed this dilemma in detail in *The Development of Aggression in Early Childhood* (Lanham, MD: Jason Aronson, 2008).

2. In our parenting education work we devised a 10-point scale of the quality of the parent's child-rearing efforts, which we described as *from growth-disturbing to growth-promoting,* meaning child rearing that interferes with or optimizes the child's developing emotional health. The more growth-promoting the parenting, the better the child's developing emotional health. See H. Parens, Toward preventing experience-derived emotional disorders: Education for parenting, pp. 121–148 in *Prevention in Mental Health* ed. H. Parens & S. Kramer (Northvale, NJ: Jason Aronson, 1993) as well as the DVD, *The Urgent Need for Universal Parenting Education: A Documentary* written and produced by H. Parens with media production by P. Gilligan, from the Thomas Jefferson University, Medical School Media Division, Philadelphia, PA, 2008.

3. Since 1970, our work with parents and their young children has formally turned to education for parenting. We have developed two methods for this work. First, we use a group method for teaching parenting to people who are already parents (H. Parens, L. Pollock, & R. C. Prall, Film #3: *Prevention/Early Intervention Mother-Infant Groups* [Audio-Visual Media Section, Eastern Pennsylvania Psychiatric Institute, Philadelphia, PA, 1973]). A group consists of seven to ten mothers (and fathers, where feasible) with all their very young children, who meet for a 1 1/2-hour weekly session with two mental health professionals knowledgeable in child development. In our group, members continued in the group, which was open-ended, from infancy until their children were five. In a natural setting, we talked about the behaviors occurring in the children that were puzzling or troublesome to the parents. We also discussed any questions the parents had about their children or their parenting. Some groups of this kind have met for several years, others are of limited duration, in the course of which we have seen mothers of all educational levels acquire much understanding of their children's emotional experiencing and the psychodynamics of their behaviors, and from that develop a good basis for growth-promoting child rearing. (See 37 years' follow-up remarks by mothers and their grown children of our original group in *The Urgent Need for Universal Parenting Education*). Such parenting education groups have been carried out for years by a cluster of mental health professionals associated with the Psychoanalytic Center of Philadelphia in the Philadelphia area.

The second method is to teach parenting to students—parents-to-be—from kindergarten through grade 12. We have developed a curriculum encompassing the emotional sector of parenting (H. Parens, E. Scattergood, A. Duff, & W. Singletary, *Parenting for Emotional Growth: A Curriculum for Students in Grades K Thru 12,* [1997*]*). Preliminary field applications of this method by us and ongoing applications of such derivative educational materials developed and used by Educating Children for Parenting® have been very well received by students and have shown gratifying results.

4. H. Parens, *The Development of Aggression in Early Childhood,* rev. ed. (Lanham, MD: Jason Aronson, 2008). See pp 202–210 for my description of a dramatic complex crisis of rage 13-month-old Mary experienced toward her mother and how she struggled to deal with it.

5. H. Parens, & A. A. Weech, Jr., Accelerated learning responses in young patients with school problems, *J. Amer. Acad. Child Psychiatry* 5(1966):75–92.

6. This includes theories of aggression proposed by psychiatry, psychoanalysis, psychology, sociology, ethology, and genetics (see H. Parens, Introduction to the revised edition, pp. xxii-xliv in *The Development of Aggression in Early Childhood*).

7. For a more complete detailing of our model of aggression see H. Parens, *The Development of Aggression in Early Childhood,* chapter 3.

8. H. Parens, Aggression: a reconsideration, *J. Amer. Psychoanalytic Assn.* 21(1973):34–60. Also shown in H. Parens, L. Pollock, & R. C. Prall, Film #2: *Toward an Epigenesis of Aggression in Early Childhood* (Audio-Visual Medical Section, Eastern Pennsylvania Psychiatric Institute, Philadelphia, 1974).

9. J. Piaget, *La Construction du Réel Chez* l'Enfant (Neuchâtel: Delachaux et Niestle 1937). J. Piaget, *The Child's Conception of the World* (Paterson, N.J.: Littlefield, Adams, 1967).

10. The documentary in question is entitled *The Urgent Need for Universal Parenting Education: A Documentary.* It was written and produced by H. Parens with media producer P. Gilligan of the Thomas Jefferson University, Medical School Media Division, Philadelphia, PA, 2008.

11. I like to point out the obvious: that infants are born into a world they have never seen or experienced before. Gradually, progressively, they have to learn what all the things around them are made of and serve what purpose, etc. Infants are of necessity more or less vigorous explorers of their new world. Imagine how excited Spain was when Christopher Columbus told them this was not the "West Indies," but a "newly found world."

12. In *The Development of Aggression in Early Childhood* (1979), I said that in *An Outline of Psycho-analysis* (1939, 185), Freud referred to a "Roux experiment" which, I then said demonstrated just this. In my efforts to confirm this information, I recently discovered that the model Freud described has nothing to do with what I then said it did. I find that Freud was referring to the experiment conducted by Wilhelm Roux (1850–1924), the "Father of Embryology," who demonstrated the vast effects of pricking an embryo that stirred cell division and left its mark on the organism.

13. H. Parens, *The Development of Aggression in Early Childhood* (Lanham, MD: Jason Aronson, 2008).

14. "Primary narcissism" is a term coined by Sigmund Freud in 1914 in his essay "On narcissism: An introduction" published in the *Standard* edition of Freud's writing, volume 14:69–102. This term, I have come to suggest, is the psychological manifestation of living organisms' biological imperative to live and to survive, because of its inherent self-value. This is the biological imperative that leads living organisms to "fight to the death" or to take flight to safety, the well-known biological concept of "fight or flight" in the face of a threat to life.

15. I discuss this in greater detail in H. Parens, Rage toward self and other in early childhood, pp. 123–147 in *Rage, Power and Aggression,* ed. S. P. Roose & R. Glick, (New Haven: Yale University Press, 1993).

16. John McDevitt, in "The emergence of hostile aggression and its defensive and adaptive modifications during the separation-individuation process," *J. Amer. Psa. Assn.* 31:5(1983):273–300, was the first I know to have observed that hate is enduring and is not possible until about 18 months of age when thought processes are sufficiently developed to make it possible for such feelings to stick. Hate carries well beyond the time of the events that gave rise to it. Our own studies (Parens, Scattergood, Duff, & Singletary, 1997) have confirmed McDevitt's explanation.

17. R. W. Wrangham, & D. Peterson, *Demonic Males: Apes and The Origins of Human Violence* (Boston: Houghton Mifflin, 1996).

18. J. Anderson Thomson, Jr., MD, from the University of Virginia, Department of Psychiatry, wrote an article on terrorism that he entitled, "Killer apes on American Airlines or how religion was the main hijacker on September 11." This passage comes from page 4 of that article.

19. Freud, "On narcissism: An introduction" (1914) in the *Standard* edition of Freud's writing, volume 14:69–102.

20. E.H. Erikson, Identity and the life cycle. *Psychological Issues* 1(1959):1–170. Proposed by Erik Erikson as the second stage of the development of "self-identity."

21. Phyllis Greenacre spoke of it as "a force of growth" in her article Notes on the influence and contribution of ego psychology to the practice of psychoanalysis, which appeared as pp. 171–200 in *Separation-Individuation: Essays in Honor of Margaret S. Mahler,* ed. J. B. McDevitt & C. F. Settlage, (New York: International Universities Press, 1971). Donald W. Winnicott spoke in 1950 of a "life force" in three short articles published under the title "Aggression in relation to emotional development." It is included in his *Collected Papers,* pp. 204–218 (New York: Basic Books, 1975).

22. A. Storr, *Human Aggression* (New York: Atheneum, 1968) and A. Storr, *Human Destructiveness* (New York: Basic Books, 1972). In these Storr was among the first to propose two trends in aggression, one destructive, the other nondestructive.

23. Among my many documents (published and unpublished) on my theory of aggression, I have a PowerPoint presentation I titled, "The multitrends theory of aggression." I had by then identified it this way for some time.

24. H. Parens, *The Development of Aggression in Early Childhood,* (Lanham, MD: Jason Aronson, 2008)

25. In rare instances in childhood, some children with brain disorders—such as those that cause epileptic seizures—may have rage reactions that may not be triggered by experiences of excessive unpleasure. These we assume to be uncommon.

26. H. Parens, *The Development of Aggression in Early Childhood,* (Lanham, MD: Jason Aronson, 2008)

Chapter 5

Dealing Constructively with Excessive Unpleasure Experiences

The younger your child when you start to use these strategies the greater your chance of success. But whatever the child's age, it is never too late to start.

> Three-month-old Kathy has been making fussing sounds for a minute. She quiets. Thirty seconds later, she begins to fuss again, this time a bit more loudly. Again, she quiets. About 20 seconds later her fussing starts again, intensifies, and now she begins to cry. Mother's attention is now diverted from her friend and turns to her baby. As Mother prepares to care for her, Kathy's crying intensifies, and we hear some complaint in that crying, some impatience, and anger. As Mother decides on feeding and prepares to do so, Kathy's reaction mounts further, and she is now crying angrily. If Kathy's mother were not to respond to her at this point, Kathy would probably experience excessive emotional pain.
>
> Eight-year-old Mike is not coming down for dinner when he's being called now for the third time. His mother asks Mike's older brother to please go get him. Nick goes up. Some fussing is heard. Finally Mike comes down, grouchy, troubled. At the table he's short and nasty to his older brother. Dad, looking at Mike, asks what's going on. "Nothing!" Dad, says, "Hmm. Seems to me something is going on." "Nothing," Mike says again. Dad says, "Mike, it's OK if you don't want to tell us now, but try to calm down and eat your dinner, and stop being nasty to the rest of us." Later, Dad makes a point of talking to Mike. Alone with Dad, Mike is more receptive to Dad's wanting to know what's troubling him. There's this big kid in school who's been teasing and picking on him in the school yard. And they talk. Dad tells Mike, he had a bully problem too. And they talk more.

> Fifteen-year-old Jan seems grouchy the last couple days. Mom has been waiting to hear from Jan what is going on that's making her feel bad. After some resistance, against which Mom pushed gently, Jan tells her she's really upset by her grades. She's trying to bring them up, but the test they got back on Tuesday (a few days ago) was not better. As Mom sympathetically pushes a bit more and tells her that she just has to keep doing the best she can, Jan starts to cry. And she tells her mother that the boy she likes, likes her friend Dee. Mom opened the opportunity to help Jan talk about this pain we all know, and with this, Mom helped Jan deal with, or "metabolize," as I like to say, meaning "make less painful," the pain she is experiencing.

Our aim in this chapter is to help parents prevent, where possible and reasonable, excessive emotionally painful (unpleasure) experiences and reduce the frequency of their occurrence. Also, since some experiences of excessive unpleasure are unavoidable, we want to help parents find reasonable ways to do what they can to decrease their intensity and duration and to lessen their negative impact on the child. We all know only too well that emotional pain, even intense emotional pain like physical pain, is part of life; and that intense emotional pain is difficult to handle on one's own. To be able to share it with someone meaningful to us can help enormously.

As I have already emphasized, excessive unpleasure—"this is more than I can take!"—is the key experience factor that generates or leads to the expression of all forms of hostile aggression, from neonatal rage reactions to later reactions of anger, hostility, and hate. Thus, preventing and lessening excessive unpleasure experiences are the most direct ways of preventing the generation or mobilization of excessive hostility in the child, infant, or teenager. In doing so, parents need to:

1. Know what their child's experiencing of excessive unpleasure looks like and imagine what it feels like.
2. To achieve this, it is essential for parents to open themselves to feeling what their child or teenager is feeling; that is, parents have to engage their capacity for empathy—that ability to feel what another is feeling—an essential for growth-promoting parenting.
3. Of course, parents need to accept the fact that their child, especially the young child, turns to them for the relief of pain, emotional as well as physical. For this, the parent needs to be emotionally available—to be open to and tuned into what the child is experiencing—and be responsive to the child or adolescent's need for help.
4. And next, the parent must try to identify the source of pain and distress and attempt to deal with it.

5. Finally, he or she must comfort the child or adolescent during experiences of excessive emotional pain and help the child or adolescent cope with his or her painful experiences.
6. Furthermore, it is helpful to follow up with talking together later, the same day or the next, to see to what degree the child or teenager has been able to deal with this challenge of emotional pain. Challenging experiences often can benefit from being brought up at a later time, revisited, if the child or adolescent is open to it. If not, don't push; let the child try to cope on his or her own.

RATIONALE

If from infancy on, experiencing excessive unpleasure is the prerequisite for the production of all forms of hostile aggression, then, as I said before, preventing and lessening excessive unpleasure experiences are the most direct ways of preventing the accumulation of excessive hostility in the child. Bear in mind that we are more concerned with preventing *excessive* unpleasure (excessive emotional pain) than unpleasure in general. Many times, unpleasure in moderate doses, such as in frustration or a moderately trying challenge, engenders adaptation and promotes healthy development and learning. True, the younger the child, the less he or she is likely to be able to deal successfully with his or her unpleasure. But the adolescent too can deal with it much better when he or she knows he or she has parents who want to help to turn to.

Let's remember that there are times when hostility is adaptive and is needed in coping with life situations. Because of this, we do not want to—not that we could—do away with the capacity to be angry, very angry, and at times appropriately hostile and hating. Nor do we want to suggest to the child that being angry, feeling hostile, or even rage is a sign that the child is bad; it is a sign that the child is feeling emotional pain, unpleasure to the degree suggested by the feelings expressed.

The generation of hostility in us is unavoidable, even under the best of home circumstances. For instance, growth-promoting child rearing often requires limit setting from about six months on (the time when infants begin to bite and many to crawl) through the teen years; this brings with it experiences of unpleasure, and in some kids, excessive unpleasure. Furthermore, life events often bring disappointments, sometimes exceedingly painful disappointments and even catastrophes.

It is excessive hostility within the child and adolescent that creates havoc. This is what we want to prevent. As I said before, preventing excessive hostility is much easier than lessening excessive hostility that has previously been generated within the child, and especially the teenager. This is because lessening excessive hostility before it stabilizes in the psyche is much easier than to try to reduce stabilized excessive hostility that is embedded in the personality, a hard-earned lesson that society has learned from working with delinquent teenagers and adult criminals.

Preventing experiences of excessive unpleasure and lessening those experiences of excessive unpleasure that are unavoidable are two of the cardinal parenting activities that can lessen the chance of a child's becoming excessively hostile. The task is not easy. Because benign experiences of unpleasure lead to adaptation and to efforts toward mastery of self and environment and, therefore, are constructive, parents have to learn to differentiate between *benign* and *excessive* unpleasure.

So, too, we must distinguish between what is benign anger and even hostility, and what is excessive hostility and rage. Giving thought to what one feels to be benign and excessive is essential. Discussions of this between parents can be productive; they won't always agree, but they should decide what works for their family. Once this is done, trust in one's own feelings and judgment is an inherent requirement of growth-promoting parenting.

When the child experiences unpleasure, the parent's helpful actions can be highly instrumental in lessening the intensity of the pain. This is the magic of tender loving care (TLC), which some sadly believe "used to be," the single most factor that has made professional nursing so effective. Parenting TLC also lessens the likelihood of unpleasure becoming the usual way of experiencing specific events and life in general. It will also lessen the likelihood of hostility becoming an automatic reaction and too large a part of their child's personality.

WHAT YOUR CHILD'S EXPERIENCE OF EXCESSIVE UNPLEASURE LOOKS AND FEELS LIKE

To prevent or lessen the intensity of excessive unpleasure, parents have to have a pretty good idea of what their child's—whatever the age, infant or adolescent—experience of excessive unpleasure looks like and what it might feel like. Just as each child has his or her own particular way of expressing the experience of pain, of physical or emotional pain, each child has his or her own threshold for experiencing pain as excessive. Children vary in such thresholds from birth on.

Because such thresholds for pain tolerance are biologically determined, probably by the child's genes, that threshold tends to stay constant throughout the years. But, in some kids, that threshold may change over time; the child may as an adolescent have grown to tolerate emotional pain better depending on his life experiences. For instance, a teenager who has done well in school and has been able to make friends nicely over the years, will feel good about herself or himself. This will make the child's ability to tolerate pain better even though the teenager's gene pool has not changed. Good and bad experiences over time can raise (make the child tolerate pain better) or lower (make the child more susceptible to pain) the inborn threshold. As days and weeks pass, most parents come to really learn when their child's pain is too difficult to tolerate. Jan's mother read her daughter well and her approach to Jan was very helpful toward reducing the accumulation of pain in Jan.

In addition to the variability that may come over time, the threshold for experiencing pain as "too much" will vary within a given child from day to day, from morning to evening. For reasons that are not always clear to us, some days we are more easily upset than others. Many factors contribute to where our thresholds of irritability or pain tolerance may lie on any given day, at any given time. A parent may well think, "Hmm. Yesterday she seemed to handle it OK; what's up today?" This changing threshold makes it important for parents to be able to recognize the child's ways of communicating that he is experiencing excessive unpleasure. It's not rocket science; most parents do so intuitively. I am addressing it to emphasize its importance to the well being of the child.

First, as I said earlier, it is essential that parents open themselves to attempting to feel what the child is feeling. We are speaking, of course, of empathy. All parents are capable of empathy; most parents are marvelous at it. It is one of the most important capabilities required of parents to produce growth-promoting parenting. Ask yourself: "What is my child feeling right now?" There are many instances when that question ought to be asked, but a parent may be out of sorts, upset, or angry with the child, and perhaps even unwilling to ask it. Nonetheless, it is essential for recognizing the experience of excessive unpleasure in the child. We cannot say too often that empathy—the ability to sense and resonate with what another person is feeling and experiencing—is a cardinal requirement for growth-promoting parenting.

Children, from very early in life, express what they feel by means of both, bodily and facial behaviors and the sounds they make. Their expression of feelings is most readily visible in their faces.

Start by asking, "What is my child feeling and experiencing right now?" There are two principal ways to enhance the ability to answer that question. First, listen to the sounds the child is making. Even the newborn will make emotional sounds that are recognizable. Then look at the child's facial expression and bodily gestures. Try to guess what feelings are expressed through the sounds, the facial expressions, and the gestures. If you sounded, looked, and gestured like that, what would you be feeling? There's a strong chance that this is what your child is feeling.

If you continue to be puzzled, try the process the other way around. How would you react—in sounds, facial expression, and body movements—if you were frightened, hurt, sad, or enraged?

Parents get to know their babies by letting themselves feel, without thinking about it, what the baby is conveying to them. For instance, when a mother feeding her baby feels her infant stop the smooth, rhythmic sucking and swallowing and notices the tensing and contorting body in her arms, her attention is quickly drawn to the baby. She will think to herself, "Oh, oh, what's going on?" Without being aware of it, she prepares to act. She will already be open to several possible courses of action and, without much awareness that she is doing so, will decide to stop the nursing, chat with the baby, place the baby on her shoulder, try to facilitate a burp, and so forth. Much of this has gone on without conscious thought, through a wide-open channel of emotional communication.

The same goes with children through the years. Maintaining an open channel to feeling what one's child is experiencing, which comes so naturally to so many parents, is critical for the well being of one's babies. Though more critical for babies, experiencing the feelings of one's school-age kids and adolescents is enormously enhancing of their well being as well even when the children do resist confronting their own feelings. In fact, the parents being tuned into their children's feelings, facilitates their children's learning to tolerate their own feelings, even when these are painful.

One of the major obstacles to empathizing is that too many parents wrongly believe young children do not feel distress and pain, or that these will not be remembered in such a way as to emotionally affect the child. That is not the way it is. Young children do experience pain, even premature newborns. And they are likely to remember it emotionally for years to come, even if they can't tell you what they remember of it. Here's what we've learned during the past decades that explains why to think young children don't feel pain and that they won't remember it is not true.

There is a large literature coming from psychologically informed infant observation over the past 60 years[1] that documents, even in film and in the past couple decades in video recordings, that days-old and weeks-old infants experience pain, even bewildering pain. Procedures on premature newborns document that even they feel pain as recorded in their physical and emotional reactions.

That children won't remember their experiences of pain in later years, even into adulthood, has proven to be wrong by the findings of brain researchers as well as mental health researchers and clinicians who have done psychodynamic psychotherapies now for nearly a century. That humans remember intensely painful experiences[2] from very early in life is now also asserted by neurobiologists. Two findings of much importance to parents follow from some of the work carried out in the past several decades: (1) pain and the amygdala and (2) a greater understanding of the functions of memory.

1. *Pain and the amygdala:* Neurobiologists[3] have established that there are specific parts of the midbrain[4] that play a key role in the regulation of emotions; the amygdala is central to this regulation. They assert that the regulation of emotions is highly affected by traumatic experiences (i.e., emotionally painful experiences including fear and anxiety), which become encoded in the amygdala. When in infancy emotional pain is intense or excessive, the reactivity that follows becomes patterned, stabilizes, and can last a lifetime; this reactivity becomes part of the individual's character. This is why early childhood trauma has a long-lasting effect.
2. *Two types of memory:* what is experienced is also encoded in memory. An interesting problem has been clarified by contemporary studies of memory. While clinicians often see much evidence of significant early life trauma in patients, convincing clinical evidence pointing to trauma that arose in family life, especially in parent-child relationships, patients often cannot remember events to document such traumatization. Yet, explanation of such clinical evidence is sound, rigorous, and asserted by different schools of psychology that often do not agree on key matters of psychology. Studies of memory of the past several decades have clarified this dilemma, the link between the clinical evidence of trauma and the patient's failure to remember it. While the study of memory continues and, as is always the case in science many questions remain, it has been established that there are at least two basic forms of memory:[5]
   a. There is *implicit* (or *procedural*) memory, which is encoded in the mind at an unconscious level and is not readily accessible to the person who is trying to remember, and it may in fact never be accessible to the individual at will.
   b. There is *explicit* (or *declarative*) memory, which is encoded in the mind at a conscious level and is accessible, though not always easily, to be remembered at will.

These more recent studies of both our understanding of the registration in the brain of the child's experience from birth on and the encoding of these experience events in memory is critical for parents to be aware of. It is not true that infants do not experience pain and it is not true that they will not remember.

Yes, if the psychological pain is very intense, be it due to intense fear, intense shame, horror, bewilderment, or whatever, the child or adolescent will repress (quite common) or disengage from the experience causing this reaction by what we call dissociation (a quite serious, often crippling self-protective defense mechanism); then the person may not remember. But then, this will be at a heavy price to the person's mental health.

Healthy development begins at the beginning, in earliest infancy—in fact, even before that. As we will insist throughout these pages, mistakes in parenting can most often be repaired. And with good care most traumas can be reduced. Our aim is to facilitate parenting by informing our readers, by adding to the great care and devotion they bring to their parenting work.

A note of caution: I am not recommending that parents attempt to prevent all pain, discomfort, or distress—which is in fact impossible. I want to point out here that pain is not always bad; nor is anxiety, nor depression. In moderate doses, these experiences call for efforts by the child to adapt and develop increasingly reasonable pain and frustration tolerance, plus increased skills in coping with it and learn how to take steps to prevent it. The six-month-old who suffers from separation anxiety really has to make efforts to cope with it. What is needed is that when possible, parents must intervene at the point when the child conveys that his feelings are becoming too difficult to bear. Again, the parents' own gut responses—their instinctive feelings—should be taken into account and trusted.

CHILD TURNS TO THE CAREGIVER FOR THE RELIEF OF PAIN

From the earliest months of life, if not, in fact, from the first days of life, infants turn to those who nurture them for the relief of pain. Recent studies have revealed that infants recognize their mother's voice, their mother's smell, the feel of their mother's body, the feel of being held, the ways their mothers and fathers hold them. They begin from very early on, not only to identify, but also to respond to, the ways they are cared for, good as well as bad.

One can see evidence in all mammals, humans included, for their turning to primary caregivers for the relief of pain. The rapidity with which this natural self-protective reaction develops in the infant depends on the degree of capability with which he or she is born. Ethologists (who study the behavior of animals) have taught us that some newborns come into the world quite more capable than others. Just considering mammals for instance, newborns of cows, horses, and sheep are quite more developed than those of dogs and cats.

Infants of cows and horses can stand within minutes of being born; those of dogs and cats can only do so after days. Ethologists call those more "mature" at birth *precocial;* and those less mature, *altricial.* Think of "precocious" and you can remember which is which.

Humans are among the most *altricial* of organisms. This means that it takes much longer for the human newborn to learn to turn to the caregiver for help when he or she needs it. The newborn calf knows where to turn for nursing within minutes after birth. The human infant can't even move there and seems to not even know to turn there. Fortunately, Mother Nature equipped that infant with emotional-sound reactions that tell the caregiver "I need help"; he or she fusses, makes the sounds we make when we feel pain; if the pain mounts, the infant cries. That infant is totally dependent on what the caregiver does. Sure the cow can turn away from her young; but the infant calf is sure to follow and latch on; and if the mother-cow keeps moving away, the calf may even look elsewhere for those things you get milk from. The human infant can't do that. Those of us who observe infants come away with the impression that the human newborn's thinking system is not yet sufficiently developed to think "What can I do?" That infant is totally dependent on the caregiver to keep it alive.

When the mother responds to the infant's "I need help," the infant learns the degree to which he or she can trust that the caregiver will, or may, or will not respond with care. By the time the infant is about six months old, the infant has learned to trust or to not trust the caregiver to help.[6] This impacts heavily on whether the infant, then the child, then the adolescent will trust that turning to others for help can work well or decide that it is useless.

In our *Parenting for Emotional Growth* project (see chapter 1), parents would occasionally bring another young child along, sometimes to do a favor for a neighbor who needed someone to watch her child for a while. One mother, Mrs. S., brought in 3 1/2-year-old Kathy.

> Somehow, Kathy was standing on a couch. For some reason she decided to jump off. She crashed to the floor and hit her head hard on some hard toy. I winced. I was concerned and so were mothers who saw her crash. Kathy sobered but there was no "ouch" and she made no appeal for help. Surrounded by caring people, Mrs. S. saw her crash and was moving to get up. Kathy turned to no one. She just got up and walked away. I saw a red mark on her forehead. Why did she not even whimper, cry, or show any sign of pain? Sure, 3-year-olds are embarrassed when they fail at what they are trying to do. Observing kids, one sees a good deal of that. But they wince; they express pain when they crash onto a hard toy. They may not call mother for help, but one can see the reaction of feeling pain.

> Most 3-year-olds tend to whimper, and go to mother for some TLC. I wonder why she turned to no one.
>
> Mrs. S, who had brought Kathy, said that she's seen her do this. "What is it?" Mrs. S. asked. "She doesn't even cry." As we talked about this, the mother who had brought Kathy told us that Kathy's mother is having a hard time keeping up with the kids and all she has to do. Her kids tend to not be cared for well; they sometimes look like they need to be washed. Further exploration suggested that Kathy did not turn to people for help when she hurts herself. Mrs. S. felt bad for her. I put forward the idea that Kathy had learned to not ask for help because if she did, help would not be given. We talked further about this distressing development, or rather, lack of development of trust in Kathy, in kids.

So the turning to the caregiver for help is less secure in the human infant and is totally dependent on the caregiver's responses. Much infant work documents (see chapter 2) that infants are responsive to the way those who care for them feel about them. They can experience being comforted, being tended to tenderly, or being handled roughly, angrily, or indifferently. They can tell when they are held by the one or two people who "love" them, as compared with others. All of us, from the earliest days of our lives, can feel when we are with someone who likes us and feels warmly and lovingly toward us. We can also tell when we are with someone who is indifferent to us and fails to read our wishes, messages, and feelings. This perception is highly influential in determining the person the child will turn to for the relief of pain. The child turns for relief to the people to whom she or he is most emotionally attached. This has a number of advantages, including the insurance of attachment and socialization within families.

BE EMOTIONALLY AVAILABLE AND RESPONSIVE TO THE CHILD'S NEED FOR HELP

Having empathized and sensed that the child is turning to you (even when the child's or adolescent's appeal for help is not evident or directly stated), you need to be emotionally available.[7] That means not only that the parent has to be present, but also emotionally tuned in and responsive to the infant's need for help. Although the parent may be engaged in some other activity, he or she should be ready to assess the child's need and determine whether she or he ought to disengage from that activity and respond to the infant's appeal for help.

Parents, of course, always have too much work to do. There are times when it will not be possible for the parent to be responsive to the child's appeal.

For instance, mother may be in the middle of cooking, or writing out an idea she must commit to paper immediately, or some other activity that she cannot leave at the moment. At these times, a word that conveys the child is being heard and understood, but will have to wait a moment longer, can be helpful to the child and his feeling that he has been heard and that his pain is not a matter of indifference to the caregiver. Even young infants can be asked to wait for reasonable lengths of time and can be comforted by means of the mother's voice, a glance, or other responses. If the mother is able, her response to the infant's appeal can be immediate. It is not necessary, however, that parents respond with alarm or drop whatever they are doing and immediately turn to their infants whenever the infant complains. Judgment and common sense dictate how quickly the parent needs to respond to the infant's appeal for help.

It is important for kids to learn that they can turn to others whey they need help. Sure we want them to be able to stand on their own two feet, but they also need to learn that at some point, everyone needs help. And the child, like Kathy, or any teenager who has not learned that when needed she or he can turn to others who are capable of helping, may not trust teachers, police officers, and may later become the adult who does not trust doctors or lawyers who are well trained to help.

TRY TO IDENTIFY THE SOURCE OF THE EXCESSIVE UNPLEASURE

Next comes identifying the source of pain and distress and attempting to deal with it. Parents hardly need to be told this, because they find it quite natural to wonder "What's wrong?" I know that I am telling the reader things many a reader already knows and may think is obvious. Every parent knows that there are times when it is easy to identify what is wrong, and there are times when it is difficult, or even impossible. It is especially then, after many efforts do not succeed in calming a crying infant, that a parent may resort to the erroneous theory that the child cries because he needs to exercise his lungs.

Where possible, of course, once it is identified, the source of unpleasure is removed. However, there are many times when an identifiable source of unpleasure may not be entirely removable. Take, for instance, the young child who has a fever and picks at his ear, suggesting an earache. In such a situation, children of all ages become aware of the fact that the parent is trying to identify the source of unpleasure and put a stop to it. Even where the parent does not succeed in stopping the pain, the child is comforted by the fact that the parent is trying. Every parent perceives or comes to learn—except when the parent is upset—that her child feels valued when she makes an effort to help him, even when that effort does not succeed in removing the pain.

Most parents tend to comfort the child automatically, even before knowing what is causing the pain. That tendency is highly valuable because it promotes the child's feeling of being valued, of being in an environment that wants to help and can be helpful (even when it fails to be so). It enhances learning to be kind to oneself, to be helpful and kind to others, and it strengthens positive attachment and confidence in others. While it may tax the parent, when the child seeks comfort, a positive response is warranted. *Children do not seek comfort when they do not need it.*

The parent has an opportunity to be helpful to her child in what we in clinical mental-health work identify as "working through." Working through is a process in which an unpleasant experience—be it a trauma or an emotional conflict—is gradually dealt with in ways leading to an understanding of the nature of the trauma, reducing its impact, or resolving the conflict, and rendering the experience no longer excessively painful. We speak of it as "gaining mastery" over an experience in which we felt helpless. This can be done by talking about what happened immediately after the experience has subsided and then again talking about it later, even more than once.

Of course, there are times when kids don't want to talk about things that upset them; it's just too upsetting then to talk about. Respecting that however, does not mean that one should not try to bring it up at another time; it's good to try to do so when the child is calm or when the child is upset because something similar is in process of happening.

In *Psychodynamic Psychiatry and Psychology*,[8] nearly 100 years of clinical experience has documented the value of talking about upsetting experiences to someone who is willing and able to listen empathically. By talking about painful experiences one gradually, step by step, works through the painful experience. Such talking with someone who is empathic helps us metabolize the ill effects of the painful experience. This bears on the fact that talking things over is known in all walks of life to facilitate solving problems and make life better. To be sure it doesn't always work; but more often than not, it does.

Here is a simple example of working through.

> On the way home from a visit to neighbors who also have a 3-year-old, Mother says to 3-year-old Timmy, who seems a bit upset: "It was hard that Johnny didn't let you play with his new helicopter. But, you know, his daddy just gave it to him. Maybe next time you can ask him if he'll let you play with it." When Timmy responds that Johnny is bad, his mother listens to his complaint sympathetically. Then she tries to explain again that Johnny was just not ready to let Timmy play with it this time. She soothes his hurt feelings by letting him

> express them, being sympathetic, and explaining reasonably and truthfully why she believes Johnny would not let him play with his new toy helicopter.

There are, of course, much more serious issues that can benefit from talking together and working through, such as why Mother needs to leave Timmy to go to work, or why she had to go to the hospital for several days, and so forth. Interestingly, exploring a child's or adolescent's feelings by talking sympathetically about them also brings with it the message that it is desirable to try to express in words how one feels.

When children are allowed to express their feelings and even to complain—which is usually advantageous, unless it is abused—the child may bring the subject up himself or herself for the purpose of further working through and mastering the painful experience. Usually, when children bring up an event that caused them pain, it is because they have insufficiently mastered it and want a further opportunity to do so. Therefore, it is generally useful to allow the child, preschooler, or adolescent to talk about an event that caused pain and to help the child emerge with a better sense of being able to deal with such events. This helps the child or teenager acquire and further enhance his or her feeling capable of mastering painful, difficult, and challenging events. This counters the tendency for unresolved reactions to painful experiences to remain in a child's psyche and continue to impact on that child's emotional development.

We want to emphasize that it is highly protective of the child's well being when parents attempt to prevent experiences of excessive unpleasure where this is reasonably feasible. At the same time, we want to reiterate that parents cannot, and should not, always prevent benign experiences of unpleasure. Benign unpleasure experiences lead to adaptation and learning. (So may excessively painful ones; but the price for these may be very high and the outcome potentially very harmful.) Here's what benign unpleasure can do and note how early in life:

> Eighteen-week-old Jane reaches for a block just beyond her grasp. She reaches, strains, stops, stares at the block, readies again with effort, and groans, but can't get to it. She stops. She stares at the block again, looks puzzled and a bit frustrated; but pressured from within, she thrusts her entire body forward, brings her entire arm down reaching for the block, grasps it, and brings it to her mouth for exploration. She was frustrated by not being able to get hold of it. This produced a mild degree of unpleasure, propelling her to make the effort we saw—and she succeeded.
>
> Think of 10-year-old John who is grumpy and embarrassed that he missed a couple balls while playing with his Little League team. He struggles to catch a ball by repeatedly throwing it in the air and catching it. He doesn't always catch it. But, if he persists, no doubt he'll get there.

> Fifteen-year-old Jack is doing his algebra homework. He's stumped by a problem he just can't seem to get. He grumbles, uses an expletive that when in private often comes out of his mouth at such moments, but he persists. He is determined that he's going to lick this thing. Suddenly a light goes on and he gets it. His relief, his pleasure breaks into a smile. From frustration to victory.

Optimal emotional development requires both reasonable gratifications and frustrations. Parents do not need to frustrate their children in order to toughen them. Life frustrates all of us well enough, in and of itself. Furthermore, children know when they are being intentionally frustrated. This undermines the child's trusting the parent and experiencing the parent as someone he can turn to. To top it all off, it makes the child unnecessarily angry with the parent. However, we do not encourage parents to try to protect their children against reasonable frustrations. It is not desirable to protect the child against all hurt, frustration, and disappointment. Under favorable conditions it can be what motivates the child or adolescent to try harder and learn.

We all know it is not always possible to avoid experiences of excessive unpleasure. The important factor is that, a parent's efforts to make his or her child feel better is never lost on a child. Experiences of unpleasure invariably make the child feel the need for soothing, for proof of being loved, and for proof of the parent's interest in and caring for the child—even when the parent's actions (or the child's experience of them) have been the source of the excessive unpleasure. We have learned that gratifying the need to be comforted within the experience of excessive unpleasure is highly growth promoting. Every parent has had the experience of a young child sustaining a benign injury, in response to which the child comes to the mother for help. Often, the mother's kissing the hurt body part, be it a finger, a hand, or a nose, may be all that is required to make the distress and feeling of hurt go away. We all know that the mother's show of tender loving care has magnificent pain-reducing and healing powers.

The less the excessive unpleasure experience, the better it is reduced, shortened, resolved, and worked through, the less hostility will be generated and mobilized in the child, teenager, and even the adult.

NOTES

1. Rene Spitz and John Bowlby in the 1950–1980s, the present work of Ed Tronick, Beatrice Beebe, others during the first decade of this new century, and many researchers in between, have reported such documentation.

2. This, by the way, applies to species other than *Homo sapiens* (humans) as well. It is well known by dog owners who own an animal that was traumatized as a pup. It

has been studied in monkeys by Harry Harlow, Steve Suomi, and others, and in apes by Jane Goodall and others.

3. Regina Pally has pulled together much of this research and developed a scholarly treatise detailing *The Mind-Brain Relationship* (London: International Psychoanalytic Association/Karnac, 2000). See also Joseph LeDoux's *The Emotional Brain* (New York: Simon and Schuster, 1996) as well as Allan Shore's *Affect Dysregulation and Disorders of the Self* (New York: WW Norton, 2003).

4. What is known as the "old brain," or most basic part of the brain, that in essence all mammals have.

5. Lotte Koehler has pulled together much memory research and applied it to the development of what is being considered *The Autobiographical Self* (L. Koehler, "On the development of the Autobiographical Self and Autobiographical memory—Implicit and Explicit aspects"), which she presented at the International Self Psychology Symposium Dreieich on May 27, 2005.

6. Erik Erikson taught us that in the late fifties. E. H. Erikson. "Identity and the life cycle." *Psychological Issues* 1(1959):1–170.

7. Margaret S. Mahler put this principle forward in her work on the development she called "Separation-Individuation." See M. S. Mahler, F. Pine, & A. Bergman, *The Psychological Birth of the Human Infant* (New York: Basic Books, 1975).

8. In a simplified explanation, the "psychodynamic" approach is to look for the meaning of experiences, to look at the nature of causes and effects of the experience, at the strategies we use, consciously and unconsciously, to cope with them, at ways to improve strategies for coping, etc. We think of these operations as the dynamics operating in our psyche, therefore, "psychodynamic." It is an approach based on experiential causes and effects, in contrast to—but not apart from biological causes and effects. For example, "my mother's sick (cause) and I'm really worried (effect)." Or, "he hit me (cause), so I hit him back (effect)."

Chapter 6

Recognizing and Securing the Child's Need for Sufficient and Reasonable Autonomy

Many years ago, in the course of training residents in child psychiatry, we made a visit to the home of Mrs. Jones during which we had the troubling occasion to observe the following situation.

> A 22-month-old boy was continually being reprimanded by his mother for touching things—ashtrays, picture frames, knickknacks, a radio, a television—all of which were easily within his reach in the living room and kitchen. Mother was enormously frustrated by her child's constant need to touch things. She frequently scolded him and was constantly on her feet, pulling him away from one thing after another. Gradually the child's frustration mounted, he became angry, sulking, and a very distressing battle of wills developed between the two of them.

To a greater or lesser degree, every parent of a nearly two-year-old child has similar experiences. This is where the challenge of getting our children to comply with our rules, regulations, wishes, and hopes begins (see chapter 8). It starts very early in life and does not stop until children turned adolescents leave home to fend for themselves in the world of adults.

It is in the child's and the parents' best interest to recognize that the development of a healthy sense of self, so vitally important to feeling like a competent individual, is propelled by strong internal forces. I detail the play of these sense-of-self-developing forces in chapter 8. While the child needs to be guided in order to develop into a competent adult, excessive frustration of her or his strivings to develop a sense of self often becomes a generator of heightened hostility in the individual.

During our child observations, we have gotten the impression that inborn, inner pressures to act drive the child to actions, which, even the child herself or himself at times, seems surprised by. However, even if troublesome, the child's experience of these inner pressures to act, which are both biologically and psychologically driven and are essential for coping in life, needs to be protected and progressively organized by the child. We must provide the necessary guidance and protection in ways that will enhance the child's ability to be constructively determined and assertive in achieving his or her goals. But at the same time, we want to do so without, where possible, causing an undue generation (production) and mobilization of hostility within the child.

In order for this to occur, it is necessary to understand and respect one's child's needs for age-appropriate autonomy and opportunities for exploration and for doing new things, while at the same time we need to set reasonable limits and help the child to master her or his inner pressures and wishes.

A major protective strategy proposed decades ago by the pediatrician Ben Spock, "baby proofing the house"[1] will prevent much unnecessary frustration of the child's seemingly obligatory explorations, as well as much unnecessary parents' needing to set limits, and thus prevent unnecessary conflicts between parent and child, all of which produce pain and heighten hostility in both toward one another. Had the mother of the 22-month-old we observed sufficiently baby proofed the house, the torturing conflict between the child and his mother might not have happened or at worst would have been much less than what we witnessed. When possible, it is advantageous for parents to help the child in his or her explorations when the child needs and asks for it. When it seems reasonable to the parents, it is advantageous to allow the child to learn and explore on his or her own, especially when that is what the child, toddler, or adolescent wants. Children at all ages need age-appropriate opportunities to do things on their own, in order to become independent (autonomous) problem-solvers. Finally, it helps if parents find safe and reasonable ways to enhance the child's progressive explorations and attempts to learn about the world and how to master it. The child's becoming an independent explorer and autonomous problem-solver can evolve dramatically over the years and make him or her feel competent to cope with life's challenges—which begin very early in life.

RATIONALE

Studies show that during certain periods of wakefulness from even the first days and weeks of life, infants tend to be busy moving about and exploring their surroundings. They do this visually at first, by looking about themselves.

Soon, when the capability for it emerges, they begin to physically explore their own bodies, their caregiver's, and their environment. We consider this thrust to activity to be an effort to master everything, one's own body and the heretofore unknown environment into which the child is born.

As every mother of an average one- to two-year-old knows, there are many instances when she will have to intervene in the child's behalf because the child's explorations may lead to harm to herself, the mother, or some valued possession. Parental interventions of this kind are necessary for the well-being, protection, and socialization of the child. With all children, such parental and other adult (such as teachers) interventions are needed as the years pass, well into adolescence.

From the middle of the first year of life on, parents will find that interfering with an infant's thrust toward exploring often leads to a reaction of frustration or anger. Where such interferences occur frequently, frustration and anger will mount. Too much frustration of the thrust to explore and master all kinds of things, of strivings toward autonomy from the first years of life and thereafter, is experienced as excessively unpleasurable and generates anger and hostility toward the frustrator.

It is important to recognize that too much frustration of autonomy strivings—especially in the form of exploration and the mastery of self and environment—during the first years of life, may interfere with the thrust to learn, to develop learning skills that serve adaptation, and with it may interfere with the optimal development of intelligence.

Therefore, through the length of childhood and adolescence, it would seem highly advantageous for parents to provide an environment that will allow for sufficient and reasonable autonomous activity. This does not mean that parents should allow the child or adolescent to do anything he or she might wish to do. But it does mean that, while parents make it as safe for their child or adolescent as they can, parents should be open to their child or, certainly, their teenager, to do things the parent might feel too bashful, or too timid, or even too frightened to do. Like in all challenges that confront parents, parental judgment and reason should prevail. Often, the opinion of trusted, knowledgeable friends, or that of a child development professional may serve well.

WHAT MOTIVATES THIS TYPE OF BEHAVIOR?

A number of factors operate within the infant to bring about the kind of activity we saw in the 22-month-old boy we mentioned at the beginning of this chapter. There are a number of ways of looking at it, and varying explanations have been put forward. This is ours.

From about the middle of the first year of life, we saw the following type of activity in everyone of the normal children in our project[2]: a notable increase in energy that propels locomotion (crawling and walking); a notable increase in interest in and curiosity about the infant's immediate surrounding environment, with what seemed to be an increased need and push to explore that environment; all in all, a notable inner pressure to do this. We have proposed that a maturational spurt of motor (physical) energy is occurring in the child, which includes an upsurge of aggression that gives character to the activities just described. This aggression is nondestructive, and it plays a critical role in the development of mastery of one's self and the environment, including caregivers and things within the infant's field of vision. This nondestructive aggression (see chapter 5) fuels strivings toward becoming an individual and strivings toward autonomy. Furthermore, it plays a large part in learning about the self and the environment, as well as in the development of skills and adaptation.

I want to emphasize that the motivation for these activities and strivings toward autonomy arises from within the child. These inner pressures and strivings for autonomy are biological and psychological. The child is driven by these inner pressures, is as much subjected to this inner force as are the objects the infant explores and may break. It's like the child's motor engine is turned on, and the child is propelled to act, not yet knowing how to apply the brakes and just learning to steer himself to whatever thing attracts his or her attention.

In the example cited above, like many a parent, Mrs. Jones was not aware that her young child was driven by inner forces over which he was just in the process of developing some control. Children under these conditions seem at times to behave as though someone turned a switch on. They are being driven by the released energy, and they have to progressively learn how to stop that energy from pushing them into activity.

Parents commonly believe their child's inner drive is intentional, something the child has control over. They see their child as willful and intentionally provocative. Surely, at some point in the course of development, every child's activity is intentional, and many a child does become willful and obnoxious. However, it is important for parents to recognize that there is a motivational force at play, over which the child, in the first two years of life, is just beginning to learn to control. Then the child needs the parent's help in developing these controls. We have found children to be occasionally bewildered by things they do when their inner drive pushes them to get their hands on things around them.

One 14-month-old, in reaching for a lamp he was drawn to, pushed it as he was exploring it. His interest and curiosity changed to surprise and fear when the lamp fell with a crash. Although it did not break, the child reacted with distress and started to cry. Think also of the 18-month-old who got hold of mother's paper cup of hot coffee and took a sip before mother could get to him. His shock on contact with the hot coffee just made him drop it—with, of course, messy results. Every parent has seen her child react with fear when he or she has unexpectedly damaged something. Although this fear at times is due to the threat of parental disapproval, the child's fear is especially due to her or his own feeling of losing control. With this comes the terrible fear of not being safe and in certain troubling home circumstances the fear of becoming violent and destructive of others and even oneself.

WHAT CAN THE PARENT DO?

First, with regard to the child's autonomy, parents decide what is desirable, and the limits of what is permissible and what is not, in accordance with their personal and their community's—ethnic, religious, cultural—standards of behavior. But this lasts predominantly from infancy to the preadolescent years, given that the teenager will more or less challenge the parents' standards of behavior under the influence of their newly forming community, the peer group, as the peer group's standards of behavior increasingly bear a strong influence.

In chapter 8, I raise more centrally the questions of "What kind of persons do we want our children to become? What kind of member of society? What degree and type of compliance do we expect from them? Do we want a child who will blindly obey what we say we expect of him or her; or do we want a child who will comply with what we expect, but retain a measure of judgment about what we are expecting him to do?" Some cultures demand absolute obedience; others expect compliance but do not want their children to just do what they are told without weighing the potential consequences and moral character of their actions. In all these considerations, the degree to which we want our children to assume a sense of autonomy has a direct bearing. What we want of our children will dictate the degree to which we foster or disallow their developing sense of autonomy.

In this regard, perhaps it comes down to these overly simplified questions:

1. Do we want our children to grow into confident, self-reliant, contributing members of society, or do we want them to become pawns of the state ready to execute whatever orders we give them for what is assumed to be the benefit of the state?

2. Do we want them to become hostile and hating adults ready to turn their hostility and hate into killing others in war and genocide, or do we want them to them to live as peaceful members of society, rearing reasonable children in warm families, but also ready to fight for their home and country if necessary?

Yes, these are simplified questions, but they are pertinent to the question, do we want each of our children to have a stable sense of autonomy and self-reliance and be responsible to society, or do we want them to be pawns of an authoritarian government and society ready to execute its laws, whatever they are?

Now, as I already said, the motor inner drive we have just talked about—which serves adaptation and the development of intelligence—challenges both infant and mother; it begins to emerge during the middle of the first year of life. Children are truly unable to control these inner pressures at the outset. And this is in part why we start from quite early on to teach them what they can and cannot do; this is when we begin to help them learn to become disciplined. Reasonable guidance from their parents is required to help them gradually learn to control these inborn pressures. Normal development soon also brings with it other types of inner pressures, physical and psychological, that will require of the child to progressively exercise self-control. Reasonable parental guidance will of course continue throughout childhood: from infancy into the toddler years when greater bodily capabilities invite taking on greater challenges to mastering oneself and the environment; into the elementary school years when peer activity invites taking on yet greater developmental challenges as in sports, riding wheeled vehicles, climbing trees, as well as that driven by sexual interest, etc.; and well into adolescence where physical and psychological experiences entice the individual to new adventures of all kinds, including sports, sex, alcohol, and drugs. In addition, the large adolescent challenge of shifting the center of one's universe from the nuclear family to the peer group[3] tends to create greater or lesser challenges for both adolescent and parents.

The second thing is well known to all parents and has been talked about for decades. Benjamin Spock and many other pediatricians have rightly advised parents to baby proof the house. It is possible, without making one's house threadbare and unattractive, to put breakable, valuable, and dangerous items out of the reach of children. This will facilitate the caregiver's challenging job and protect the child's sense of well-being. It will provide an environment less likely to interfere with the child's curiosity, the exercise of his beginning skills as an explorer and a student of the universe in which he lives, and the development of the skills this kind of interest and exploration brings. It will decrease the frequency of experiencing excessive unpleasure and excessive frustration at the hands of a mother who is attempting to protect her valuables as well as her highly valued infant. Thus it will prevent the unnecessary generation and mobilization of hostility and make life easier for mother and child. House proofing to match the child's developing ability to evaluate what can and cannot hurt her and her ability to control her body, as well as its inner pressures, will prevent crises that produce pain and heighten hostility.

However, as all parents know, even the best house proofing for babies and our best strategies for making life safe for children and adolescents will not prevent some falls, breakages, resistance, and unpleasant encounters between child and parent. Unavoidable everyday crises will result from the need to limit a child's activities, to deny a child's wish, to say "no." All parents have experienced battles of wills with their infants, toddlers, school-age kids, and teenagers. Where good handling of battles of wills can be achieved in the early years, it is highly likely that they will occur less and less as time passes. Where they are handled in an authoritarian manner, they may seem to get resolved obediently during the early years but may be overturned during adolescence, sometimes in a vigorous rebellion. We will talk about handling such events and crises in the chapters that follow on compliance and on setting limits constructively.

A third consideration of importance to child and parent follows here. Much exploratory-mastery activity, school-learning activity, and development of skills, be it in sports or artistic endeavors, serves strivings toward autonomy, individuality, and the development of self. At times these efforts are best exercised when the child tries things on her or his own. At other times, the child needs the help of a teacher, the first teacher of every child being, of course, the care-giving parent. From infancy on, it is enormously helpful (to both child and parent) when the parent can determine whether the child wants to "do it myself" or wants help. Given the chance, children of all ages usually communicate clearly whether or not they want help.

As in all parenting, reasonableness should determine the parent's behavior. If there is a risk in letting a child do what she wants—for example, the two-year-old who wants to climb on a chair to help mother or father cook, or the 14-year-old who insists on driving mom's car—generally ought to be disallowed. If the nine-year-old wants to help father fix a leaking water faucet, it may take more time, but the benefits can be large to the child's feeling of competence, increasing individual skills, and relatedness to her father. If time is short, the child should be told so, and occasion taken another time to allow the parent to help the child do something she or he has not yet learned.

Of special importance to this issue of enhancing strivings for autonomy is to let the child do things by herself or himself. Children need age-appropriate opportunities to feel independent and autonomous (I can decide or do this). At the beginning, the parents virtually do everything for the child: make all the decisions, feed the child when he or she is hungry, and help her or him get to bed. This gradually expands to the child's letting parents know that he or she prefers certain foods, and later still, that he or she wants to choose certain clothes. Again, when it seems reasonable, children should be allowed to make independent decisions of an age-appropriate nature.

Parents of young children sometimes want to help when the child may not want help. The child may then experience the offered help as an intrusion or even as indicative that the parent doesn't believe the child can do this. This causes frustration of autonomy strivings, unpleasure, and annoyance in the child, much to the dismay of the parent, who really just wanted to help. Help is great—when it is felt needed by the person being helped. Otherwise it may be experienced as interfering with the child's own efforts to master and grow. Then, the effort to help can generate hostility.

Of course, it is helpful when parents devise age-appropriate ways of enhancing a toddler's bustling curiosity and interest in the world the child is discovering day by day. So too, some elementary school-age kids and adolescents may strive better when their efforts are facilitated by parents' support and encouragement to take on new challenges. Most children of all ages are deeply curious and interested in learning about things that are novel and that they see others engage in. From very early on kids seem pressured from within to know things, in order to have a feeling of mastery over them. Finding ways to allow safe, reasonable, and supervised exploration is highly desirable from early childhood on. We believe that good learning habits begin in the toddler and are then generally carried into their schoolwork and beyond.

Now let's talk about one of the major challenges for both child and parent, one that invariably generates and mobilizes hostility in both child and parent: the complex task of getting children to comply with our expectations, which brings us head on with the difficult challenge to help them develop discipline which, in turn brings with it the need for limit setting and punishment. We'll take this up in two chapters. In chapter 7 we'll take up the question of achieving compliance by our children with our expectations—which are society's expectations—and in chapter 9, we'll take up strategies for developing discipline, for limit setting and for punishment.

NOTES

1. Benjamin Spock is responsible for having introduced this valuable concept in his book *Baby and Child Care,* which has undergone many revisions since 1957.

2. We did not see this mid-first-year activity in one child who was born with cerebral palsy, which even with very good care, sadly, seriously hampered her development.

3. In going from being a child to becoming an adult, one must make the decade-long journey of adolescence, during which major challenges have to be addressed. Among these, foremost is making the shift from the nuclear family as center of one's universe to that of the peer group. This is in order to be securely engaged in that universe of peers from which a mate will be chosen to continue the sequence of generations and the preservation of the species.

Chapter 7

Compliance

Compliance Versus Obedience

One of the most challenging tasks pertaining to our handling aggression constructively in our children and adolescents is that of obtaining compliance from them, to achieve this task in growth-promoting ways.

What do we mean by compliance? In child rearing, in some corners of the world, another goal is aimed for, it is to obtain obedience. The central concern I hold is that the two, compliance and obedience, are vastly different concepts that have vastly different consequences. Given that we do not all use these concepts, *compliance* as well as *obedience,* similarly, I must define the way I use them. And, because of the relevance *compliance* and *obedience* bear on "what kind of kids do we want our children to become," a question crucial to society as well as to parents and the children, I have turned to the *Oxford English Dictionary* for the authoritative definitions I shall use for these concepts.

Compliance is "acting in accordance with, or the yielding to a desire, request, condition" stated by another. This dictionary states that it is "a consenting to act in conformity with, an acceding to, practical consent. . . ." The dictionary defines *comply* as "to fulfill, . . . to be accommodating, . . . to do the civil or polite [thing], . . . to make oneself agreeable" (492–493). Interestingly, the obsolete sense of the word the dictionary states is: the "practice of civility . . . agreement, harmony, amicable relations" (492). This conforms to my grasp of the word "compliance."[1] For our purposes here, I understand compliance to be the child's accepting and conforming, even if against initial or continuing resistance, to the parent's expressed wish that he or she behave in accordance with the parents expectations of the child. In this, the child yields but also chooses, for a combination of reasons, to do what the parent wishes.

The *Oxford English Dictionary* defines *obedience* as "submission to the rule or authority of another; compliance with a command, law, or the like." Interestingly, the *OED* includes *passive obedience*: "[to allow oneself] to be treated according to the will of another; in which [one] suffers without remonstrance or resistance. . . . Unqualified obedience or submission to authority, whether the commands be reasonable or unreasonable, lawful or unlawful" (1,962). This definition too conforms to my grasp of and concern with the concept obedience. Here then, I propose that to obey is to yield to authority and to do as ordered or commanded; it allows no opinion or question; it disallows argument and requires no explanation. "Don't even think; do it!" It is authoritarian.

WHAT KIND OF CHILDREN DO WE WANT?

The principles by which we rear our children determine what kind of children and then adults they are likely to become. In chapters 2 and 3, I spoke of the positive correlation social scientists have found between the way we treat our children and the aggression profile they develop. And many such scientists have documented correlations between harsh handling of children—be it physically or emotionally harsh (as in humiliating) handling—and delinquent and criminal behaviors. It is well known that humans with large loads of accumulated hostility and hate are likely to turn it against others. Such persons can readily be set into discharging their hate against a designated chosen victim.

Similarly, anthropological studies[2] have documented that harsh treatment of children—where fathers are harshly authoritarian and strict, even brutal disciplinarians—correlates strongly with these children becoming more hostile, hating, and destructive over time. These anthropologists also found that the harsh treatment of children is programmed in societies that more than others rear their children to engage in warfare. This seemed to also be at the core of the Nazi ideology, which ruled Germany from 1933 to 1945. W. Bohleber[3] tells us that aiming to make "Arian" men "hard and manly, . . . Nazi ideology [carried with it] sternness toward the ill, the weak, and foreigners, the inability [or disallowance of the ability] to empathize, [and brashly proclaimed its] aggressive ideas of purity and fantasies of national grandeur" (5, 10).

Whether we expect compliance or obedience in our children bears on the question: what kind of kids, and later adults, do we want our children to become? We do have choices. It is noteworthy that, according to Lotte Koehler (personal communication) who knows his work well, the late German social historian Hans Kilian found that most cultures have highly similar views on what is morally right and what is wrong, what is believed to be desirable and undesirable. Let me again pose the questions I put to the reader in chapter 7:

1. Do we want our children to grow into confident, self-reliant, contributing members of society or do we want them to become pawns of the state ready to execute whatever orders we give them for what is assumed to be the benefit of society and the state?
2. Do we want them to live as peaceful members of society, rearing reasonable children in warm families, but also able and ready to fight for their home and country if necessary; or do we want them to them to become hostile and hating adults ready to turn their hostility and hate into killing others who have different life views?

I assert that these differences are strongly facilitated by expecting compliance or, instead, by demanding obedience.

WHY IS ACHIEVING COMPLIANCE SUCH A CHALLENGE?

Achieving obedience in children is not difficult: just crush their emerging sense of self and their strivings for autonomy, which some parents and teachers see as their stubbornness or their self-centeredness according to Koehler and Bohleber; some have even declared that to achieve obedience, "the child's will or stubbornness must be broken."[4] Threaten them and punish them harshly. They will obey!

Achieving compliance is more difficult. Here is why.

If as I have proposed all the trends in aggression are in the service of the child's achieving his wishes, aims, and goals and to gain mastery over himself or herself and the environment in which the child exists, aggression, then, is in the service of the child's adaptation to life. In adaptation to his or her particular life, there is a direct but complex relation between the child's aggression and the development of his sense of self, of others, and his relationship to them.

The development of the sense of self—"I am Joseph or Josephine"—is essential to not only adaptation, but also specifically to developing a sense of "I can do this or that" or "I can make this happen," to setting up goals for oneself, feeling reasonably self-confident, persevere, take on responsibility, be a contributing member of society, and more. We all think about this; we even ask our children, "What are you going do when you grow up?" We want them to feel: "I am capable of doing this or that. I don't need someone to do it for me." We all want our children to become competent individuals, which means that each must have a sufficiently stable sense of autonomy, the sense of "*I* am able to do" or "*I* am able to make this happen."

But there is a powerful inborn factor at work in developing a sense of self and of autonomy. It is *primary narcissism*, a term coined by Sigmund Freud.[5] By this term, Freud spoke of an inborn sense of being valuable and of being meaningful. This sense of being valuable at birth is focused on the self because the newborn's very immature ability to perceive is centralized on his or her own feelings and needs; what comes from within his or her own body. The newborn's own feelings and needs give rise to his or her first sensory perceptions. These are the infant's first step in developing the ability to perceive, that is, to think.[6] Thus, the foremost domain of life the newborn perceives is himself or herself. As Kohut[7] has emphasized (and I have, too), primary narcissism is a healthy sense of self value. Freud did not mean a sense of being better than or superior to others, nor of being prideful.

What in essence is primary narcissism, where does it come from? There is a biological imperative in all living organisms to maintain its own life and stay alive. Primary narcissism, I have come to suggest,[8] is the psychological manifestation of this biological imperative to maintain life, to survive, because of the organism's inherent self value. This inherent self value is the biological imperative that leads living organisms to "fight to the death" or to take flight in the face of deadly force, the well-known biological concept of "fight or flight" in the face of a threat to life.[9] Living substance fights to stay alive.

There is a biopsychological link between the self's primary narcissism and aggression.[10] One could say that primary narcissism uses the force of aggression to maintain the self's life. In fact, Phyllis Greenacre speaks of the inherent form of aggression I call *nondestructive aggression* as a "force of growth" and Donald Winnicott speaks of it as "life force." As I reported in 1979, a number of psychoanalysts saw the need to consider a trend in aggression that serves adaptation. The long and short of it is that the self's primary narcissism uses the force of nondestructive aggression to fuel the child's developing sense of autonomy, that factor that leads the toddler to say "me do it!" when he or she wants to do something the mother is trying to do for the child. When the parent allows it, many a toddler will want to "me do it!" While we all like to have things done for us, to be served in various normal settings, this does not take away from our need to feel competent to do whatever we decide we need to do.

So, once the young child is able to move about—usually from about four to six months of age on evidenced in the child's beginning to crawl—developing his or her sense of self and the sense of autonomy, the child begins to orient to the universe in which she or he lives. But while the infant's familiarity with this universe is already rich, it is nonetheless very sparse: the infant is really only beginning to know its mother and father and those who buzz around him or her and take care of the baby. But once able to move about, the now accessible universe becomes enticing, exciting, and the infant often feels he must explore it. Just as "nature abhors a vacuum," as we say in medicine, so too the infant abhors living in a universe he or she does not know, at least not well enough. Enticed, excited, the infant starts to actively explore his surroundings. And if it has not yet been necessary, now it will become necessary for the primary caregiver, most commonly the mother, to set limits. And this is where this challenge begins, for both child and mother.

The challenge emerges when, seeing the child is doing or is about to do something that will put him or her or something the mother values at risk, mother tells the child "You can't do that!" The child's behavior suggests to him or her this means, "You can't do what you want to do!" The challenge lies in the fact that the mother's task and the child's wish are in conflict with one another.

The mother's experience is, "I need to protect my child from doing something that may cause him, or me, or something I value, harm." Or "I have to insist, for his own good, that he has to do what I am telling him to do. As a responsible mother, I have to do this."

The child's experience is something like, "My mother won't let me do what my sense of autonomy drives me to need to do. I didn't choose to do what I'm doing—I've got to do it." And the child feels, "She is stepping on my sense of self." And this, experienced by the child as an injury to his or her sense of self, to his or her healthy narcissism, causes more or less intense emotional pain and thereby generates hostility in the child toward the mother (or father) who is setting limits. Where these conflicts between child and parent are too frequent and too intense, the level of hostility generated in the child and in the mother or father will be high.

The conflict between young child and mother is real. To be a responsible mother she must at times step on her child's emerging sense of self and of autonomy. I'll take up the challenge of limit setting in the next chapter.

COMPLIANCE VERSUS OBEDIENCE AND PERSONALITY FORMATION

Whether we parents, and later educators, expect compliance or obedience, and how we achieve each using the strategies needed to do so, discipline, setting limits and punishment, has far-reaching consequences not only for the child's developing sense of self, but also for the child's personality formation.

Some of the things we do in rearing our children have greater weight than others in how we impact their personality formation. For example, whether we treat them with manifest (emotional and physical) affection, or we hold back on showing our loving feelings in our care of them; whether we believe they understand what we say to them, or we believe that children don't understand us until they're in the first grade or even later, so why talk to them before then; whether or not we talk to them and we listen to what they have to say; whether we expect them to learn in school and do their homework, or feel these are not important; all of these carry much weight in how our children will grow up. Other things we do, of course, play their part too. But it is psychologically clear that in the things we do, we choose the kind of society members we hope they'll become.

COMPLIANCE

In all cultures parents are challenged to secure from their children sufficient compliance with family expectations—which, as Freud observed in 1939,[11] in turn are the expectations society has of its members. Such compliance plays a major part in preparing our children for a productive life, in organizing groups into societies and in making these societies functional and able to secure their survival. But in behavioral science we have found that compliance, like many other behavioral traits and other things in life, can carry with it a more or less undesirable price if it is either excessive (and becomes obedience), or if it is insufficient.

For those among us who do not assume that human nature is inherently destructive, we must recognize that compliance, to agree to do what an authority expects one to do, in rearing our children often tends to go against the nature of one's healthy narcissism and one's healthy sense of self, which inherently seeks autonomy and competence: "I want to do what I want to do." To adapt well when we are young, however, our combined healthy narcissism and sense of self is not always the wisest guide to secure survival and a good life. The three-year-old who wants to chase his ball into the street values his ball, but he had better not just blindly run after it; nor, should the teenager who wants to please his friends agree to drink a bottle of vodka to show how manly he is. More than just their healthy narcissism has to have input in their decision to act. Listening and complying with "Don't do that" or "You must do this" is often very healthy and even life preserving.

Expectation of compliance starts very early, even before that ball-chasing three-year-old. The seven-month-old infant who bites his mother's breast cannot yet anticipate and conceptualize he would cause her pain. The mother's reaction begins to teach him that he did so.

Many a seven- or eight-year-old, having been in school for seven hours, feels he's put in a full day and, once home does not want to do his homework. But we parents know that in order to grow in his ability and into a person who develops good work ethics, he must do his homework. Now or later, that he can choose, but by evening, he must get his homework done.

For the teenager, the balance of facts is different. She is able to think about the reality she lives in. But she is challenged by her peers to do something they all know, but for a variety of reasons need to deny: too much alcohol can kill you. The teenager is individuating, separating from her nuclear family. She has to gradually move into her own changing universe, which more and more during adolescence is the world of her peers. Mother Nature dictates this shift in the center of the adolescent's universe: from the nuclear family to his or her peer group, because this is where he'll or she'll find a mate. And side by side with this, the adolescent has to progressively be able to make it on his or her own. Adult authority, the parent-equivalent authority, is what the adolescent is trying to free himself or herself from. The quality of the more than one decade-long relationship to the parents will be transferred to that of the parent-equivalent authority. If the child trusts the parents—due to the positive quality of their long-term relationships—the teenager is likely to trust parent-equivalent authority, and resistance to that authority will be modest. Where the adolescent's relationships to the parents is burdened with abuse and neglect, the relationship is insecure, trust will be weak or even replaced with mistrust;[12] so will parent-equivalent authority not be trusted, and the hope for love and trust in others will often be sought for in the peer group.

As a member of a society, the individual cannot function at his or her best, be confident, self-reliant, and use rational morality-based judgment, if the demands of that society disallow excessively the individual's sense of self and healthy narcissism. Humans are pack animals. Well or not, they collaborate in packs to survive; for better or worse, each member of the group makes his or her individual society-surviving contribution.

In time of war, when it is recognized to be for the good of the community, of one's family, of one's compatriots, compliance may take on the color of obedience. War-contingent compliance, even under conditions of war does not demand abdication of the sense of self; it engages the self to safeguard the common good. In obedience, the sense of self is more or less abdicated: the self submits to authority without having an opinion or daring to question. And in passive obedience, the self is completely abdicated: it submits in "unqualified obedience . . . [even] whether the commands [are] unreasonable . . . or unlawful" (The *Oxford English Dictionary,* 1,962), as was adopted by many who embraced the Nazi ideology.[13]

The abdication of the self can only be compelled by disallowing, suppressing, or even crushing the child's inborn primary narcissism and thrust to autonomy. If these are disallowed, it leads to a lesser or greater degree of narcissistic injury in the form of frustration, which generates in the child *hostile aggression.* If these are "suppressed," it will lead to a greater feeling of narcissistic injury and generate in the child more intense negative feelings of *hostile* destructiveness. If they are crushed, it will further intensify the narcissistic injury, which will generate high level hostile destructiveness, possibly in the form of rage, that generally cannot be discharged against the crushing authority due to dread of strong rejection, or even annihilation. In addition, due to internal developmental dynamics, when the child is enraged he in turn dreads that he will be destroyed.[14] The intense hostility, hate, or rage remains internalized in the child creating internal turmoil and anxiety.

To cope with these intense feelings of hostility, hate, and rage, defense mechanisms are activated to reduce the anxiety they stir within the child, and within any of us. Among the mechanisms commonly activated, most troublesome for family life and society are the (1) displacement of these unwanted feelings, and (2) identification with the aggressor. Both of these invoke the subsidiary mechanisms of what I have called[15] (3) reality-distorting defenses, which include, "reductionism, caricaturing, depreciation, vilification, . . . and generalization" of the "other" who is selected as the subject upon whom the high-level hostility is displaced and these defense mechanisms are enacted.

In displacement, we direct our accumulated feelings of hate and rage onto others, rather than to those who caused the feelings in the first place. Innocent others then become victimized. In identification with the aggressor, we act like the harsh abusive parent or authority by whom, one was victimized. In reality-distorting defenses we falsify the characteristics of the factually innocent other, in order to give oneself reason for maltreating, even killing him.

Regarding identification with the aggressor, Anna Freud suggests that this defense results from transforming oneself into being like the frightening abuser: "If I act like a ghost, I'm not afraid of ghosts." Lotte Koehler[16] suggests that it may also result from taking on the role of identifying with the powerful victimizer. Both explanations are sound. A colleague (who asked not to be identified) found this in a very young painfully traumatized patient who told him, "You're trying to make me not be so mad, but when I'm mad I feel strong!"

To harshly control and rigorously regulate children's inborn dispositions, which create in them the tendency to need to do what they want to do, has been a guiding principle in some even highly civilized societies. What has not been recognized is that such efforts to make the child obedient for the purpose of making the child civilized will predictably bring with it abdication of the sense of self, of one's judging function, and generate heightened levels of accumulating hostile destructiveness in the child.

Note that when children are reared harshly to make them obedient, the same basic reactive process is triggered in them as when children are harshly abused or neglected at home: repeated, prolonged *excessive psychic pain → high level hostile destructiveness.* It is very likely that harsh rearing, or intense abuse or neglect in childhood prior to World War II,[17] played their part in there being highly sadistic Nazis in Germany, equally sadistic Jewish "Kapos"[18] in the death camps, and sadistic French special police, *la Milice,* who, like such hostile individuals in most European countries brutally pursued Jews, gypsies, and other "undesirables," to incarcerate them in concentration camps or sent them east to the Nazi death camps, where many died of starvation and disease. The lowest common denominator, *high level excessive psychic pain → high level hostile destructiveness,* is produced by harsh maltreatment, whatever the kind. Children so maltreated are highly likely to rebel in adolescence or be easily engaged into or mobilized to victimize others.[19]

But doesn't obedience make us better workers and citizens? It is well established that obedience can lead to the development of high-level discipline, which when channeled well can produce very productive students, workers and citizens. But obedience obtained by crushing a child's will or stubbornness can also have seriously troubling consequences for the individual and for society. For the individual, the abdication of the self, of the denial of one's inborn primary narcissism, of one's strivings for autonomy, which are required for adaptation, will not only lead to the individual's becoming loaded with accumulating hostile destructiveness, it may also damage his sense of reason and morality. I'll take up below some of the problems it has created for society.

While some children will accept the message conveyed by the authoritarian parent that the harshness is for the child's own good, this conviction is vulnerable to challenge over time, and the accumulated load of hostility generated by the harsh treatment remains a psychological energy-draining and symptom-formation burden, which tends to challenge the individual from early childhood on through adolescence and still into adulthood. The history of civilization has also demonstrated that the formation of very productive students, workers, and citizens can be achieved with the discipline obtained by constructively instilling compliance.

Compliance with authority is highly facilitated where basic trust is attached to authority. This is when the trust comes not from a show of power, but by virtue of the parents' valuing the child's inherent sense of self, which instills in the child the sense that the authority has the child's best interest at heart. Compliance is highly unlikely where there is little or no trust in authority. How then does obedience achieved by the parent crushing the child's sense of self ensure trust in the parent?

Would it not lead the child to question: is all authority trustworthy? The child will naturally begin sooner or later to judge, to evaluate what authority demands, in fact what everything around him means and is. He will often wonder, "What shall I do?" The child's evolving judgment too depends on the child's history in the family. In some families and societies, children are encouraged to use their judgment, from quite early on. In other families and societies, children are discouraged from using their judgment; quite the contrary, they are commanded to obey, not to think, and not to judge. And they may be led to actions that are likely to follow them for generations, for centuries.

What gives rise to children's accepting to be obedient, to be excessively compliant?

Obedience (or excessive compliance) may result from:

1. In earliest childhood, fear of rejection and abandonment, which lead to intense anxiety, even dread.
2. From about two on, fear of the loss of love from his or her parents, which, when basic trust is not secure, the child feels can happen anytime. This is felt by children whose emotional attachment to their parents is insecure, when the attachment feels to the child to be in jeopardy.
3. Fear of parental (or other) authority, usually because the threat of punishment is perceived to be large. For instance during the Nazi era, many Germans who did not accept the 1935 Nuremberg (Nazi) Laws complied with these due to their fear of well-established threats to life and freedom; being sent to a concentration camp for noncompliance with this authoritarian rule was then a well-known reality.
4. Unquestioning (often unreasoned) obedience due to passivity. This may result, as I noted before from the crushing of one's inborn feeling compelled by strivings for autonomy to do what one wants to do. Or it may come from having been taught and learned that "I can't trust my judgment; if I listen to myself I'll get into deep trouble." This may result from identification with parents who hold dogmatic views or from parents presenting themselves as the ones who are "always right [and the child always wrong] and know what's best."
5. It may come from ethnocentric and fundamentalist education that fosters the conviction that one's own group, be it racial, ethnic, national, or religious, is superior to others.' We saw this in Stalinist Communism when children would report their own parents who would not comply with communist dogma. Ethnocentric and fundamentalist education commonly leads to some forms of malignant prejudice. This compliance tends to be rationalized, that is, to be based on biased, even falsified reasoning. This rationalized compliance is fortified by self-righteousness, which as

> Strenger[20] describes may become "malignant self-righteousness." In fact excessive compliance (obedience) often is rationalized and may become robotic (passive obedience).

One more thought—given the example I use of obedience (or excessive compliance) based on fear of punishment as occurred during the Nazi era. Many Germans were in profound disagreement with Nazi dogma, and many were incredulous that this was going on in their own highly civilized country, but too many were not. Too many were in strong favor of these policies, including the notorious 1935 Laws by which Jews and other "undesirables" lost crucial human rights, which eventually led to the Holocaust. These Germans were not passively obedient; they were taking on this dogma as their own. It is well known that this dogma was congenial not only to many Germans, but also to many French, Poles, Russians, Hungarians, and other European peoples as well[21]—with the exemption of Denmark and Bulgaria's people who refused to comply with the Nazi demand for Jews, gypsies, and others—where anti-Semitism and other virulent brands of malignant prejudice were quite common. In Russia and Poland, virulent, murderous anti-Semitism was loose in these lands long before it erupted in Germany.

The point I want to make here is that we have to distinguish obedience (or excessive compliance) from being oneself an advocate of prejudice. An advocate of prejudice is not complying with another's authority; he or she is himself or herself advocating such belief and behavior; so does militant ethnocentrism, which is the initiator of racism, ethnic superiority, and religious and national superiority.

THE PROBLEM OF EXCESSIVE COMPLIANCE (OR OBEDIENCE)

Excessive compliance (or obedience) with or to authority has played a central role in the history of civilization. It is remarkable, yet not strange at all, that the various major religions' holy scriptures and liturgies affirm very similar views on what is right and what is wrong. Problems arise when what we know to be right and wrong is applied only to one's own or selected societies and not to that of others. As Ben Kiernan's History of Genocide[22] and studies of prejudice hold,[23] since Biblical times humans have shown again and again, often with reason, that we discriminate against members outside our own ethnic, religious, or national community. In this, excessive compliance (obedience) with (to) authority has played a central role. In fact, Kiernan observes that

> In the first book of Samuel (15:1–16:1), God recalled Amalekites had "lain in wait" for the Israelites on their journey from Egypt, and he told Saul: "Now go and smite Amalek, and utterly destroy all that they have, and spare them not; but slay both man and woman, infant and suckling, ox and sheep." . . . But Saul spared Agag, king of Amalek and his kingdom's best stock. When God found that Saul "hath not followed my commandments," Samuel "hewed Agag in pieces before the Lord." God punished Saul for refusing to "utterly destroy the sinners the Amalekites" by denying Saul's descendants the throne of Israel. [And Kiernan tells us that] Demands for obedience and genocide recur in Judeo-Christian (and Islamic) scripture, [while at the same time] so do models of dissent and nonviolence" (2007, 6–7).

I noted before that anthropological studies[24] as well as that more recently reported by Bohleber (*The children of the perpetrators*) and powerfully portrayed by film director Michael Haneke (*The White Ribbon (Das weisse Band)*), all have found that where fathers are harshly authoritarian and are strict, even brutal disciplinarians, correlates strongly with their children becoming hostile and destructive over time, and that harshness in rearing children has even been programmed in societies that put a high priority on surviving by and engaging in warfare. Evidence for this quite well documented assumption comes from many corners. For instance, learning that I was writing about this, a colleague whom I esteem greatly reported to me that he had recently read a piece pertinent to it. While it is not strong scholarship, I want to quote him and let him take responsibility—a responsibility he accepts—for what he wrote to me:

> I will try to dredge out the story about brutal discipline and its effect on human adult behavior. I cannot recall where I read the story, even though it was recently. . . .
>
> . . . The story described a systematic training program for new recruits into the Japanese army in the period preceding Japan's onslaught at the beginning of World War II. The process was designed to eradicate any personal thoughts or opinions in the recruits, especially any considerations of the feelings and desires of others. The program consisted of rigid rules over every aspect of human behavior and was brutally enforced by beatings, ridicule, food restrictions, [and] sleep deprivation so that the desired end-result was soldiers who obeyed without thought any orders given them. Some of those who survived this deliberate evisceration of their feelings then became the trainers of the next group of newcomers.

American soldiers who had the misfortune of falling into the hands of Japanese troops—as in the march from Bataan—experienced merciless treatment. In other situations, such as the campaign to capture the island of Saipan (where I worked for two years) the Japanese soldiers never surrendered even when trapped inside a cave and facing death by fire from flamethrowers. They had orders to stay and fight even when out of ammunition.

. . . I'll still try to recall where I read it.[25]

Let's not underestimate the degree to which, in trying to achieve compliance or obedience, in the application of strategies of discipline, limit setting and punishment, these are invariably heavily emotionally laden and subjective and that the border between harshly strict discipline and child abuse is well known to be a steep, slippery slope. Here is a tragic example of this problem occurring in early childhood:

In November 1993, a major American newspaper[26] carried the front page, headline report from which a few sentences follow:

> "L. M. was only 23 months old when he died after a beating . . . in July. . . . M. L. was three when [he was found in June] in the basement [of his home], battered, naked, dehydrated, and suffering from a broken leg. S. S. was two when he died of massive head injuries received during a beating . . . in September 1991. . . . And . . . R. T. still bears the scars from being dunked, at the age of two, into a tub so hot that it seared off her skin. . . . All four tragedies, prosecutors contend, had something in common: The violence was triggered by a toilet-training accident.
>
> "Getting children out of diapers is one of the most frustrating and time-consuming hurdles that all parents face. But for some, it is so frustrating that researchers now are linking toilet-training accidents with many of the most serious—sometimes deadly—cases of child abuse"(1).[27]

The challenge to parents of getting their children to comply is only too well known. Of themselves, harsh discipline and punishment do not tend to work as well as parents hope it will. What makes discipline or punishment work is not when it is forceful or intense; it is when the child feels a loving attachment to the parent and it is the parent's disapproval that makes the parent's efforts works, not the punishment itself. I'll say more about this in chapter 9.

Disciplining and punishing harshly to achieve obedience are risky ways to try to get compliance because harsh rearing is often equated by the child or adolescent as maltreatment and abuse. No matter how often father may say, "I'm doing this for your own good," children feel, "If my father really loved me he would never do this to me." When they do, it is generally because they cope with the harshness of the parent by identification with the aggressor. Two facts then follow from being harshly disciplined and punished:

1. The harshness is perpetuated from generation to generation by identification with the aggressor, which through identification with the harsh parent tends to bring with it the rationalization that "proof that my father was right is that it worked for me, and it'll work for my children."
2. It tends to develop children who are harsh in their personal relationships and in whom harshness toward unknown others—which facilitates malignant prejudice—is seen as justified and righteous given that it is condoned by their parents and, the child then deduces, by the society of which her or his parents are the representatives.[28] This documents what anthropologists have found in warrior cultures[29] where children are treated sadistically to make them "good (sadistic) warriors," even if at the expense of their family and other social relationships.

Let's also note that experience in the past several decades has taught us that harsh punishment does not bring the results aimed for. Law enforcement has found that a large percentage of individuals who have spent time in jail tend to repeat crimes once released. Recidivism is a well-known problem for law enforcement agencies; these agencies themselves have pushed for programs of rehabilitation. Although studies vary in results, some push for more extensive rehabilitation programs given that increasing severity of punishment does not lessen recidivism.[30] We have found that the harsh punishment of losing one's freedom does not stop criminality. On the contrary, it tends to heighten the individual's load of hostile destructiveness (i.e., hate and retaliation against society), which is one of the key driving factors in criminal recidivism (see chapter 2).

Decades of research and clinical work on child development, parenting, and aggression, have led me to conclude that harshness in interaction with our children is not the most successful strategy for getting healthy compliance from our children and adolescents. But while harshly achieved excessive compliance (obedience) has played a disastrous role in the enactment of dictates of militant ethnocentrism and fundamentalism—a driving factor in both Nazism and Stalinist Communism where individual rights and even life were threatened by noncompliance—we know that when compliance is blatantly insufficient it may equally lead to delinquency, prejudice, and crime. I'll next look at the problem of insufficient compliance. But first another related important consideration.

THE EVOLVING PRINCIPLE OF HUMAN RIGHTS

As a student of the psychodynamics of human behavior, I have long held that social conditions have changed progressively over time and that civilization is "growing"—not just in numbers, but rather that it is growing as a "live entity," as the young do, from being an infant, to a child, an adolescent, etc. According to Lotte Koehler, the social historian Kilian held a similar view.[31] Considering the fact that both, excessive compliance (obedience) as well as insufficient compliance have often outweighed or disregarded decency, reality-based morality, and the principle of human rights, it matters a great deal that in its evolution, civilization has come to recognize the drastic consequences tragically highlighted during the twentieth century by its series of genocides:[32] civilization's failure to secure equitable human rights for all.

In broad strokes, I would say that, the principle of human rights to the present has, in some regions on our globe more than others, undergone dramatic changes. From the beginning of the modern era, which Kiernan tells us historians extend from the fifteenth century to the present, Western civilization, driven by the then governing principle of class and racial rankings (that is, by inequalities among people), as well as by self-appointed religious and ethnic superiority and by virtue of its increasingly massive weaponry and military might, its insatiable hunger for materials, wealth, power, and dominance on reachable continents, that Western civilization developed programs of colonization that spanned several centuries even into the present. During the colonization of Africa, the Middle East, Southeast Asia, Australia, and North and South America by Western European powers, the conduct of the overtaking powers toward the indigenous habitants of the lands they invaded and seized was replete with mass killings and scandalous disregard for these inhabitants' human rights. Religion, ethnicity, and nationalism are all part of our inherited communal identities. But ethnocentrism, that is, racism, and ethnic and religious fundamentalism, gave rise to crimes that culminated in genocides of increasingly large dimensions.

While variable individual and group factors have made these massive killings and genocides possible, large among these factors are: (1) passive obedience (or excessive compliance) to authority, and (2) ethnocentrism with malignant prejudice that arise from rationalized inequitable standards of human rights. The American, French, and Russian revolutions, the American Civil War, men and women from all walks of life serving in the military service of World Wars I and II, and the five genocides/mass killings of the twentieth century have highlighted the disastrous consequences of inequitable standards of human rights. But over the past three centuries inequitable standards of human rights have been increasingly challenged, even while manifestations of these continue to occur everywhere. Despite these sporadic manifestations of inequitable human rights, the movement away from class distinctions, racism, anti-Semitism, male chauvinism, Islamophobia, and other forms of inequities, while not replaced by generalized humanism nor by "liberty, fraternity, equality" so aspired to by the French,[33] nor by America's self-evident truths "that all men are created equal," Western if not global civilization seems to be moving in this direction.

This movement toward equal human rights as a principle of governance and of constitutional rights held by the United Nations—even while resisted in large domains of humanity—as a principle of universal application, inherently places limits on what can be declared morally justified, I would say have *morality-adherence.* The reduction or denial of equal rights to citizens of any given land, increasingly viewed internationally through the lens of human rights, is regarded as immoral. The Nuremberg trials held after World War II conveyed to the world that the standards enacted into law by the Third Reich's propaganda machine, declaring large sectors of its society as undesirables—while following colonization standards exercised by European and other powers for centuries before them—were standards based on a highly compromised, rationalized morality. Unleashed by malignant prejudice, these standards led to the largest historically recorded perpetrated mass of crimes against humanity. Good citizenship, the Third Reich held, required of parents to expect their children to hate and condone criminal behavior toward its undesirables. Its societal expectations degraded into immorality. The international community increasingly is aligning itself on the side that asserts, that the expectations parents have for their children have morality-adherence.

To be sure, the problem of mass killings and genocide is driven by much more than just passive obedience and malignant prejudice. Some mass killings, such as that in Rwanda-Burundi, are part of a precedent of a warring history. Others, especially that of the Holocaust, are not and were based solely on malignant prejudice against Jews, Roma, and other undesirables. Unlike the Holocaust, at the center of some of the war-driven mass killings is the role of revenge for past crimes committed against the then-victims-now-turned-perpetrators by the then-perpetrators-now-turned-victims.[34] So too, territorial imperatives have triggered and driven large interethnic conflicts in what is now the United States, in what led to World War II, and in the current painfully entrenched Palestinian-Israeli conflict. The historical cycle of violence that comes with these inter-ethnic conflicts is well known and is made difficult to resolve by two difficult to surmount socially generated problems: (1) what many have noted and I have called *the Janus Dilemma* of interethnic conflict:[35] what to the victim is a crime against humanity, to the perpetrator is an act of valor, of heroism; and (2) the significant change it imposes on a community and its members' sense of identity: "Who am I if I don't have my enemy against whom to specify who I am?"[36] These monumental challenges have much more to do with territorial imperatives that lead to interethnic conflicts and crimes against humanity than passive obedience. Nonetheless, passive obedience to dictates of militant ethnocentrism often based on reality-distortion—such as, "Jews [or whatever scapegoat] are responsible for the economic collapse of the late 1920s [or whatever perceived community problem]"—has surely played its part in this sort of rationalized denial of human rights.

In short, excessive compliance or obedience, often passive obedience, has created vast social problems and led to deplorable human behavior from bullying to crimes against humanity. But then, the converse of excessive compliance, insufficient compliance has also created its large share of deplorable human behavior.

FROM EXCESSIVE COMPLIANCE (PASSIVE OBEDIENCE) TO INSUFFICIENT COMPLIANCE

A phenomenon of notable consequence to German society has followed from harsh rearing that demanded passive obedience of its children. The crimes against humanity unleashed in Germany, but committed by European Nazis[37] from 1935 to 1945, created all kinds of problems now recorded for three generations among those who, during the first generation were victims and those who were perpetrators, and their respective descendent second and third generations.

W. Bohleber[38] speaks to an issue directly pertinent to this book's aim, which is to explain why achieving compliance in our children is far more advantageous to society than trying to instill in them passive obedience. Here, I document a unique example of consequences that may follow from harsh child rearing that leads to such obedience. German psychoanalysts L. Koehler and W. Bohleber, independently, hold that those who were reared harshly to obedience became well suited for carrying out Nazi ideology.[39] In addition, these harshly reared people in time harshly reared their own children.

Bohleber tells us that the guilt and shame the Nazi generation's actions generated in its children, led this second generation to be unable to speak to its own children, the third generation, about what its grandparents did during the Nazi years. The second generation became "the silent generation." The guilt and shame borne by the silent generation due to the Nazi principles and the crimes against humanity so many Europeans who adhered to them committed, led to a serious consequence, which is highly pertinent to the thesis of this book. It led to many of the second generation's failure to guide its children to reasonable compliance with universally accepted mores.

Bohleber speaks to the failure of the second generation. He tells us that "During the xenophobic riots in Rostock, 14- to 15-year-olds who threw stones and Molotov cocktails at a home of asylum-seekers were astounded that nobody stopped them: 'It can't be true that I can simply throw a Molly and the police does nothing . . . it's a lot of shit that they just let you do it'" (14). The silent generation parents could not prevent their children's criminal behavior nor could they guide them to acceptable moral social conduct. Bohleber writes that

> In a very detailed case study Bergmann and Leggewie[40] described two youths from Hesse, who wanted to set a home for asylum-seekers on fire. They threw Molotov cocktails, but . . . no great damage was done. Both youth come from an orderly, lower middle-class background, both are employed. [These youth] describe how nobody . . . remonstrated with them after the deed. Just having been released from prison, one of the boys was told by his mother, "I'll pay for your lawyer." Instead of punishing his son, one father had bolted with psychosomatic complaints, leaving his wife and two sons behind. Questioned about his father, the young culprit had said: "I have no father. As far as I'm concerned, he's dead." It seems there was nobody . . . who would confront them with the gravity of their offence. (14).

Dan Bar-on has brought to light how some of the silent generation experienced their parents' denial and rationalization of their participation in the Nazi crimes against humanity. Bar-on[41] extensively studied the problem of post-atrocities "silence." In doing so he started the remarkable project of giving adult children of survivors and children of perpetrators opportunities to come together and in this context, express to each other the byproduct of their Holocaust experiences, each from their respective side of the criminal tragedy. Bar-on, reporting on what some adult children of perpetrators said, tells us that these adult offspring feel that, "Their [parents'] love of order and discipline, obedience and adjustment at any price has deprived them, ourselves, and society of its vitality. . . . Consequently our concern with the past was and is a search for new vitality in our lives" (1993, 291).[42]

Noteworthy, Bohleber gives us two quite contrasting byproducts of having been reared in accordance with harsh upbringing whose aim is unquestioning obedience to authority. These are poles apart: (1) identification with the aggressor and (2) antiauthoritarianism. He observes that "the Nazi doctrine of sternness lives on . . . a durable heritage. . . . Stern [I would say, harsh] parenting ideals, coupled with an ideology of eliminating what is weak or ill, force the child to identify with his parents [in order to] eliminate his own weakness and helplessness[43]. . . . In this way attitudes and behavior patterns of violence and sternness and the inability to empathize are perpetuated and passed on to the next generation" (11–12).

On the other hand, in reaction to having been reared harshly, in order to be made strong and a warrior who passively obeys authority, can lead the adult offspring to a rejection of authoritarianism, which in parenting, then, may manifest itself in a reluctance to set limits and demand that the child comply with societal expectations. Bohleber especially holds that the second generation's silence, not only prevented its own and the third generation's coping with and working through their family's shame and guilt, but it also complicated the rearing of the third generation children, seemingly leading to what some believed was an antiauthoritarian child rearing. As a result, "with the best of intentions, children were allowed to do as they pleased, parents . . . communicated almost no rules and set no limits" (12, 15).

Thus, from harsh demands for obedience the pendulum swung too far into antiauthoritarianism and insufficient compliance with societal expectations.

THE PROBLEM OF INSUFFICIENT COMPLIANCE

Let's look more closely at some of the consequences of insufficient compliance, a problem long present in all societies that has led to delinquency and even crime, including singular (individual criminals) and collective crimes (for example, racial and ethnic mob crimes such as lynchings in the United States, pogroms in Russia and Poland, and more recently against migrant groups or "asylum seekers" as occurred in Germany and diverse developed countries). Many factors contribute to such individual and collective delinquency and crime.

Let me start by saying that by *insufficient compliance* I mean the child or adolescent's obstinate disregard for the parents' (or other authority) clearly and frequently stated expectations—assuming that these expectations are age-appropriate, reasonable, and morality-adherent. Insufficient compliance carries with it defiance of parental (authority) expectations.

As children develop and confront new challenges, it is quite common for them to challenge the compliance hoped for by their parents. In time, however, kids can achieve reasonable compliance. Of course, children vary from birth on in their degree of malleability; some infants find it very difficult to abandon their own inner driven behaviors, which then require of the parents greater efforts to achieve compliance. We'll address this aspect of the issue in chapter 9, on limit-setting. And below, we'll consider normal expectable categories and levels of compliance, as well as the developmental line for the ability to comply, that is, when can a child be expected to understand the implications of not complying?

For now let me note that the ability to comply with age-appropriate expectations is not achieved by the age of six years, this generally results from a child's not having acquired sufficient trust in the parent's commitment to love, protect, and respect the child. Not trusting authority to be caring and benevolent, the child does not acquire a positive regard for the parent's authority and, self-protectively, disregards it. This negative experience of authority eventually tends to be replicated with other adult authority—whether or not that authority is malevolent. Kids like this, wanting no relationships with adults, may in time turn to the peer group for mutual love, protection, and respect, some among them ending up in gangs. There, interestingly, these noncompliant youth, must and are willing to adhere with the gang's rigorous rules of conduct.

But another striking phenomenon large consequence to society seems to have emerged in the last several decades that derives directly from *insufficient compliance.* It is that, in many countries in the western world, much disruption in our educational systems arises from a level of insufficient compliance, even total noncompliance, on the part of many students in our schools.

Sure, teachers have always had to deal with some insufficiently compliant students, but never to this degree. This large increase in insufficient compliance is especially marked at middle- and high-school levels but manifests even earlier. The consequences that follow from student noncompliance in classes are seriously compromising to their education and their future. For many, it jeopardizes opportunities for life improvement that compulsory education brings.

In addition, the problem of insufficient compliance also leads to teacher-student as well as student-student problems of unprecedented dimensions.[44] Insufficient or noncompliance leads many teachers to use coercive and shaming (humiliating) strategies to enforce compliance, but also, compelled by their anger and even rage, toward seriously recalcitrant, even defiant, students, teachers at times cause such already troubled students great harm. Among students and between teachers and students, this has led to increased levels of bullying, with escalations into violence among some of them. With this there have also been a number of bullying-induced suicides, as well as an increase in gang formation and in juvenile delinquency with a dramatic rise in substance and alcohol abuse, and even occasional horrific crimes such as what happened in Columbine. Among the factors that contribute to this upsurge in noncompliance in schools, a number of us believe one of central concern for parents is the following.

It is assumed by a number of child mental health professionals that this new level of insufficient compliance on the part of our youth may have arisen with the advent of a social development that reflects a highly desirable advance in civilization, namely, the women's liberation movement. A central part of the human rights movement, the demand for equal rights by women[45] progressively opened the way for many women to attain higher education and enter the workforce on all fronts and levels of performance, professional, business, industry, etc. It is a long awaited advance in civilization that to this day is continuing to spread over the globe—some, still against harsh resistance. The benefit of this movement to the well-being of women is unequivocal. But it may have brought with it unanticipated problems, among them the one I want to address now.

I cannot speak on this topic with statistical support nor with strong authority. But I want to put forward a pertinent hypothesis to which much professional clinical and nonprofessional anecdotal evidence points. With so many women in the workforce, while they are at work, who is taking care of and bringing up their children? Efforts to deal with this question have led to the development of daycare and preschools programs that have multiplied, indeed have become a new industry. And, I put forward this question as a hypothesis: might this phenomenon in one way or another have led to the level of insufficient or even noncompliance we see in our youth?

Having now for decades been privileged to help train women who have chosen the fields of child psychiatry and of child psychoanalysis, while teaching them child development, I witnessed the great distress some expressed when they became aware of the needs young children have for familial, personalized emotional nurturance and care, packaged in with their physical care. They recognized that physical care could securely be provided by others than themselves, but could others also provide the kind of emotional nurturance that generally only parents give their children, that kind of emotionally invested nurturance on which children's emotional health depends?

One mother of our original research group (see chapter 1) put the issue in highly sensitive words. She was telling the group of mothers and research staff that she realized while she was taking care of her neighbors' children for several days now that, while she really likes these young kids, she realized that she couldn't let herself feel about them the way she feels about her own three kids. She couldn't she said because if she did, she would find it very difficult to send them back to their own parents at the end of the day. She couldn't invest in them emotionally to the level that she did her own kids. Only biological or adoptive parents do that.

Studies of children in orphanages,[46] of attachment,[47] and of psychoanalytic child development,[48] as well as studies on this question from other related disciplines, all document the critical need for emotional engagement and emotional investment in human relationships from infancy on and throughout life. While physical care is essential for health and well-being, it is not what makes us all thrive. Profound emotional engagement is what brings with it a child's eventual self-valuation, optimal physical and emotional development and life-long physical and mental health. Parental quality emotional engagement is essential to making our children thrive. Unfortunately this does not often come from others than the child's own emotionally invested parents.

Many efforts have and continue to be made, to deal with the problem brought about by the fact that now both mothers and fathers have joined the workforce in large numbers. The problem is not insurmountable, but it must be recognized for us to effectively deal with it. Many men, sympathetic to the rights of their wives to become who they wish to be, have more and more engaged in the care of the children, even very young ones, from their infancy on. This is highly desirable for family formation. Many fathers, who might otherwise not have done so, have become closer to their children from even the first days of the child's life on, forging a stronger attachment between fathers and their young children to the benefit of the child, the father, and the mother. Families vary; couples vary in their willingness and ability to care for their young children. Some men are wonderful baby holders; others seem to be unaware of the discomfort experienced by the baby as a result of the father's having no clue that reciprocal molding is necessary for a baby to feel comfortably held.

Following on my work and research in child development and parenting, I have been asked: What should we do? How should we deal with women's rights and this newly created dilemma? What should we recommend to parents? "How many hours a day should the less than one-year-old child be in daycare without jeopardizing his well-being?" was a question that created a serious debate in the 1980s–1990s. Unfortunately, the issue was so emotionally laden and politicized that it interfered with the kind of research that could help us securely make meaningful recommendations. Research documenting support for daycare for less than one-year-old infants was equally balanced with research documenting the adverse effects of it; the bias of many a researcher was discernible even in the way he or she would report on it.

Early in my research on this issue, based on the many studies I have known, I weighed in on the side of the adverse effects of daycare for children in their first year of life. One mother taught me well. We had talked together about the possible disadvantage to her baby of her putting him in daycare from several weeks after birth on, as had some of her friends had done. Conflicted by our recommendation and wanting to do as her friends had done, she was neglecting and even maltreating her baby, we found. We agreed that this baby might be better off if this mother went back to work outside the home, and we recommended to her that seeing the strong understandable need she experienced to go back to work, she ought to do so. Both the baby's needs and the mother's needs are important; tending to only the needs of one—mother or child—can create significant problems for both. But then, what should we do?

Study of the question led me during the last three decades to lecture to professional audience about the need for "an individualized prescription for each family." Each family has to determine what would best serve the entire family and the individual members of the family. The challenge is large. But retreating to coercive dictation that women must choose to have babies or join the workforce is unworkable.

I am not advocating a universe filled with self-centered individuals who clamor only for their rights. Rather, what can we do to see to it that each of us has the right to make the best we can of our individual and our collective life? But, given the advantages of it, we must do so without sacrificing our children's learning to comply with reasonable authority.

But how has this dilemma led to so much noncompliance in students in school?

One observation made by child psychiatrists and psychologists who have treated children of such two-parent-working-outside-the-home families is that quite a number of these children feel they come second to their parents' outside-home-work commitments. Their parents most likely do not feel this way, and while it may in some instances be true, in others it certainly is not. Nonetheless, this is the way many children feel. Parents are troubled by this, either because they do not feel this way, or because they do, but they feel that their kid is only a selfish spoiled brat. For those who do not feel their work is more important than their child, this text can help. Those who feel their child is a spoiled brat, the problem requires more than what I am about to say here.[49]

Those who do not feel that their work is more important than their own children, often coming home tired, tend to feel guilty because their children in one way or another have let them know that they feel neglected. Some parents, unconsciously then, try to quiet or lessen the guilt they feel, by backing off in the face of their children's protests from the reasonable demands and expectations that mom or dad have for their children. While the children may feel rewarded that they don't have to do what other kids do, they are unaware of the eventual cost to them of not learning to comply with their parents' expectations. In short time, sensing their parents' inability (out of guilt) to stand up to their resistance to compliance, some children tend to increasingly dig in, intensify and even assert their noncompliance, feeling then an enlarged sense of autonomy and power, which heightens the child's narcissism. This narcissism, however, now threatens to become the narcissism of the spoiled kid who has increasing difficulty dealing with the disappointment and the anger of not getting what he wants.

Negative consequences follow from this dynamic. Let me mention just a couple of them. First, having difficulty not being able to cope with not getting everything one wants creates pain each time such a disappointment occurs. But disappointments are unavoidable in life. Learning to cope reasonably with them makes life much more pleasant; one protects oneself against repeatedly feeling painfully injured and pouting or having a blooming fit. All parents who have a child whose narcissism is that of a spoiled kid know this well. The child feels miserable and the parent gets very angry with the child, all of which further burdens their relationship.

A second result follows from a child who, in defying his parents' reasonable-enough expectations develops an inflated sense of autonomy and power. No doubt, this child will at times find, as do all kids, that he or she can't deal with a frightening situation and experience much anxiety. Since the child feels more powerful than his parents, he will not turn to them for protection when frightened as most children automatically do. After all, he's more powerful than his parents; his parents are weaker than he, so how can they help him? To cope with the anxiety, the child will then use psychological defense mechanisms that are likely to interfere with sound and positive adaptation. He may rationalize that he is even more powerful and the danger is not real, and falsify the world around him. He is likely to not believe that adults can help him, protect him—after all, his parents can't. Not only is turning to adults for protection out the window, but also in some cases, so is compliance. And there are more problems as well, but let's get back to the question of insufficient or noncompliance.

Many children who defy their parents' reasonable-enough expectations will, when they go to school, feel that they do not have to comply with the teachers' expectations that they will listen in class and do their homework, nor eventually of the policeman's expectations that they obey laws. The path to school failure and to delinquency is facilitated.

Fortunately, some children recognize the problem created for them by their parents' inability to demand reasonable compliance. At 14, a young girl I was treating psychotherapeutically spoke of how lucky she is that unlike her friends' mothers, her mother did not demand that she be home by 10 p.m. even on school nights. Of course, many reasonable parents do not allow their children to go out on school nights at all. Interestingly, when she was 17, in the course of our continuing psychotherapeutic work, she said that she was troubled by the fact that her mother did not expect her to be home by a certain time at night. "Doesn't she care what happens to me?" The much valued gratification of her autonomy at 14 did not outbalance her need to be cared about and reasonably protected. Perhaps psychotherapeutic treatment helped her sort things out better than she might have done on her own, but psychotherapy is no substitute for responsible parental guidance and care. These children may, and many do, find their way to realize that compliance with authority is valuable and they see their parents' failure to protect them; these children's own resilience leads them to find constructive ways to secure their education and their future.

I have stated my hypothesis simply. But we all know that compliance/noncompliance, like any psychological character trait is governed by multiple contributing factors and cannot be stated to derive from just one. In addition, children vary in their coping with any one given real-life condition or situation. For example, children of single-parent families tend to not react as negatively to mom's working outside the home, because they grasp the reason that mom has to do this; she is the only one to put food on the table and buy all the things she and the kids need. In fact, many will pitch in with home chores, some even without being asked to do so. So often, in spite of their complaining about mom's not being at home, we see an older sibling become the temporary caregiver for his or her younger siblings when mom is at work. Kids are well known to surprise adults with what they can do when the conditions require it. The reader can see that I cannot assert my hypothesis with no reservations.

Then add this. Where the parent-child relationship is quite good, but when mom goes to work, the child may nonetheless feel that mom's work is more important to her than the child and the child feels neglected; but this child may, with the passage of time and especially as a teenager, feel proud that mom, through her work is recognized by society as a productive citizen, whether mom's a doctor, or lawyer, or a CEO, or runs a store, or is a seamstress, or whatever.

I put this hypothesis forward not to weigh against the advancing tide of the rights of women but to facilitate its achievement, while at the same time seeing to it that we secure our children's well-being, and optimize their development and their ability to comply with reasonable and well-intentioned authority—because we all know that growth-promoting guidance can enormously better their lives.

Given the miscarriages of excessive compliance and the unacceptability of insufficient compliance, as standards of human rights have evolved, so must the standards of healthy compliance we expect from our children. We assert that children must learn to comply with their parents and society's reasonable and growth-promoting expectations. Several questions arise from this assertion. (1) What are reasonable and growth-promoting expectations? (2) At what age can we expect compliance; what is its development time table? And (3) how do we best achieve compliance with the expectations we have of our children?

REASONABLE AND GROWTH-PROMOTING EXPECTATIONS

We all have expectations of our children. Many of us fantasize what kids we're going to have and how many; some of us do this even before we are ready to have children. We all want them to make us be proud of them, to have society's approval of them and of us. We all have a program for them to achieve this even before they are born; some of us more firmly so than others.

In years of work with kids and their parents, like others, I have discovered the obvious: kids come into the world with minds of their own. Some seem to know what they do and don't want from the outset; others are more malleable. All parents quickly find that their infants don't seem to have the same program for themselves in mind that we do. Some babies more than others; in fact, some don't seem to like our program at all. This is so with wake-sleep cycles, eating, and a number of things even from the very beginning. How do we get them to accept our program?

Well, we have to weigh the pros and cons of these matters. The parents' program and the kid's program are, more or less, at odds. Many parents are troubled to find that the baby does not just accept their mother's (or other caregiver's) expectations, whether it's with regard to eating or sleeping. Of course, it's not uncommon for the parents themselves to have programs for their child that are at odds with each other, each parent having different ideas on how to achieve what each thinks is best. Let's not consider this dilemma; it would take us too far afield from our present concern.

Mental health professionals know that both parent and child have to compromise. Unfortunately, some parents, in an authoritarian way, assume that the child must accept the program they have for the child. This works in some cases; in most, except when harsh measures are used to break the child's will, it does not. Many individual factors in both the baby and the parents are at play, which create this program dilemma. Most common in these built-in character factors is rigidity of adaptability in the parent (resulting from her or his genetic make-up and life experiences) or in the child (which is generally a genetic factor). Some parents and some babies are quite more malleable than others. Whatever the factors, parent and child must compromise. Margaret Mahler, a well-known child psychiatrist and psychoanalyst, held that the mother is the one who must and most often yields in compromise, which she felt is the way it should be. But it is clear that mother also has to hold the line on the baby's complying reasonably.

Many books have been written about how to deal with this dilemma, such as on when to feed, what to feed, how to help infants regulate their sleep-wake patterns, when and how to put the baby to bed; when and how to toilet train, etc. The reason so many books have been written on these subjects is that it is really difficult to be sure, which of our expectations we should demand of the child, and which to yield on. This starts at the beginning of the child's life.

And it goes on. Even in the later years of adolescence, parents' expectations are challenged. Here are two instances of parental expectations being challenged even in young adulthood. One father, a physician, was very unhappy that his son wanted to be a mathematician; he wanted his son to become a doctor. The father developed all sorts of arguments to support his efforts to convince his son to go into medicine. "Economics, [he said,] look at how little money you'll earn as a mathematician." To be sure, physicians fare better financially than do most mathematicians. The son yielded. The long and short is that I have known fairly well two physicians who became doctors because their parents wanted them to, and neither really enjoys medicine, their life's work. Some may see this as a reasonable compromise; many among us do not.

Another instance showed the reverse. A college graduate was convinced his father wanted him to become a doctor as was the father. To be sure, the father would have loved to have his son become a physician. But he saw that this was not his son's inclination and he had a higher priority for him. He wanted his son, a highly intelligent hard-working student, to do what his son wanted to do. This father understood well enough that he could not be sure that being a physician would gratify his son the way medicine was gratifying him, the father. Can any father really know what will make his son happy with his own life? Not everyone loves being a doctor or a lawyer—I have also seen several lawyers leave the law after years of practice because they were not gratified by its practice. For those who are fortunate enough to be able to choose their life's work, so long as it is socially accepted, parents' expectations have to yield to the child's.

To be sure, we all know that it is undesirable to *not* have expectations of them. Children know that having expectations of them is part of our valuing them, of wanting what's best for them, even when at times they argue that by our expectations we show that we don't care about their well-being. And furthermore, they have expectations of us, their parents. Yes, at 14, the girl I mentioned earlier, with evident pleasure said to me, "I can do whatever I want; my parents are OK with that"; but then at 17, she was troubled: "I don't understand . . . doesn't my mother care what happens to me?" And consider Bohleber's comment that "the Rostock 14- to 15-year-olds, who threw stones and Molotov cocktails at a home of asylum-seekers, were astounded that nobody stopped them: 'It can't be true that I can simply throw a Molly and the police does nothing . . . it's a lot of shit that they just let you do it'" (1995, 14). Sure, most kids, most of the time, want to be allowed to do whatever they want. But even in early life they have expectations of us. For instance, when five-year-old Jane fell down the steps screaming, the first words out of her mouth when her mother came running to see if she was OK, were: "Why did you let me fall!" Still thinking magically as a five-year-old will, she expected her mother to prevent her falling. Our children have serious expectations of us. What expectations should we have of them?

Our expectations cannot all have equal weight. We should have categories based on degree of obligation such as "This you must do," "This you cannot do"; and "This I really wish you would, or you would not do"; and "This, you choose what you want to do, but you know what we wish you would do."

Before expecting that the child can grasp the notion of "obligatory," "this you must do," and "this you cannot do," we have to recognize that the young child has not yet developed the ability to anticipate or to judge what the consequences of her behaviors and actions truly might be. We'll look at this in the next section on the timetable for the development of the ability to comply. But before we get to the timetable, here are a few key examples of categories of expectations.

Categories of Expectations

Obligatory Expectations

Obligatory expectations are the things you must do or must not do. You have no choice; you can complain, but no arguments are accepted. Here are a couple examples I especially hold to.

- Unless you are truly sick, you have to go to school every school day.
- You have to do your homework; if you need help, you have to ask for it; we'll be glad to help or if we can't help we'll get someone who can.
- We all have to obey the law in the neighborhood and at school. For instance, you don't mess with other people's mail; you don't intentionally break your bully's window. You cannot have a knife with a blade larger than three inches; if you do, you can't take it to school or carry it around in your pocket.

These examples obviously cannot apply to young kids. Each family has to determine at what age they feel they can begin to expect this from the child. Each family has to determine what is obligatory for their family, be it praying everyday and going to religious services every week, never hitting your little sister (or brother), keeping your room sanitary (i.e., all food or liquid remains are to be cleaned out before the day is over), or whatever. One cannot make all expectations obligatory because it diminishes the child's recognition that some expectations matter more than others. Besides, the child will soon discover that some expectations are not as reasonable or as serious or as important as others. And to make the less important ones obligatory, lowers the value of what is "obligatory."

Desirable Expectations

"This I expect you to do or to not do. If you don't comply you will lose a privilege." With this, the parent does not feel the behavior is totally unacceptable; it's not what you want, but it does not run counter to what you feel is so important for your child to comply with.

- Some families of teenagers insist on knowing where the kid is when not in school or at home, or that the child be home by a certain time on weekend nights. Not complying earns a scolding and may lead to the loss of a privilege. In chapter 8, we talk about how to weigh in on limit-setting and punishment and that the child's age and personality traits have to be taken into account.
- You live in this house. There are many chores that need to be done. As a responsible member of the family, you are expected to help clear the dinner table, put the dishes in the dishwasher or help washing them, or empty the dishwasher or dry the dishes. Again, age is determining of what we can expect our kids to help with. Parents might be surprised to know that when kids feel respected, loved, and valued, they are willing to help at home, some even when as young as five years of age. In fact, they feel good about helping. And when parents express appreciation for the help, many a child reacts, beaming with a feeling of accomplishment.

Here the child has some choice. Not complying earns him a degree of disappointment from the parents—which never feels good to kids or adolescents. A simple, "What would you feel like if you expected me to help you, like picking you up at (your friend) Johnny's or Suzy's and I don't show up. How would you like that?" This is good enough to convey your disappointment; it gives the kid a chance to reflect on the effects of his or her not pitching in with assigned chores. Avoid (intentional) shaming in expressing disappointment. A reaction of "You'll never amount to anything" is too harsh; in fact, it's abusive, harmful, and will lead to resentment. We talk about this later in this chapter.

Wished-For Expectations

"I really wish you would do this, or you would not do this." Here, it's a hoped-for expectation. The parent has to deal with this disappointment privately; especially since in many instances, the parent's wished-for expectation that a child cannot fulfill can make the child feel guilt and shame at letting mom or dad down. For instance:

- A child of average intelligence works well enough in school to make Bs. The reasonable enough parent wishes for the child to try harder in order to get As. Some children will respond to such wishes, knowing that this is what mom or dad really wish. Children can read us pretty well; they see our facial expressions and hear our vocal reactions to their announcing they got another B in math. "You can see that I wish you'd try harder, can't you? But so long as you try the best you can, that's what counts." This is far better than, "Oh well, no point pushing you to try harder." With this the message may be understood to mean, "I know you can't do better, even if you tried," which is very discouraging to a child.
- "It would be very nice if sharing your toys with your little brother (or sister) wasn't so hard for you." Most parents wish their children would be generous with each other and treat each other well. This tends to be problematic for kids given that we rarely, nor should we, ask them if it's OK with them if we have another baby. Firstborns don't tend to welcome a new baby with whom they now have to share their mom and dad and everything else.

All parents have such wished-for expectations. But being disappointed that our child is not the model child we wish she would be is not really fair. Can we ourselves always count on being a model parent or model person?

So, I have only pointed out here that our expectations have to have variable weight; some are nonnegotiable, others are. Our children have a right to have a voice in these matters. But it is the parents' responsibility to decide on which expectation they do and on which they do not.

TIMETABLE FOR DEVELOPMENT OF THE ABILITY TO COMPLY

The ability to comply with parental expectations requires mental abilities not yet present at birth. The child's ability to control her inner push to do what she wants and to get what she wants requires the development of adaptive functions such as being able to put the brakes on the inner pressure, to delay getting what she wants, even to tolerate not getting what she wants. And it requires the development of cognitive functions such as the child's being able to think about the effects of what the child wants, to reason what the consequences might be, to integrate past with present, and to apply this to and to anticipate similar future events, to understand similarities and differences, and more; all in all to think at a level where the parent's expectations can be assessed by, and make sense to, the child.

Getting children to obey parents when they use coercive training methods can be achieved earlier than when children achieve the ability to comply. Threat of punishment in young children is very efficient in getting obedience even when the child cannot yet think. But as I have emphasized, it does so at serious cost to the adaptability of character, emotional disposition, independent functioning, creativity, and can even impair moral judgment. Compliance demands greater responsibility on the part of the child, which requires greater individual mental development.

We now know from studies of child development, psychological[50] and psychoanalytic,[51] as well as from brain research,[52] that soon after birth elements of two types of experiences are registered in the brain: those that occur frequently and those occasional experiences that are intensely painful.[53] Registered in the brain, they become part of our memory bank—although the part of our memory bank where these memories are stored makes them inaccessible to recall except under certain conditions. But near birth infants can't yet put their experiences into ideas or thoughts. What is foremost recorded of experiences that give rise to early memory formation is their feeling component—what is felt physically and emotionally. Even though the infant within weeks of birth cannot conceptualize experiences into words, thoughts, or ideas, the feelings that are recorded in implicit memory[54] resonate with, and are activated by the kinds of experiences that gave rise to these feelings in the first place. And these repeated feeling-experiences then amplify and stabilize those that are already recorded in implicit memory. Even though implicit memories cannot be recalled on demand, from their unconscious recesses of the mind, these feelings will play a large role in the person's baseline personality and moods for years to come.

As Erikson taught us,[55] by six months or so, an infant can sufficiently predict whether or not when he cries, mother (or other caregiver) will come to help, or will not come to help the baby, or will react negatively to the baby's appeal for care. These experiences over time lead to the development of basic trust or basic mistrust, which, in turn, brings with it the infant's feeling that he is deserving of trust (i.e., is "trustworthy) or that he is not deserving of trust and is not a good enough baby. While this learning is based on classical conditioning,[56] the early experience of feelings and moods being recorded in primitive centers of the brain (the amygdala and hippocampus) stabilize very early in life.

The classical conditioning mode of learning predominates during the first two years, registering experiences as these are felt and perceived by the infant. Thus prior to the third year, one can coerce an infant to be obedient.

If you don't do what I say, you will get punished. If you do something I do not approve of, you will be punished. But one cannot yet expect the less than three-years-old to elect to comply with, or be able to weigh the consequences of not meeting parents' expectations, when they are not threatened with harsh punishment. Infants may comply with parents' expectations but this is on the basis of wanting to please the parent, not on the basis of weighing the meaning and merits of complying.

The period from two to eight years of age is one during which basic adaptive and a number of critical cognitive abilities develop. During these years, the ability to grasp the meaning of and develop ideas about life events, to bring together past and present, and from these predict the future, to identify cause and effect (this happened because or this caused that to happen) increasingly become possible. The integration of appraisal of and giving meaning to experience and events,[57] is prerequisite to understanding the expectations the parent has of a child. The development of the ability to recognize that, mother has thoughts of her own that are different than the thoughts I have in my mind, develops by four to five years of age.[58] To recognize that not everyone thinks what I think, is essential for weighing another person's expectations and their possible consequences, positive and negative. This capability is essential for predicting a child's ability to comply; compliance just cannot yet be securely predicted before the age of four. Obedience, on the other hand, does not require the ability for this level of mental processing because it demands that the child not think, or that the child simply adopt what the parent thinks.

J. Kagan and N. Herschkowitz[59] tell us that, during the two- to six-year-old era, five thinking (cognitive) abilities progressively develop on which the ability to comply depends. These include:

(a) *The reliable integration of past and present:* from four years of age on, children begin to and progressively use thinking of past experiences in order to understand and interpret what they are currently experiencing (190).
(b) *Anticipating the future:* "the ability to relate the present to . . . the future also matures during [the] four- and seven-year-old [period]" (190).
(c) *The appreciation of causality:* ". . . A five- or six-year-old who makes an error reflects on the possible reasons for the mistake, and on occasion, corrects herself. . . . six-to-seven-year-olds are usually reflective following a mistake; that is, they take more time studying [the next time the task needs to be done]" (193–194).
(d) *Enhanced semantic [recognition of the meaning of words, phrases, ideas] categories:* Most of us can remember experiences from about five or six

years of age on. The reason is that we then began to record experiences in word concepts, in stories about or narratives of events. At about six we begin to be able to link and delink events from the feelings they generated in us. A child then "might remember the fact that he was mad at a parent a week earlier and [do something annoying to the parent now] without any feeling of anger" (198).

(e) *Recognition of the relations or differences between what they expect and others expect:* By seven, a child tends to compare the standards of behavior others expect of him with those he holds for himself. He is able to compare his behavior with what parents expect. Generally, well-cared-for children tend to make efforts to avoid criticism from parents and teachers (206).

Much new knowledge of brain development and the assumption that this development correlates with the development of adaptive, cognitive, and emotional abilities, while not proven to date, is believed by many scientists to be plausible. In this spirit of caution then, in terms of brain development, Kagan and Herschkowitz tell us that "the psychological competences that appear during [the two to eight years] era, require the coordination of many maturing brain sites," and that brain "connectivity [between different sites] is enhanced in three dimensions . . . : [nerve fibers] connecting the right and left hemispheres, [nerve fibers] connecting various areas within each hemisphere, and [nerve fibers] linking cortical to subcortical structures . . . resulting, by seven or eight years of age, in a massively interconnected brain" (210–211). As Koehler[60] sums up, "Up to the third year . . . the right hemisphere of the brain is dominant, [but] it will process what it receives and no more. . . . [It is the left hemisphere that will] elaborate and make inferences about [the event experienced, and it will] strive to provide an understanding not only of the event, but also of the underlying cause of the event. In this way, one can develop a mechanism to cope with future occurrences" (10). This is achieved only when the necessary brain sites are interconnected.

And the degree to which brain interconnectivity is critical to the development of adaptive, cognitive, and emotional functioning from two to eight years of age can be appreciated when, as Kagan and Herschkowitz note, "the rate of increase in total cortical surface accelerates [from] the second . . . birthday [on], and the human brain attains 90 percent of its adult weight by eight years of age" (208). Correlating this with what we see in observing children's behaviors, the two- to eight-years period is the critical period for establishing a well-developed foundation for the ability to comply with parental expectations.

The further development of compliance as a reasoned principle of functioning, that goes beyond family expectations and is integral to further maturation of personality, will occur during the 8- to 14-or-so-year period. In terms of brain development, this correlates well with the fact that "the volume of the prefrontal cortex increases slowly from infancy to about eight years of age and then undergoes an accelerated growth from 8 to 14 years of age. The integrative functions of the prefrontal cortex . . . participate in working memory, planning, control of inappropriate actions, and conscious awareness of feeling tone, . . . and is important in [the integration of different modes (such as visual, auditory, feeling, thinking) of perceiving experience] (Kagan & Herschkowitz, 213–214).

We also know from psychoanalytic child development that conscience formation and the development of morality, a significant contributor to achieving compliance, organizes during the three- to six-year period. Then, learning to abide by rules of play and fairness reaches a new level of organization during the 6- to 12-years period, which most children under six do not yet have and therefore, can't play games governed by rules and consequences, as is required in playing checkers and cards games (beyond War and Go Fish). The 9- to 12-year-old can, and his progressively developing moral judgment and guidelines for conduct begin to influence his behavior in human interactions.

Then as the 12- to 18-year-old progressively shifts the foremost center of influence in his life from his family to his peer group, that peer group increasingly dictates and modifies his beliefs and behavior, and with it the adolescent's conscience undergoes some revisions. Generally, the better the relationships in the adolescent's core family, the more will her conscience retain its original basic structure, but will now add to, and begin to integrate the old with the new elements of conscience. The poorer the family relationships, the more will her peer group influence her conscience revision, perhaps even leading to its reformation, to correspond with the peer group's beliefs and behaviors (see chapter 3).

What do we make of these notes on adaptive, cognitive, and emotional development? Adding decades of research (see chapter 1) and of clinical work with children and adolescence, I come up with the following timetable, as a guide, for understanding when a normal-average child may be expected to comply with parents' expectations.

Before two years of age, parents begin to tell the infant what expectations they have of the child with regard to eating, sleeping, not biting, not hitting, not taking other kids' toys, and the like. Limit-setting will increasingly be needed as the 8-to-24-month-old child is driven to explore his environment, to check out and test his newly emerging abilities, as well as many things and encounters novel to him.[61] Given that the child's ability to learn will be based on classical conditioning, and the need to hold on to the mother's (and father's) good feelings toward the toddler, some simple but meaningful expectations of the child's behavior will be feasible. Simple cause and effect can be explained and may be grasped by the child, such as "You can't throw your sippy cup; it could make a big mess." When the caregiver expresses feelings of disapproval, the less than two-year-old will get the message, but verbal explanations should be given along with the parent's demanding compliance (more on this in chapter 9 on limit-setting). Because feelings are understood even by infants, words at this early age carry their meaning by the feeling and tone we put into using them. This is "how to behave" starts to be conveyed by parents to the child during the first year of life even when the baby can't yet understand words.

During the second and third year of life, the child is responsive to the parent's demand for compliance (more or less) because she doesn't want to lose mother's love and care; but also, if her basic trust is secure, then it is because she feels that mother means to help her well. In this, the child will subdue her strivings for autonomy, which by their inherent healthy aggressive nature tend to resist demands for compliance made by the caring parent.

The period between two to eight years of life is the era when compliance is most easily and most favorably developed. Foremost important principle: the better the child's basic trust, the more favorable the parent-child relationship (already well-established during the first two years of life), the more likely will compliance be achieved. Where basic mistrust predominates, where there is much parent-child conflict in the relationship, compliance will be more difficult to achieve, although all reasonable efforts to achieve it are strongly recommended.

If a good degree of compliance is not established during the two to eight years period, achieving compliance in the years that follow will generally be more difficult.

During this two to eight years golden era for compliance, the child will progressively develop the cluster of abilities required, to grasp and assess the merits of complying with the parent's expectations. While limit-setting has already been required, from two years of age on, given the young child's increasing efforts to test and master the environment and himself, the need for limit-setting will increase. Of course, the degree to which limit-setting is needed will depend on the child's inborn dispositions including, the child's energy-level, the intensity of his curiosity, and the degree of aggressive pressure of his strivings for autonomy. Testable explanations and reasons for the demands made will generally facilitate compliance. We detail strategies for this challenge further in chapter 8.

From four to eight years, that remarkable period when most children begin to learn to recognize and write letters, then words, then eventually to read and write, demonstrates the child's growing ability to read meaning into symbols. This extends into the child's progressively grasping the meaning of parents' intentions and expectations. And then beyond six or seven years, the child will grasp meaning whether it is stated simply or with humor, with patience or with annoyance, or even with sarcasm—that undesirable tendency some parents have. Parents can increasingly expect compliance from six- to eight-year-olds. In some well-put-together kids who have already demonstrated a strong need to have their own way, the challenge of setting-limits that continues for some years to come, will require greater patience and persistence on the part of the parents. Encouragement and reasonable praise for good performance are likely to go farther and faster, than harsh demands and punishment. More on this in chapter 8.

When a good, healthy, level of compliance is achieved by eight or so years of age, the way to achieving compliance with school and social expectations is well-paved. Healthy compliance is based on a willing acceptance of parents' expectations, on an unconscious agreement to adopt the parents' beliefs and codes of behavior, all essentially based on a positively valued identification with the parents. The converse holds as well. When an insufficient level of compliance by age eight years prevails, most commonly due to basic mistrust of parents care and intentions—although one occasionally finds a child whose uncertain sense of self and of autonomy makes compliance unfeasible[62]—compliance with school and society is likely to be insufficient.

What is achieved by age eight years, we might say "the foundation years for compliance," does not close the door on further possibility of its development. The continuing development during the 8- to 14-years period of adaptive, cognitive, and emotional functioning allows for the acquisition of new skills and abilities that may bring about a new trend in compliance. The challenge, however, of establishing compliance where a good foundation of it was not achieved by eight years, is that patterns of reactivity that led to insufficient compliance will have to be undone, before patterns of compliance take sufficient hold to become predictable. Much more work will now have to go into achieving healthy compliance.

Dramatic life events with much meaning for an elementary-school-age child, say the role of a loved teacher who has won the child's trust, may bring about a significant reversal of old patterns of noncompliance reactivity. The sudden loss of such a teacher, by the child's internalizing the teacher's expectations, can virtually overnight transform the child into one who will comply. Or, the influence of newly acquired friends who convey the merits of compliance may have a beneficial effect.

During the 14- to 19-years period, we cannot predict achieving compliance in adolescents whose compliance profile up to now has been weak, even less so with those who largely have been noncompliant. In adolescents of this age, the hope of instilling sufficient compliance with societal mores and rules of conduct can only be achieved by remedial educational, therapeutic, or dramatic means—the latter for instance, as coming across, and being influenced by, a former noncompliant person who has paid a heavy price for past delinquent or even criminal behavior. Some adolescents whose upbringing have been replete with neglect, or over-restrictive or harsh handling, may go through a period of rebellion from which, with the help of better adjusted friends or benevolent adults, they may modify their tendency from noncompliance to sufficient compliance.

NOTES

1. I am saying this because in my clinical work as a psychiatrist-psychoanalyst, I have found that patients (and colleagues) sometimes confound me with the fact that we don't always mean the same thing when we use certain words. The word *aggression*, the key word of this book, is a fine example; amazing, the different meanings given to the word. It makes me appreciate Lewis Carroll's complaint through Dorothy's voice in the Wizard of Oz, paraphrasing, "How can you make words mean so many different things?"

2. M. M. West and M. J. Konner. "The role of the father: an anthropological perspective," pp. 192–207 in *The Role of the Father in Child Development,* ed. M. E. Lamb (New York, NY: John Wiley & Sons, 1976).

3. Werner Bohleber, a German psychoanalyst, in his 1995 paper on "The children of the perpetrators—The after-effects of National Socialism on the following generations," which he presented in Toronto, May 4, 1995 (personal communication).

4. Psychoanalyst Lotte Koehler, who grew up in Nazi Germany, tells me that some child rearing books in Europe—such as "The German mother and her first child [which had] already appeared before Hitler took over the power in 1933"—have as much as declared this to be desirable. Also, Bohleber remarks that "according to Nazi ideology . . . the boy's will was to be broken . . ." to make him obedient, but also "hard and manly" (10).

5. Freud, "On narcissism: An introduction" (1914) in the *Standard* edition of Freud's writing, volume 14:69–102.

6. Jean Piaget proposed this to be the first stage of the development of intelligence. J. Piaget, *The Child's Conception of the World* (Paterson, N.J.: Littlefield, Adams, 1967).

7. H. Kohut, *The Analysis of the Self* (New York: International Universities Press, 1971) and *The Restoration of the Self* (New York: International Universities Press, 1977).

8. H. Parens, "Toward understanding prejudice: Benign and malignant," *The Future of Prejudice: Psychoanalysis and the Prevention of Prejudice,* ed. H. Parens,

A. Mahfouz, S. Twemlow, & D. Scharff (Lanham, MD: Jason Aronson, 2007): 21–36.

9. The "fight-or-flight response" was first described by Walter B. Cannon in 1915, and published in 1929 in his book *Bodily Changes in Pain, Hunger, Fear, and Rage* (New York: Appleton). Cannon's theory states that animals react to threats with a general discharge of the sympathetic nervous system, priming the animal for fighting or fleeing. This response was later recognized as the first stage of a general adaptation syndrome that regulates stress responses among vertebrates and other organisms." Taken from en.wikipedia.org/wiki/Fight-or-flight_response.

10. Which I detailed in *The Development of Aggression in Early Childhood* (Lanham, MD: Jason Aronson, 2008), chapter 3.

11. Freud, An outline of psychoanalysis. *Standard Edition* 23 (1939):141–207.

12. As Erik Erikson taught us. E. H. Erikson, "Identity and the life cycle." *Psychological Issues* 1(1959):1–170.

13. Bohleber, *The children of the perpetrators.*

14. Psychoanalytic developmental theory holds that in early life, the experience of feelings of intense hostility and rage (hostile destructiveness) are experienced by the young child as enormously powerful while the child's adaptive capabilities, his ego functions, are still weak. As a result the young child fears that his own destructiveness may destroy him too.

15. See chapter 5, p. 94, in Parens, et al., *The Future of Prejudice.*

16. Personal communication (2009).

17. In fact, a recent film directed by Michael Haneke, *The White Ribbon (Das Weisse Band),* portrays exactly this thesis. In a German village before World War I, a pastor's harsh, authoritarian rearing of his own children leads to their progressively committing crimes against targeted villagers. In a soon-to-be-published article, entitled "Voyeurism, violence, and the power of the media: The reader's/spectator's complicity in Jelinek's *The Piano Teacher* and Haneke's *La Pianiste, Caché, The White Ribbon,"* Margarete Landwehr, Ph.D., suggests that Haneke's mission is to hold up a mirror through film of our history so that we may better see ourselves. Haneke proposes that this film reflects this critically flawed societal trend that led to the crimes committed by the Third Reich. In a companion article, I will discuss how the psychodynamic mechanisms I am here talking about bring clarity to Haneke's portrayal of what happened.

18. During the Holocaust, "Kapos" were individuals from among those incarcerated in the camps (detention, concentration, labor, and death camps) who were selected to act as leaders of any given barrack that housed them. Some were as brutal as the Gestapo (Nazi Police).

19. As I wrote in chapters 2 (34) and 16 (282–285) of *The Future of Prejudice,* in addition to the role of hostile destructiveness in the dynamics of the malignant prejudice that drove the sadistic behavior of the Nazis (Gestapo especially) and the Milice in France, militant ethnocentric education—which for example teaches that "The Jews killed Christ" and "Infidels deserve to die"—buttressed by what Carlo Strenger calls "malignant self-righteousness" played a strong determining part as

well. C. Strenger, "The psychodynamics of self-righteousness and its impact on the Middle Eastern conflict," *International Journal of Applied Psychoanalytic Studies* 6 (2009:178–196.)

20. C. Strenger, "The psychodynamics of self-righteousness."

21. I speak about this in some detail in my memoirs, *Renewal of Life: Healing from the Holocaust* (Rockville, MD: Schreiber Publishing, 2004).

22. Ben Kiernan's *Blood and Soil: A World History of Genocide and Extermination from Sparta to Darfur* (New Haven, CT: Yale University Press, 2007).

23. Parens et al., *The Future of Prejudice* contains a number of studies on prejudice.

24. West & Konner, The role of the father.

25. Sent to me by Sam Chirman, M.D., a lifelong friend whose family was incarcerated with mine in Rivesaltes, a French concentration camp, and therewith shared with me some of the tribulations visited on us by the Holocaust.

26. The *Philadelphia Inquirer,* November 9, 1993. Front page, feature story by Martha Woodall.

27. This reference comes from Parens, Scattergood, Duff, & Singletary's *Parenting for Emotional Growth: The Textbook, Unit 2,* 100–101.

28. Strenger, C., "The psychodynamics of self-righteousness."

29. West and Konner, The role of the father.

30. See en.wikipedia.org/wiki/Recidivism and www.going-straight.com. The latter website is sponsored by Paul Karsten Fauteck, Psy.D., forensic psychologist and former prisoner, who strongly favors rehabilitation.

31. Personal communication (2008). Indeed, Kilian is reported to have contributed an article that was reviewed in *The Annual Survey of Psychoanalysis* (8[1956]:391, ed. J Frosch & N Ross, 391. New York: International Universities Press, Inc.), in which Kilian details a view of the development of civilization in parallel with the phases of libidinal development of the human child.

32. While there is disagreement as to whether these should equally be considered to have been genocide, Kiernan has recorded five genocides during the twentieth century: the Armenian genocide of April 1915, the World War II Holocaust of 1940–1945, the Killing Fields of Cambodia between 1975–1979, that of Rwanda-Burundi April-July 1994, and that in Bosnia in 1995. And the Darfur genocide, continuing to this day started early into the twenty-first century.

33. It is still hailed as France's idealistic triadic hope, the disgraceful Nazi collaboration of the Vichy France government in its contribution to the Holocaust during the second World War, notwithstanding.

34. We see this in all forms of interethnic, international, and even in interindividual conflict. A striking example occurred in and was a large motivator of World War II. In his *The Rise and Fall of the Third Reich,* William Shirer (1960) reported on his observing Hitler emerging from the same wagon train in which at the order of French General Foch the Franco-German armistice was signed ending World War I, and which Hitler had insisted the WWII armistice declaration would be signed—sweet revenge—that "I [Shirer] observed his face. . . . It was grave, solemn, yet brimming

with revenge. There was also in it, as in his springy step, a note of the triumphant conqueror . . . a scornful . . . joy . . . at this great reversal of fate—a reversal he himself had wrought" (742). Salman Akhtar, who knows its history well, describes the continuing cycle of violence-revenge in the interethnic centuries-old conflict between the Hindus and Muslims of India (see *The Crescent and the Couch* [Lanham, MD: Jason Aronson, 2008], chapter 13). Akhtar justly points to the fact that this interethnic massive community, as is common in all interethnic relations, is not just colored by hate, but also by love: "In the end [Akhtar says], their story is one of a close but ambivalent sibling bond" (231). This, I believe however, is not the case with all such interethnic conflicts.

35. Chapter 16 in Parens, et al., *The Future of Prejudice,* 288.

36. As I wrote in 2007, (*The Future of Prejudice,* 288), "Bar-on et al. (1997, 63–64) struck at the heart of the matter: [he, an Israeli and his Palestinian collaborators] found that in order to make efforts at peace and coexistence work, it is important to recognize that 'the peace process can bring about a severe crisis of identity. Who are we if there will be no enemy who tries to kill us?' [D. Bar-on, S. Sagy, E. Awwad, & M. Zak, Recent research and intervention activities in the Palestinian-Israeli context: an overview, 57–69 in *To Live Together: Shaping New Attitudes to Peace through Education,* ed. D.S. Halperin, (Paris: UNESCO: International Bureau of Education, 1997).] "Pertinent to this challenge is the recent NPR broadcast (August 23, 2005) comment by Dr. Eyad El-Sarraj, psychiatrist, president of the board of directors of the Gaza Community Mental Health Programme, a sound political activist, on the question of the effects on the Palestinians of the Israeli withdrawal from Gaza. He observed along lines similar to those of Israeli Bar-on, that elements of a crisis of identity comes with this withdrawal, that the Palestinian will have to revise critical aspects of his self concept, shifting the focus of his everyday motivations from preoccupation with the enemy in his house to that of coping with his fellow Palestinian in solving the problems that exist in-house" among his own people—"Who am I if I do not have my enemy" (Parens 2007, 288)?

37. I first applied the term "Nazis" to include European perpetrators as well as the Germans, who collaborated to carry out the Holocaust, in 2004 (in my memoirs, *Renewal of Life: Healing from the Holocaust).* In doing so I assert that, while Germany's Nazi (National Socialist) regime, by instituting its 1935 Nuremberg Laws—which stripped specified minorities of citizenship and all kinds of other human rights—initiated, engineered, and carried out the largest crime against humanity in recorded history, all but two countries in Europe—Denmark and Bulgaria—collaborated in carrying out this monstrous crime. It is moral dishonesty to hold only Germany of the Third Reich responsible for it; the German Nazis could not have carried this crime out without the collaboration of many non-German Europeans. Historians have recorded these facts (see Michael R. Marrus & Robert O. Paxton, *Vichy France and the Jews.* (New York: Schocken Books, 1983), as well as Saul Friedlander, *The Years of Extermination: Nazi Germany and the Jews, 1939–1945,* (New York: HarperCollins, 2007).

38. Werner Bohleber, a German psychoanalyst, in his 1995 paper on "The children of the perpetrators—The after-effects of National Socialism on the following generations" which he presented in Toronto, May 4, 1995 (personal communication), speaks to the problem addressed here. Specifically, the cases reported by Bergmann & Leggewie (1993—note 40 below) document what I am saying in the text.

39. Lotte Koehler, in personal communications has made the same assertion.

40. Bergmann, J and Leggewie, C (1993). Die Taeter sind unter uns. Beobachtungen aus der Mitte Deutschlands. *Kursbuch* 113:7–37.

41. D. Bar-on, *Legacy of Silence: Encounters with Children of the Third Reich* (Cambridge: Harvard University Press, 1989); Children of Perpetrators of the Holocaust: Working through one's moral self, *Psychiatry* 53(1990): 229–245; and Encounters between descendants of Nazi perpetrators and descendants of Holocaust survivors, *Psychiatry* 58:3(1995): 225–245.

42. Quoted by Bohleber (1995, 8). Lotte Koehler informed me that Gabriele Rosenthal, in her book *The Holocaust in Three Generations: Families of Victims and Perpetrators of the Nazi Regime* (London: Cassell & Company, 1998), found, in studying three generations of five families of victims and two families of perpetrators, the highest rate of suicides occurred in their third generation. The consequences of malignant prejudice-driven traumatization, in both victim and perpetrator, reverberate through their history.

43. This in essence is what Anna Freud described as "identification with the aggressor" in her *The Ego and the Mechanisms of Defense* (New York: International Universities Press, 1936).

44. Twemlow, Fonagy, & Sacco have done extensive work in schools that point to this problem. See the following: S. W. Twemlow, P. Fonagy, & F. C. Sacco, A social systems–power dynamic approach for preventing school violence, 272–289 in *School Violence: Assessment, Management, and Prevention,* ed. M. Shafii & S. Shafii (Washington, D.C: American Psychiatric Publishing, 2001); S. W. Twemlow, P. Fonagy, & F. C. Sacco, Feeling safe in school, http://www.backoffbully.com (2001/2002); S. W. Twemlow, P. Fonagy, F. C. Sacco, M. Gies, R. Evans, & R. Ewbanks, Creating a peaceful school learning environment: A controlled study of an elementary school intervention to reduce violence, *American Journal of Psychiatry* 158:5((2001):808–810.

45. In the United States, the world's first women's rights convention was held in 1848. The movement persisted during the first half of the twentieth century with an increasingly demanding voice that led to the launching of the women's liberation movement at its Chicago convention in 1968. www.ibiblio.org/prism/mar98/path.html.

46. For example, S. Provence & R. Lipton, Infants in institutions (New York: International Universities Press, 1962).

47. Starting with (1) John Bowlby's work in the 1950s and 1960s and beyond culminating in his major three-volume work, *Attachment and Loss,* vol. I (1969), vol. II (1973) and vol. III (1980) published by Basic Books; (2) M. Ainsworth, M. Blehar,

E. Waters, & S. Wall, *Patterns of Attachment: A Psychological Study of the Strange Situation* (Hillsdale, NJ: Erlbaum, 1978); and (3) a large number of researchers on the topic.

48. Such as (1) Rene Spitz (1946, 1965; [add full ref.]); (2) Anna Freud, *Normality and Pathology in Childhood* (New York: International Universities Press, 1965); (3) E. H. Erikson, *Identity and the Life Cycle,* Psychological Issues, Monogr. 1. (New York: International Universities Press, 1959); (4) M. S. Mahler, F. Pine, & A. Bergman, *The Psychological Birth of the Human Infant* (New York: Basic Books, 1975); (5) D. Stern, *The Interpersonal World of the Human Infant* (New York: Basic Books, 1985); and many others.

49. The child may be a spoiled brat; this may require more parental guidance than I am discussing in this text. If it is not that the child is a spoiled brat but, rather, that the average-expectable emotional needs of rearing a particular child demands more of the parents than the parents assumed when they decided to have a child, the resulting problems may be large and the parents might find it enormously helpful to seek help from a child-trained mental health professional to sort things out and institute a psychotherapeutic process to help both parents and child find more constructive and adaptive ways of dealing with what has already developed in the child and how to proceed henceforth. The consequences of not resolving such a situation positively may have life-lasting consequences for all concerned, parents and child.

50. J. Kagan & N. Herschkowitz, *A Young Mind in a Growing Child* (Mahwah, NJ: Lawrence Erlbaum Associates, 2005).

51. (1) J. Bowlby, *Attachment* (New York: Basic Books, 1969) and many attachment theorists; (2) Rene Spitz, *The First Year of Life* (New York: International Universities Press, 1965); (3) Mahler, Pine, and Bergman, *The Psychological Birth of the Human Infant;* (4) H. Parens, *The Development of Aggression in Early Childhood,* (5) Stern, *The Interpersonal World of the Infant;* and others.

52. Reported by (1) Lotte Koehler in her "On the development of the autobiographical self and autobiographical memory—implicit and explicit aspects" given at the International Self Psychology Symposium, Dreieich, Germany, May 27, 2005; (2) Kagan & Herschkowitz, *A Young Mind in a Growing Child;* (3) J. C. LeDoux, *The Emotional Brain* (New York: Simon & Schuster, 1996).

53. Stern, *The Interpersonal World of the Infant.*

54. Memory researchers tell us and there is agreement among them that there are two types of memory that conform well with what we find in intense psychotherapies: 1. *Implicit memory,* also called *procedural memory,* is the first form of memory that becomes recorded in the brain. It is not retrievable at will; it seems to reside in the person's unconscious mind and may emerge, after much effort, not as fully developed ideas but as images of experience. For example, in the course of a clinical psychoanalysis, a painfully traumatized patient while putting into words what came to her mind, suddenly crying and in anguish, put into words a fantasy of a child crying bitterly and who is trying to cling to her caregiver who pushes her away. This opened a series of spontaneous powerful fantasies of an infant, who, crying and pleading for comforting is pushed away repeatedly; and finally the infant quiets, is curled up in the

corner of her crib, her cover over her head; hopeless. 2. *Explicit memory,* also called *declarative memory,* is the second type of memory, which we generally are able to remember at will or with minor effort. Explicit memory generally carries with it the ability to remember an experience in words, in ideas, in time, as well as with feelings. By five to six years of age, the capacity for explicit memory is sufficiently developed that most people can remember their past to about those years.

55. E. H. Erikson, *The Life Cycle* (1959).

56. Classical conditioning has been shown to already occur in the unborn child, during the third trimester of fetal life. This intrauterine learning Kagan and Herschkowitz tell us "can be preserved through the early postnatal months. [These authors go on to describe a study of] a chimpanzee fetus [who was subjected to] a 500 Hz tone CS [as a conditioning stimulus] followed by a vibroacoustic US [unconditioned stimulus] that provoked physical movement [in the fetus], over 150 trials over a 30-day period. Presentation of the CS alone 58 days after birth provoked a conditioned [physical movement in the infant ape]" (*A Young Mind in a Growing Child,* pp 57–58).

57. Koehler, "On the development of the autobiographical self."

58. P. Fonagy & M. Target, Playing with reality: I. The theory of mind and the normal development of psychic reality, *International Journal of Psycho-Analysis* 77(1996):217–233.

59. Kagan & Herschkowitz, *A Young Mind in a Growing Child.*

60. Koehler, "On the development of the autobiographical self."

61. M. S. Mahler et al., *The Psychological Birth of the Human Infant*; H. Parens, *The Development of Aggression in Early Childhood* (1979 [2008]).

62. Some children with harsh obsessive-compulsive disorders, or with autistic spectrum disorders such as Asperger's Syndrome, may find it difficult to comply with even quite reasonable parental expectations due to excessive, disorganizing anxiety, and not due to basic mistrust of their parents.

Chapter 8

Achieving Compliance: Discipline, Limit Setting, and Punishment

Optimizing the way we achieve compliance is the prime goal of this chapter. We achieve compliance by means of *discipline, limit setting,* and *punishment.* As I did with regard to *compliance* and *obedience,* I must define how I use these terms.

Discipline has a twin application. (1) From the parent's position, it is the parent's efforts to help the child develop the ability to behave in ways that are acceptable to the parent and to the social group in which they live. (2) For the child, it is to develop the ability and the skills to do what is expected of him and to do what the child demands of himself—which means to develop self-discipline. Note then, that discipline requires collaborative action between child and parents and that it is an undertaking that fosters the development in the child of a sense of competence and self-reliance. Discipline is usually brought about when the child's behavior challenges the parent's wishes and beliefs of what the child's conduct should be. All parents hope that their children will ultimately internalize their views of what the child's conduct is expected to be.

Limit setting is the parent's restriction of some activity the parent feels is harmful—to the child, the parent, someone else, or something valued—or which is not socially acceptable. In this, the parent acts as an agent of the child's adaptive functioning, at a time when these functions are not sufficiently developed within or are resisted by the child. In other words, the parent does for the child what the child cannot yet or will not do for herself or himself, whether it is because of insufficient ability or lack of understanding or the unwillingness to recognize, or in defiance of, the consequences of her or his actions.

Punishment is a strategy in which—as a sign of substantial disapproval and to enforce one's limit setting—the parent withdraws a privilege or inflicts pain upon the child. I want to note here and discuss later that punishment always is a sign that limit setting has failed. Important: competent limit setting reduces and may even eliminate the need for punishment.

As I said in chapter 7, the rejection of authoritarianism now prevalent in many corners of every continent and the rising awareness on all continents of human rights, lead to the need to correspondingly program our strategies for developing compliance in our children. Rather than by harsh measures that deny their sense of self, we have to find ways to obtain compliance with authority in our children while allowing their sense of self and their healthy narcissistic need to make of their life what they want and can, while based on reasonable principles and a human rights-based sense of morality.

So, in our efforts to achieve healthy compliance with authority, the child must be loved and respected as a human being with rights, and at the same time we require of the child that he have a sense of self that brings with it a sense of reasonableness and responsibility. A child who is treated like each one of us (child or adult) would like to be treated, is much more likely to comply of his own free will with parental and community-accepted authority than the child who is not so treated. But at the same time, one does not achieve free-will compliance in a child by always being sweet and making no demands on that child or by always giving in to what the child wants. It is reasonable and realistic to hold that: when it's time to go to bed, it's time to go to bed. When it's time to get up to go to school, it's time to get up. A protesting child should be taken seriously; her complaints should be listened to, but this does not carry with it a promise that her wish will be met. Limit setting to which we turn now is critical in getting there.

RATIONALE

When I asked "What makes achieving compliance so large a challenge" (chapter 7), I said that limit setting invariably encroaches on the child's developing sense of self and strivings for autonomy. Given their psychobiological role in securing adaptation, strivings for autonomy have to be rigorous—life is full of challenges from the moment the unborn baby starts the journey out of the birth canal. These strivings for autonomy are prewired (part of prebirth brain development) and therefore are driven from within. When the parent attempts to restrict the activities of a young child thrust by that inner pressure, the child unavoidably experiences frustration. Like all experiences that cause unpleasure (psychic pain), when frustration becomes excessive it generates hostility within the child. This hostility is experienced toward the person who is causing the unpleasure, the one setting the limit. But this person is most commonly one who is highly emotionally valued by the child, be it mother or father; the hostility experienced is toward someone the child loves. In this way, setting limits often creates a conflict within the child.

But when the child resists the demand made by the parent, limit setting becomes challenging for the parent too. It causes the parent distress, even pain, when setting limits that are in the child's or teenager's best interest causes the child to feel hostility toward the parent instead of appreciation—what thanks for trying to help your kid. Consider the difficulty your 13-year-old daughter might encounter, were she allowed on a date with an 18-year-old boy she likes, but who does not know she is only 13. Mother sets limits. The 13-year-old becomes furious and stomps upstairs, shouting at her mother, "I hate you; you never trust me, and you never want me to be happy." It cannot be avoided; it must be done. But we parents do need to think of how we might best meet this challenge.

Not only do we not get appreciation for protecting the child, but more difficult is that the child's reaction evokes in the parent an almost unavoidable counterreaction of anger, which troubles the parent further and often, in thoughtful parents, makes the parent uncertain about insisting on the child's compliance. As a result, many a parent will avoid setting child-protective limits exactly because of the hostility it may mobilize in the child and, in reaction then, in the parent. Feeling hostility toward the children we love commonly produces feelings of guilt in us and self-doubt, plus the feeling that one is being a hurtful parent. One mother said that she worried that insisting on compliance would "break her child's spirit." Note that in this, the parent's worry seemed to be that her child's sense of self and autonomy would be broken. This mother's anxiety is in crucial contrast to that experienced by the mother who believes the principle that recommends harsh child rearing, that "the child's stubbornness must be broken" (see chapter 7). But by backing away from limit setting to avoid the child's anger, the overanxious parent risks making her child insufficiently compliant—with all the problems this brings (see chapter 7).

A second common byproduct of a child's resisting the parent's limit setting is that the parent may tend to set limits punitively and punish before it is necessary. A third common byproduct is that parents may set limits and inconsistently follow through with that limit setting. That is to say, feeling conflicted over setting limits the parent will do so in an unclear manner, often conveying her or his uncertain feelings about it. This may lead some children to increasingly defy any limits and expectations.

In summary, in the child, the difficulties arise because his strivings for autonomy are being interfered with. If limit setting is done in a context of increasing hostility in both child and parent, it is likely to lead to problems in the child's developing a competent sense of autonomy and the sense of self.

Secondly, limit setting quite commonly stirs up feelings of hostility toward the parent the child loves, thereby producing a conflict of ambivalence within the child. Ambivalence creates an internal conflict that is produced by experiencing coexisting (or rapidly alternating) feelings of love and hate toward a loved person. And it is important to know that conflicts due to ambivalence in early childhood have a tendency to stabilize, and may then become part of the parent-child relationship into adolescence and beyond. While this type of internal conflict, by the way, is quite unavoidable in human relationships, it is important that these conflicted feelings not get too intense nor occur too frequently.

Furthermore, feelings of hostility, and even hate—that come with troublesome limit setting—toward someone we love are experienced not only by the child toward the parent, but also on the part of the parent toward the child. Thus, in limit setting there is the risk that both child and parent become burdened by conflicts due to ambivalence.

We want to emphasize, however, that while this kind of conflict holds the potential for creating problems within the child, when the ambivalence is moderate, it can produce significant healthy growth. It will do so by triggering accommodative reactions on the part of the child that will lead to:

1. Learning how to deal constructively with his own hostility given that the child feels nice kids don't hate their mothers. No one needs to tell the child. The child feels it himself.
2. Fostering the internalizing of the expectations and mores of the parents.
3. Forging reasonable compliance to authority and instructors.
4. Molding healthy assertiveness within the child. This will not be achieved if the ambivalence experienced toward the parent is too intense.

The goal then is to not intensify excessively feelings of ambivalence within the child, nor within oneself as one sets limits; parents must maintain the anger and hostility generated in them by their child to reasonable levels. This is one large reason why avoiding harsh limits and punishment is crucial. Then, once the conflict in setting limits subsides, it is enormously helpful to talk about what happened to try to help the child learn from the distress mutually experienced, by parent and child, and when necessary, to mitigate whatever undue hurt feelings were engendered and repair whatever wounds were caused. One does so by apologies, explanations, and talking about what happened that went awry, *not* by gifts of candy or toys. This applies to kids at all ages from early childhood through adolescence.

Limit setting, then, impacts significantly on the parent and the child from infancy through adolescence. For both, there is much at stake. Now let's talk about constructive ways to set limits.

SETTING LIMITS CONSTRUCTIVELY

Competent, constructive limit setting not only fosters compliance, but also reduces and may even eliminate the need for punishment.

It is important to reduce as best we can the need for punishment for two reasons: (1) When limit setting fails it generates anger and often hostility in both child and mother; punishment then, is commonly dished out under conditions of anger and even hostility between a child and his or her parent. (2) As all parents know, as punishment often brings with it the discharge of the parent's own hostility toward the child, it tends to cloud its aim of being in the child's best interest—even when the parent insists that it is for the child's good. Even the best parents are at times driven by their children's behavior to actions they regret. By virtue of the large difficulties produced in them by growing up, the large demands made on them by the environment, the occasionally excessive demands they make on themselves, and the significant frustrations and pains that often come with their interactions with peers and others, children are at times at wits end and may push even the best of parents to the point where the parents behave in ways they subsequently regret. Parents need to recognize that when a child feels secure enough at home, it's at home that he or she may let loose, even be onerous, because it's the safest place in the world to let off steam—the place where he will get least hurt and most easily forgiven. There is no way out of it: it will be necessary for parents to discipline their children, to set limits, and from time to time to punish them.

We have found that parents tend not to see the distinction between setting limits and punishing and many then have difficulty setting limits constructively. They especially avoid setting limits when their anger arouses within them the fear that they will harm the child. But when one has a clear understanding that setting limits is intended to act in the child's behalf when the child cannot yet herself adequately do so, the parent's fear of causing harm wanes.

Every parent who has more than one child knows that children vary in how they will respond to limits. Inborn dispositions play a large part in this. So do the child's prior experiences. Some children are more malleable than others; some tend to resist guidance and direction more vigorously than others. As a result, some children will be easier than others to set limits with and some will challenge the parents' wits, love, and fortitude. Here we are speaking about children who fall within the wide range of normal behaviors. The significantly disturbed child or the more difficult child at the farther end of the spectrum of irritability may require more specifically tailored strategies. There are good books[1] that address this type of child.

When to Set Limits

I have often been asked, "When should I start setting limits?" The best answer I know is, "When limits are first needed." Here is an example from our EPPI/MCP project (see chapter 1).

> When Candy was five months old, she crawled toward Cindy, also five months old. In her exploratory push, Candy grabbed the toy that Cindy held. Even though we could not infer that Candy was intentionally taking something from Cindy, in contrast to her simply being attracted to the toy Cindy was holding, the group of mothers quite uniformly reacted with the feeling that this should not be permitted. Candy's mother immediately reacted by going to Candy, taking the toy from her, returning it to Cindy, and telling her five-month-old daughter that she was not allowed to take the toy from Cindy.

Some parents are taken aback by the thought that it is reasonable to set limits with a five-month-old child. I point out that if the child is doing something the parent does not approve of, then the parent ought to convey this to the child and set an age-appropriate and situation-appropriate limit. The setting of this limit was not done with anger or even annoyance. It was done with the awareness that this five-month-old had transgressed in a social situation, and since the mother felt that this is not desirable social behavior, conveyed this to her child by her action. Certainly, a five-month-old is too young for an explanation—although it causes no harm to say a few words—but she is not too young to get the message conveyed by mother's emotional tone and action that she is not allowed to take another kid's toy.

> At 13 months of age, Jane seemed to constantly be propelled—as are most children at this age—to want what others had. When she wanted my coffee, I did not allow her to take it, telling her that it was hot and might hurt her and that coffee is not for children. After that, she turned to her mother and conveyed to her that she wanted some juice.
>
> At this age, Jane was not so easy with her peers. She would be demanding, pulling, holding onto things, and she would become angry. This particular morning, she screamed twice and shouted in anger at two of her young peers. She was tenaciously pursuing the purse that Temmy was holding. Temmy held on for about a minute, but Jane persisted in her demand, kept pulling, and angrily scolded Temmy, who let go of her end and began to cry.
>
> Jane's mother intervened. Prior to her physical intervention, Jane's mother had been giving Jane instructions from a distance, telling her not

> to behave as she was with Temmy and raising her voice as time went by. Ultimately, when Jane pulled the purse from Temmy, mother got up, went to Jane, retrieved the purse from her, and returned it to Temmy. As she did so, she told Jane—with mild anger and a scolding tone—that Jane is not allowed to take things from others.

We have found in our years of observation that, most children begin to require limits from the time they are about six months of age. Our studies show that the requirement for limits from this time on is largely the product of a psychobiological upsurge in aggressiveness (in the form of assertiveness) in children that is part and parcel of a maturational change occurring around this time period (see chapter 1).

Parents are often frustrated by the fact that when they set limits—even with a child as young as 6 or 13 months old—they need to repeat the limits more often than they like. Thirteen-month-old Jane's mother was annoyed by the fact that (as had been happening for about five months now) Jane did not readily respond to mother's expectations and mother had to repeat them a number of times. Furthermore, mother was quite annoyed when it became necessary for her to go to Jane and put some force behind the behavioral expectation she had of her lovely, feisty daughter.

My impression is that parents seem to recognize that while the child seems driven by an inner pressure to do what she is doing, the child does not have built-in controls over it. The development of such controls occurs only over time as the child makes conscious efforts to put on the brakes. As I discussed in chapter 7, the child is pushed from within to do what most parents believe she "wants" to do; but the fact is that the child is driven and often seems compelled to do it. It's at the basis of the fact that generally none of us likes to be told what to do. This is so from the very beginning of life. Therefore, the mother's expectations often run against not only the child's endowment and inability to know how to control her inner pressures, but also against the child's wishes, healthy narcissism, and strivings toward autonomy. For these reasons, limit setting is a long process, one that requires repetition and is often tedious for both child and parents.

One more point on when to set limits: Because limits are going to be called for many more times than is wished for by either child (of whatever age) or parent, it is going to be tedious for both mother and child (at whatever age), and because setting limits invariably brings about a conflict between child and mother as well as a conflict within the child and often within the mother, it behooves parents to set limits only when they are truly needed. Again, the obligatory level of the limit has to be considered. Setting limits that are not actually necessary tends to be experienced by children of all ages as oppressive. As they grow, children are eventually able to discern whether the limit imposed by the parent is really called for or not. They may not achieve that capability when they are one year old, but they certainly will by the time they are five to eight.

Principles of Limit Setting

I said in chapter 7 that to achieve compliance with the expectations we have of our kids, the expectations we have must have meaning and be reasonable; they can't all be equally obligatory. Children come to recognize quite soon in life that not all of our expectations have the same weight. As I suggested, we therefore, should have categories of expectations with degrees of obligation: some expectations are obligatory, some are desirable but don't have the same degree of "you have no choice; you've got to do or not do this", some may be that we as parents wish our kids would do or not do. Going to school can't have the same meaning as sharing toys.

Also, a few paragraphs back, I said that limits should be set in ways that are age-appropriate and situation-appropriate. They should also be state-appropriate and history-appropriate.

Regarding age-appropriate: One can't have the same expectations for a child when he is seven months, seven years, or 14 years of age. We'll take this up more extensively in a moment.

Regarding state-appropriate: A seven-month-old who bites mother's nipple while falling asleep requires a different tone and approach to biting than the wide-awake three-year-old who, much distressed, bites her playmate.

Regarding situation-appropriate: A different tone and approach is warranted when an 18-month-old takes a toy from another child than when that 18-month-old tries to pull an air-conditioner plug or walks into the street.

And regarding history-appropriate: What we have in mind here is any particular child's history of reacting to your limit setting. If the child readily complies when limits are set, or limits are not often required, a freer hand can be allowed in setting limits—more casualness, less firmness, more time. On the other hand, if from early life on, the child, like Jane, tends to resist limits, and setting limits often becomes a mini battle of wills, a more structured and predictable pattern of limit setting would be very helpful. It's also likely that more firmness and a greater conveyance of disapproval will be needed. Or, if the child from quite early on not only resists, but also puts up a struggle when mom sets limits and battles of wills are common and at times difficult, a well-structured, clearly defined pattern of limit setting will be necessary. There is a greater likelihood that limits may fail and punishment will be needed with this child than with the other two.

When setting limits, explain why the limit is needed, have a strategy or pattern of limit setting, be reasonable and be firm. For parents, be lovingly firm. Why explain? So that your child or adolescent will know your good reason for stepping on her sense of self. It should be in order to protect her, someone else, or something you value. Don't say "Because I said so" or "Because I'm the boss"; your child will not be impressed. She'll think you're a bully. Your adolescent, in addition, will despise you. If you've already amply explained, "Because I said so" is ok.

Pattern your limit setting so that your child will learn what to expect from you. Take a set number of steps before you feel you have failed and go to punishment. It is great to avoid punishment, but not by giving in to the child who is stubbornly refusing to comply with the limits. When you do, you both lose.

The Basic Limit-Setting Model

Step 1: Nicely tell your child what to do or not do.

If your child does not comply, go to

Step 2: Repeat what you said a bit more firmly, and a bit louder.

If your child still does not comply go to

Step 3: Now tell your child this is the third time you're telling her to do what you said, and you don't like that. Remind your child how unpleasant things turned out the last time you went through this with her. Your tone is still firmer than before. Don't plead. It produces guilt and meanness.

If you still get no compliance, go to

Step 4: Now go to your child, with firmness and moderate anger tell her you really don't like her behavior. If she does not do what you said now, there will be a punishment. This is a warning of things to come; it is not a threat. Your child should know where you stand.

You can present it as the child's choice: she can do what you say or she can choose the punishment—no favorite TV program today. This heightens the child's awareness that she is in fact choosing: "I comply or I take punishment," thereby heightening the child's sense of having a say in this miserable event.

If you still get no compliance, the child in fact is choosing that you go to

Step 5: You now tell the child she will not be allowed to see her favorite TV program tonight, or the like. And you physically help her do what you told her to do four steps before.

With six-to-ten-year-olds you should not need that many steps to get compliance; four or even three may be enough. With nondifficult adolescents, you should not need more than three steps.

Let's assume that you set a limit and soon came to recognize that the limit was not really necessary. For example, a mother has just told her four-year-old he cannot play outside with the cousin he is visiting because he will get his clothes dirty. But he is already no longer clean and it is near the end of the day, and mother decides it won't really matter much now. She changes her mind. She tells him that she has thought it over and it's okay to go out. He is tickled pink.

There is much to be gained by telling your child (of whatever age) you have reconsidered the limit you just stated and find it is not necessary. Our experience is that children of all ages are appreciative of a parent changing her or his mind when that change is reasonable. In more than four decades of observing and working with infants and their mothers, I have yet to see a child or teenager turn to her mother and ridicule the mother for having changed her mind. Quite invariably, I have seen appreciation on the part of the child or teenager for this kind of thoughtfulness and flexibility on the part of the parent. Furthermore, it is a good model for the child, that he is more likely to adopt such thoughtfulness and flexibility having seen his mother or father change her or his mind when it is reasonable to do so. Some parents make the mistake of thinking that changing one's mind when reasonable to do so may be taken by the child as a sign of weakness. But the child and certainly the teenager will recognize when the parent's change of mind is due to weakness or due to reasonableness; furthermore, the parent who never changes his mind when it is reasonable to do so will quickly be experienced by the child as rigid, unreasonably rigid.

Vary your pattern according to the kind of child you have. That is, if you have a child who is a bit shy and timid, slow the pace of limit setting down. Go easy. If your child is quite vigorous and even a bit hyperactive, move into limit setting more quickly and take two or three steps instead of five. If you have a hyperactive child, you and your child would very likely benefit from professional help. If you have a difficult adolescent, more rigorous behavioral strategies will be needed and again professional help may be enormously helpful for both adolescent and parents. One more point before we consider principles of punishment.

A Critical Point in Setting Limits

Two-year-old Harry once again stood up on the chair from which his mother had just taken him off. Pushed to anger, mother pulled him off the chair somewhat harshly. Harry, now upset and crying, stretched his arms up to his mother, conveying that he wanted her to pick him up. She turned away from him with, "I told you not to

> stand on the chair. You're a bad boy." Rejected by mother, Harry shuffled across the room to his father and leaned on him. Father said, "Don't come to me. You're being bad." Harry's crying intensified; he hid his head in the sofa and I learned that for hours later he seemed upset.

We all operate under the general principle that we want to hold on to what feels good and get rid of what feels bad. Another way of stating this principle is that we all want to take in, to internalize that which feels good, and we all want to eject, deny, and throw out that which feels bad. For this reason, setting limits under favorable emotional conditions tends to favor the child's internalizing the parents' expectations. The reverse—not internalizing parental expectations—holds when limits are set with hostility and in a mean-spirited interaction.

A critical point occurs when the parent has scolded the child and the child becomes upset and turns to the parent for comforting. If the parent has gotten to the point of scolding the child—and the child has gotten to the point of being upset enough to cry, fuss, and want comforting—it is understandable that the parent is going to be angry with the child. When the child is upset, however, who do we expect the child will turn to for comforting? Of course, he'll turn to the caregiver to whom he is attached and that usually is the loved parent.

I have often found that some angry mothers will reject the child's appeal for comfort under these circumstances. I have been told, "He's trying to get his way," or, "He's trying to butter me up." I think that is wrong. What I see is that when a child is scolded by his mother, he feels threatened that his world is falling apart. Made very anxious then, he turns to his mother for comforting. Who else would he turn to for protection and safety? And, the mother (or father) should accept the plea and comfort the child. The reason for this is twofold—and this applies to not only kids of all ages but also adults. In terms of young children:

First, given the principle that we all want to retain what feels good and try to eject from ourselves what feels bad, consider the following. The mother who picks up the child who is making a plea for comforting has the opportunity to repeat her limit setting under conditions when the child is experiencing her as the comforting, loving, soothing, good mother.

> Upset because Mother told her she could not take Betty's ball, three-year-old Lucy was on her mother's lap. Mother was gently and quietly saying, "I know it upsets you that you can't have Betty's ball. But, it's hers. She doesn't want to let you play with it right now. You can't just

take it from her. I can't let you do that. I wouldn't let her take your things." Mother hugged Lucy gently. Lucy still looked a bit sad. But she slowly nodded just once and stayed, comfortable, in mother's lap for a few minutes. Then she was off, playing with Betty again.

Given how Harry's parents rejected his plea for comforting, repeated the limit in anger, and told him he's a bad child, this in fact undermined their efforts to set limits and intensified Harry's emerging feelings of hate toward them. In addition, at the same time they were intensifying their own feelings of anger toward their own child. But the principle is this: What Lucy's mother is doing will lead to Lucy's internalizing mother's expectation because it is stated under conditions of comforting and soothing in the hands of a good mother. It comes from the "good mother" and will be experienced as being done for the child's well-being. By contrast, the handling of Harry by his parents makes him wish to eject what, his "bad mother," as he then perceives her, is telling him; he does not hear what she is saying and he therefore is likely to reject internalizing his mother's expectation.

Of course this is a simple model; nothing in psychic life is that easy. That is to say, yes, Harry will eventually internalize the "bad mother's" actions and her hostilely stated expectation. It will, however, be internalized with an overload of anger, a wish to resist it, and to be rid of it, with the full play of hostility still attached to the experience. Lucy on the other hand, comforted by her sympathetic mother, is helped to lessen and perhaps even eliminate the angry feelings her mother's limit setting generated within her.

The second reason for responding positively to the scolded child's appeal for comfort is this. In the course of development, we all start out with feelings about ourselves and others—especially our family members, most particularly our mothers and fathers. Some of these feelings are good and some are bad. These feelings become part of the images we have of ourselves and those around us.

Mental health professionals speak of the "good self" and the "bad self," the "good mother" and the "bad mother." Mental health professionals assume that we all form images of ourselves, which we retain in our minds and that play a large part in our emotional life. The larger the feelings we have of love for ourselves and our mothers, fathers, and siblings, the less our feelings of ambivalence. The larger the load of generated hostility within us—the larger our feelings of self-hate and of hate toward our mothers and fathers, the larger our negative feelings of ambivalence that stabilize over time—the greater the difficulty we encounter in life. The influence of love on the one hand, and excessive hostility on the other, in the development of our relationships, our self-esteem, and the character of our conscience, is determined by the balance of these feelings of love and hate toward others and ourselves we carry within us.

This is only a partial listing of the influence of the balance of love and hostility toward our self and others. It is well-known in the mental health field that excessive ambivalence leads to pathologic formations that can have exceedingly harsh consequences to our adaptation to life, the formation of relationships, and our ability to cope, work, and derive gratifications.

Taking this into account, trying to lessen the degree of hostility we feel in setting limits becomes crucial. It is exactly at the point where a child who has been scolded and now wants to be comforted that ambivalence can be significantly lessened or intensified. For this reason especially, but not only in the course of setting limits, when your child pleads for comforting, pick her up, comfort her, then (when setting limits) repeat your expectation, explaining why you have this expectation and that you expect your child to comply with it.

PRINCIPLES OF PUNISHMENT

Of course you want to avoid it. The negative consequences of needing to punish often are large. Too frequent punishment erodes parent-child relationships. Parents know that, but it is well to bear in mind.

So is the fact that when we punish our child, we assume that it is in the child's best interest. Regrettably, as all parents know, punishment often occurs when a parent is angry, sometimes very angry, and in fact feels hostility toward her or his own child. This regrettably may override the parent's genuine aim of the punishment being in the child's best interest. Even the best parents are at times driven to actions they regret by what they feel to be their children's unacceptable behavior. Children, by virtue of the challenges and difficulties that come with growing up are highly capable at times of pushing even the best of parents to the point where their parents behave in ways these parents subsequently regret.

We parents ourselves need to be sufficiently self-disciplined to prevent our causing undue harm to our own children because there is no way out of it. It is desirable for us to discipline our children, to set limits, and from time to time we will need to punish them.

There are two basic forms of punishment: (1) the withdrawal of a privilege and (2) the inflicting of pain. The withdrawal of privilege is much safer and generally much better than inflicting pain—kids have enough pain just meeting the demands of everyday life. Unfortunately, too many parents forget that their growing up years were full of anxiety-producing challenges and even outright psychic pain.

In punishing by the withdrawal of a privilege, allow me to make a rather obvious comment. When choosing the withdrawal of a privilege, it is well to choose a privilege the child enjoys. A child may say that she does not care whether or not she can watch that (her favorite) program. Children will often say they don't care in order to lessen the sting of having a privilege withdrawn. Sometimes a child may say this to retaliate against the parent, to try to make the parent feel ineffectual. In withdrawing a privilege, rely more on what you know your child has enjoyed in the past and is likely to enjoy now, rather than on the child's response when a heated battle of wills is going on between the two of you.

Punishment is never reasonable with infants less than one year of age.

The mildest effective withdrawal of privilege is the "time out." For the young child, the child has to sit or be in some limited space and stay there for a limited number of minutes. This can work very well with children from 18 months to 6 years (more detail below). Beyond that age including into adolescence, it takes the form of "grounding," which works well too. And of course there are other privileges that matter to kids, TV, computer, cell phone, etc.

When withdrawing a privilege, be reasonable; dose the amount of punishment to the degree of unacceptability of noncompliance. For instance, don't take the TV, or the computer, or cell-phone away for more than one program at a time, or for more than one evening or day at a time.

Don't withdraw things that are needed for your child's well-being such as food or sleep. Don't disallow a TV program recommended by a teacher as an assignment. If your child has some difficulty making friends, don't punish by disallowing a peer from coming to the house.

Use your judgment: the older the child, the more difficult she is to set limits with, the more you up the punishment, etc. The younger the child, the more shy or timid, the more slowly you move into punishment.

Inflicting pain is loaded with problems. Unfortunately, some energetic young children younger than five or so, just will not comply with limits even when privilege withdrawal would seem reasonably dosed. Many of these younger kids tend to not stop until they get a swat on the bottom.

But, there have to be strict rules and limits in physical punishment:

(a) Never use anything other than your open hand. A fist is out of order. Belts, sticks, paddles, and all else are out of order too.
(b) Give no more than one *moderate* swat on the bottom of the less than six year old.
(c) Always swat on the clothed bottom. Do not make the child take off her or his pants. A moderate swat on the back of a shoulder too can put emphasis on the need for compliance.

(d) If you have to physically transport your child to his room, be firm but exert the least force needed. There's a good chance that your child will say you're hurting him; you have to make sure that your hold is not, in fact, harsh.
(e) Physical modes of punishment too easily run into becoming child abuse, and parents *must* avoid child abuse. Child abuse cures nothing; it cripples a lot, both child and parent.

I'll comment below about physical punishment in the six-to-ten-year-old and adolescent age ranges.

LIMIT SETTING AND PUNISHMENT OVER THE YEARS

It is of course critical to consider the child's age when setting limits. This is because, as I detailed in chapter 7, the state of self and the self's ability to understand, predict, know, judge, and adapt, are not present during the first two years and develop only gradually; we can assume that they become sufficiently developed by six to eight years. Note that the timetable that I, or any developmentalists, suggest is not intended to give exact ages at which all children will have developed a given ability. This is because children vary in their development schedules—due to both their biological endowment and their experiences. So the numbers given are "at about this (given) age."

Mental health research and clinical work this past century have taught us that it is in the best interest of the child and the parents for children to be permitted and helped to express their feelings and thoughts. We expect them to do so, however, with reasonableness, appropriateness, and with good judgment. It is the task of each family to determine what constitutes "reasonableness, appropriateness, and good judgment." Parents are of course informed by cultural mores to make this determination.

Let's look briefly at limit setting over the years.

Limits need to be set whenever they are called for, but only when truly needed: to protect the child, others, and valued possessions, and to help the child behave in a socially responsible and acceptable way. Limits should be clear and understandable with appropriate explanations and reasonable firmness. They are set to inform and guide the child. Where needed, limits should be enforced and backed up. But parents should also be able to back down on a limit they find on reconsideration to be unnecessary. Punish when it is absolutely necessary and after a warning has been given. However, it helps to punish with care and respect for your child. In the course of limit setting, when your child is upset and wants you to comfort him or her, do so. Then, while comforting the child (of any age), repeat your limit and give the reasons for it.

Infancy (zero to eight months)

Taking what we have learned about brain development and the development of intelligence (see chapter 7), we cannot expect the less than two-year-old to process the parent's expectations and to understand why the parent is having such expectations. But by classical conditioning, the child will resonate with the parent's feelings about what the child is doing and what the mother expects. Finding again and again that mother reacts unpleasantly, in tones alarming to the baby or toddler when the baby or toddler does a given thing or acts a given way, the less than two-year-old can learn to comply with mother's age-appropriate expectations. One can explain to the infant why one makes the given demand; it is a very good habit to get into—that is, to talk to one's baby[2]—but it's the feeling tone that will be well understood.

It's rather common that babies will bite mother's breast and bite others, or grab another baby's hair and not yet be able to let go, or reach for a cup of hot coffee, or hit (playfully or not). Infant limits begin to be needed.

What to Do?

The child cannot yet anticipate the effects of his actions, nor judge his consequences. The caregiver must take over what the child should do, act in the child's behalf, as the child's representative. Mildly toned limit setting has to be predominantly instructive: the infant needs to learn what he can't do and why he can't do it. The mother's tone will convey the expectation. As I said before, it won't hurt to explain; but it's the tone that will be understood.

Compliance at this age can only be hoped for; it cannot yet be expected.

There is no plausible justification for, nor potential usefulness in punishing the less than one-year-old infant—given that he cannot and will not yet for many months be able to, as I said, "anticipate the effects of his actions, nor judge their potential consequences."

Toddlerhood (8 to 24 Months)

Strivings for autonomy and the first upsurge of aggression (see chapter 5) will emerge at about six months or so. From then to about 24 months, due to the toddler's emerging ability to move about, the need for limit setting will mushroom. Depending on the child's inborn energy level, the intensity of her thrust (inner push) to autonomy, and her malleability (degree of flexibility[3] in her reactions to demands for compliance with parent's expectations), the degree of limit setting needed will vary. Low-energy type mothers will have their hands full with a high-energy[4] child due to their respective different inborn energy styles. A calm-reactor, slower-moving mother or father is likely to experience her or his child's brisk and energetic reactivity as annoying, to be challenging, a mismatch for her or his own reactivity style.

Now the basic limit-setting model begins to be frequently set in motion. It will feel natural to the parent. But, still, the tone will play a larger role than thought-based understanding. And then, there will be times when a limit has to be set quickly; there will be no time for the step-wise progression of the basic model. For instance,

> Thirteen-month-old Louis reaches for an air conditioner plug engaged in an electrical outlet. What does mother or father do? We have seen varying reactions. One mother firmly prohibits Louis's touching the plug or outlet, getting up quickly and telling him it's a dangerous thing. He persists, and, with mother's further prohibition, he becomes angry. She holds his hands firmly, but without hurting him as he pulls against her effort to inhibit his reaching for the plug, and with seriousness in her voice, she tells him he is not allowed to touch the plug or outlet because he might get hurt. She tells him she doesn't want him to get hurt. He gets angrier and begins to cry. When he then reaches for her to be picked up, she does so. While comforting him, she repeats her prohibition and the reason for it. She also tells him that she knows it's hard to not be able to do what he wants.
>
> Another mother seeing this type of behavior at first says nothing. But as her young child persists in touching the plug, she shouts from across the room that he'd better get away from there or she'll smack him. Because he does not comply with mother's distance communication, she goes to him, yanks his arm angrily, and loudly proclaims that he is determined to kill himself. Now frightened, he stretches his arms out to mother. She ignores him and returns to her seat.

It helps the parent deal with this major challenge, as I explained in chapter 8, when she or he understands that setting limits with the less than two-to-three-year-old means to disallow and interfere with the child's often vibrant adaptation-serving strivings for autonomy. Not yet able to grasp the meaning and reasons for mother's or father's prohibition and, therefore, not being able to weigh the merit of the parent's protective intention, the child feels that his mother (or father) is obstructing his push to do what he is driven to do, which causes him distress (psychic pain) and this generates hostility in the child toward the limit-setting loved parent. This brings about a conflict of ambivalence (having feelings of anger, hostility, or hate toward a person one loves) within the child. This psychic conflict leads to anxiety in the child, which may then lead to problems in the child's developing a secure sense of autonomy and sense of self.

However, given that nothing is simple in child rearing, we should also recognize that this conflict of ambivalence, while troublesome for both child and parent, also gives the parent the opportunity to help her or his child learn to deal constructively with the child's own hostility, a much needed help (see chapter 10). This, in turn, then leads to the child's developing a reasonable and responsible conscience (see chapters 2 and 3).

It is important for parents to distinguish between limit setting and punishment. One mother said something like, "I worry about (setting limits on my child) because I don't want to break his spirit." This suggests the misunderstanding that setting limits, because it challenges the child's sense of autonomy will break it. But given that the setting limits we advocate to achieve compliance does not disallow the child's sense of self and strivings for autonomy, but rather aims to help the child learn to govern his autonomy strivings to his own advantage, such limit setting fosters the development of a constructively adaptive sense of self. The limit is set to both protect the child from harm and help him or her behave in socially acceptable ways, which in the long run will benefit the child's sense of self and autonomy enormously. To be accepted by his peers and others he will have to behave in ways that conform to their expectations. Of course, in time we want to help our children use their judgment as to what are reasonable and unreasonable, acceptable and unacceptable peer-based expectations.

Limit setting will more and more be needed, battles of wills will heat up, and ambivalence will wax and wane. In children with low thresholds of irritability (who are easily upset), temper tantrums may emerge.

What to Do?

As Ben Spock recommended years ago, "baby-proof the house." Make it safe for the toddler to move about in the space available to him. Put your favorite pottery, breakable valued things, and knick-knacks, out of the toddler's reach.

The increase in limit setting now required will help the toddler learn basic rules of care for himself and valued things. Select and put out of reach the books you don't want your toddler to inadvertently damage. Get the toddler her or his own collection of books—and read them to the toddler; most of them love being read to and there are some wonderful books for toddlers.

Even though the toddler will not yet grasp the reasons for the limits, start the process of making limit setting instructive; the toddler is about to begin to learn what is reasonable and what is not. What is not permitted and why it is not is basic information the toddler will eventually need to know for his well-being. When appropriate, clarification of what is permitted coupled with what is not permitted can be very helpful even before thought-based understanding is developed. These will be understanding-based-learned in the next couple years, but begin giving reasons when limits are needed even while you know the toddler will not fully understanding the ideas.

Caution: do not assume that the toddler can't understand you at all. The patterning of limit setting now guides both child and parent. Both will be able to guess what will happen if the toddler does not comply. Compliance that comes at this age will be based on conditioned learning and from understanding the tone of what you say more than your words.

Do be careful. Major concerns during this toddler era are:

(a) That excessive limit setting may interfere with the inner push to learn what the world is made of, that is, to explore—which is where learning begins. It will interfere with the child's need to learn what happens if I do this or that. And it interferes with the healthy development of the sense of self and of autonomy. Learning does not begin in school; it begins at home. The child's strivings for autonomy require that the toddler begin to learn all she can about, and how to solve problems in, the world into which she was born. If this learning is too interfered with and discouraged, it may make learning a negative experience and set up a conflict about learning that the child may then carry into her experiences in school. It may discourage the spontaneous drive to learn.

(b) Insufficient limit setting will not guide the child well enough in determining what behavior is reasonable and what is not. And it can bring the problems I talked about in chapter 7: insufficient compliance. The child will then learn the hard way and may pay a heavy price for not learning to comply reasonably.

When setting limit fails, time-outs are perfect for toddlers. Given toddler's push to do things and move about, "One minute 'time-out' per age in years" is a good formula: one minute time-out for a one-year-old, two minutes time-out for a two-year-old, etc. Time-outs that are too long are experienced as harsh; they are too punitive. But the time-out decided on must be held and involve no talking to mom or anyone, no playing with toys, no reading a book; just sit and learn what mom or other caregiver said.

Physical punishment, even with our rules, is generally inferior to a time-out. But a swat on the bottom may be needed with some quite challenging, very determined toddlers. I'll say more about this in the next section (the preschool child).

Preschool Years (two to five years)

The two-to-five-year period enters the "golden era for learning to comply." It is the first stage of cognitive (thought-based) rather than just conditional and emotional-based learning why and how to comply; the parent's explanations begin to be grasped intellectually.

From two to five years, propelled by the child's increasing adaptive, cognitive, and emotional abilities and skills, the child's exploratory behaviors will become more complex and will increasingly require guidance, and increasingly challenge the parents to set limits. But it is important for parents to realize that while setting limits is unpleasant, these years are the start of the optimal period during which setting limits impacts most favorably on the child's learning to comply with expectations. In addition, it is a good time to help the child increase her or his ability to adapt constructively. Because learning is now accelerated, the child will increasingly be able to understand the parent's explanation for her setting limits, even if the child does not comply. When so indicated, the parent will also have to persist in setting the limit, while also being prepared to make compromises depending on the "obligatory level" (see chapter 7) of the parent's particular expectation.

Early self-discipline starts. This of course is the time period for toilet training, which is more or less challenging for both child and parents. As I said in chapter 7 (under the section on "The problem of excessive compliance"), where limit-setting and compromising fail, and harsh measures to enforce compliance are used, this challenge can unfortunately lead to painful, even (though fortunately rare) deadly consequences. Less challenging but also requiring limit setting are: brushing teeth, washing hands and eventually the rest of oneself, bedtime, and eating well enough. Challenging but requiring more encouragement than limit setting are: learning colors, reading letters, and then reading words. Each child will require her own program, depending on her developing abilities, talents, and skills.

Preschool experience is critical in that it sets the stage, establishes a baseline, for the child's school years that will follow. It is important for parents to be aware of and evaluate the child's experience in preschool. Is the experience positive or negative? If it is negative, efforts should be made to change what is causing the negative experience since it may color the child's view of school for years to come. Similarly, does the child have much pain on separating from the parent when taken to school? When separation to go to school is too difficult for the child, this too is a problem that needs to be solved because the pain it causes the child will set a pattern for disliking school, which may then dampen the gratification that comes with studying and learning. And, in addition, it will generate hostility in the child as well as in the parent. In the chapters that follow we discuss handling the various reactions that often come with such childhood distress: expressing anger, hostility, and hate; tantrums; and experiencing anxiety, sadness, and depression. We have learned over the last eight decades of mental health clinical work with children that early separation problems, difficulty separating from parents, need to be taken seriously. If these persist during the two-to-five-years period, professional consultation may be very helpful for both child and parents.

Learning to play with peers, not kids just playing side by side, but rather kids playing with one another begins during the two-to-five-years period. Playing wildly, unfairly, taking things from others, having difficulty sharing reasonably, shoving, hitting, teasing other kids—all require limit setting and guidance. Here specifically, these limit-setting challenges are valuable occasions for helping one's child find ways to interact with peers that will pave the way to their being able to make and retain friends for years to come.

For most kids, the first peer relations occur at home. And during the two-to-five-years era, this is one of the foremost places where parents are challenged to set limits with their kids. How to get along with one's sister(s) or brother(s)? Rivalries begin with the birth of the second child. These are unavoidable. "The grass is always greener on the other side of the fence" applies among siblings. The other sibling always seems to be better treated by the parents than the self—unless the other is a real troubled kid. Having been there before the other kid understandably makes the firstborn feel his place is usurped by that brat. In some case more, in some less, siblings always come with challenges. It's only years later, that having siblings becomes valued—for many people, but not for all.

Conflicts between siblings are no doubt as challenging as conflicts between parent and child. While, of course, the parent-child relationship will shape the child and will leave its effects on the child for life—it will also impact the parents' life—the person(s) the child will know for longer than anyone else ever is (are) the sibling(s). Sibling relationships are crucial in that we all live most of our active life with our peers, as children and as adults. The peer world is where we are most engaged over the span of our life. And, except for one-child families, it's at home that we first learn to live with peers. And it's up to parents to mediate, and often to be the referee, to see to it that their children do learn to live together in some reasonable degree of harmony. For parents who recognize that it is enormously important to help their kids learn to live together well, conflicts between siblings is the arena where they can best achieve this goal. Therefore, having to mediate and referee conflict between their kids are opportunities for parents to help their kids learn to live well with peers, both within and outside the family.

It makes parents' task easier when they see that these unpleasant events are occasions to teach kids to cope constructively. Sure, parents experience these episodes of maladaptive behavior in their kids as a burden. But in fact, in dealing with these maladaptive behaviors, we help kids to better govern their reactivity, improve their problem-solving skills, increase their self-discipline, and grow into more confident kids who have success in relating to others. I understand that the Chinese writing symbol for "danger" (or "crisis," some say) is the same as that for "opportunity." Such "crises" in parent-child life are "opportunities" to teach kids to cope better. In clinical work we often find that a crisis for an individual or family is an opportunity for change—because a crisis, during which one feels a degree of helplessness, mobilizes one's individual or family's adaptive forces. If well handled, such crises foster resilience in kids' capacities to adapt constructively. I want to quickly add, that parents don't need to create such crises for their kids to foster their resilience; life and growing up do this well enough all by themselves.

These preschool years do more than represent the first period of thought-based learning to comply. They also are the time, according to Erikson when the child develops a sense of initiative. This sense of initiative molds the developing self into a self that can make things happen. Erikson says that it becomes "a basis for a high and yet realistic sense of ambition and independence."[5] Rather than independence, I believe it is more accurate to speak of this as a capability for "self-reliance," for "I can initiate this and I can do this myself."[6]

Battles of wills may continue at the same frequency or they may now decrease. In many kids who have temper tantrums, these usually lessen when they are handled constructively (see chapter 11). The need for limit setting may progressively become less during these years as the preschooler increasingly is learning what is permitted and what is not. At the same time, limit setting may need to be subtler as the child's abilities to think, understand, and do things become more complex. Limit setting becomes more challenging as the preschooler gets into more interactional peer play, including mutual sexual explorations.

What to Do?

Setting limits that guide the child to better adaptation, socialization, and learning at home and in preschool are highly valuable. By now, the basic limit-setting model should be automatic in the mother and father and be predictable by the preschooler. By now parents know quite well the limit-setting pattern that works best for their particular child. Limit setting continues to be instructional, but also now more and more aims at the child's consolidating inner controls and discipline: to internalize parental and preschool teachers' expectations.

Setting limits when two-to-five-year-old kids are in conflict with a younger or older sibling is an opportunity to help our kids learn about fairness, reasonableness, empathy (perceiving how the other person feels—a much required skill), making compromises, and not gloating when he or she gets the upper edge, or moping when he or she gets less than he or she wanted. What a workshop. What an opportunity. Who else in settling things is going to be more thoughtful—wanting the best for both of the siblings in conflict—try to be most fair, be most sympathetic than the parent? Of course, parents have to be aware of, and be very honest (with themselves) and look out for any biases they may have in favor of one or the other of their kids. Efforts have to be made by parents to apply the same basic principles and measures, shaped by the child's age and vulnerabilities, in refereeing between their kids. It's not always easy, but it must be aimed for. While it's not uncommon for kids to think that the other sibling was mom's or dad's favorite, it is beneficial to the parent to feel that to the best of her or his self-knowledge, "I don't prefer this or that one of my kids."

The explanation for limit setting is more challenging to parents as they set limits on their child's sexual explorations. The years from two to five, due to the normal psychobiological development of children's sexual self, bring with them much interest, curiosity, and anxiety about matters pertaining to their own and others' sexual anatomy. Thinking about what to say to the child about their sexual interest, questions, and behaviors, is challenging. Finding a good book that explains sex matters well to children, or talking to a knowledgeable person, can prepare parents for the almost certain eventuality that they will need to talk to their child about what in sexual matters is and is not permitted.

Parents should allow the child to protest to their limit setting to a reasonable degree; they should not muzzle the child, but at the same time, parents should hold the line depending on the obligatory level of the expectation. We value having a heart-to-heart talk with the two-to-five-year-old after such episodes have cooled a bit. Of course, the language has to be at the child's level of comprehension. Why mom did what she did; why what Johnny did is not acceptable. And be sure to close with a statement that affirms the parent's love and respect for the child even when he or she feels angry with the child and that being angry doesn't make love go away (commonly a child's fear).

Punishment of choice for the two-to-five-year-old continues to be the time-out. In addition, where more than a time-out is needed, withdrawal of privilege can now include choice activities the child especially likes, such as a young children's TV program or being excluded from a family game. The withdrawal of privilege has to be reasonable like before: one TV program disallowed at a time or one game disallowed at a time. Just because the child is getting older does not mean the punishment should multiply; this applies only to time-outs for which the formula "one minute per year" still applies. Excessive punishment puzzles the child, may intensify his or her sense of having done something really wrong, and it may challenge the child's judgment of what is reasonable. Once the child develops the ability to judge, the excessively punishing parent will be experienced more negatively by the child than most parents wish for.

But here is another punishment issue of concern.

> When Jane was about three years old she and her mother got into an unpleasant interchange. Quite aware that she was now irritating her mother, Jane persisted in stepping playfully (to Jane) on her mother's foot. Whatever the reason, it seemed to really bother mother. Mother set limits with her, quite well. But Jane persisted in stepping on mother's foot, teasing her with it, blatantly defying mother's expectation that she stop it. As Jane was about to yet again step on her mother's foot, mother got hold of Jane's arm and gave her one swat on the bottom. Jane immediately stopped stepping on her mother's foot.

To Jane, it was a game; to mother, it was troubling. Jane disregarded not only her mother's telling her to stop, but also disregarded the distress she was progressively causing her mother. My impression is that mother's aim was not primarily to hurt Jane, it seemed more to tell Jane "Look at what you're doing. Look at what you're bringing onto yourself." Mother was insisting on reasonable toddler behavior.

I have found that in this era when all reasonable parents are appalled at and aware of the highly negative consequences of child abuse, many parents automatically reject the notion of a swat on the clothed bottom. I have a pretty good idea why they do. Physical punishment has a slippery slope. But I ask, to what degree was the swat on the bottom this mother gave her daughter damaging to her child's body or her psyche? I ask this question to engage the reader's thinking about this controversial issue: child abuse and neglect. This issue is, I believe, more complicated than many well-intentioned people assume. I too, among many, raise my voice against abuses and neglect of children, in fact, of all people. Child abuse and neglect should be outlawed everywhere. As I have written more than once, "a United Nations Children's Fund (UNICEF) report [holds] 'that an estimated 40 million children globally under the age of 15, suffer from violence, abuse, and neglect according to a UN-sponsored study led by Paulo S. Pinheiro, in what is deemed to be the first detailed look at how children experience violence all over the world, and what must be done to prevent and end this scourge' (*United Nations News 2005*). I should note that 40 million is probably an underestimation."[7] While this report does not specify that the "violence, abuse, and neglect" occur at home, my decades of clinical work and research lead me to say that abuse and neglect that are experienced at home are more psychologically damaging than when these occur elsewhere. And while I do not know where these occur most, whether in terrible events as genocides, or in recruiting children as soldiers, that which happens at home far outnumbers that which happens in schools and the neighborhood.

The serious negative consequences of abusing children physically (as well as sexually), today are well known. Much has been written about them; many studies have traced their life-long-lasting consequences (see chapters 2 and 3, this volume). None of us who are concerned with the ravages these create and the rise these give to emotional disorders in our children, to delinquency and crime, individual and collective, can condone any abuse or neglect of children.

I want to highlight here, however, as I have elsewhere[8] that equal to the harsh consequences to a child's emotional life of physical abuses (physical and sexual) and neglect, emotional abuse has for too long been left in the shadow of our awareness and concern. While not as blatant as physical abuses and neglect, emotional abuse too has far-reaching harmful consequences. Much more emotional abuse occurs at home (and elsewhere) than physical abuse. Acts of rejection, shaming, depreciation, and humiliation by parents of their children are rampant in too many homes everywhere. These insults—acts of emotional abuse—which injure a child's healthy narcissism, especially and foremost when experienced at home, tend to bring with them a poor sense of self and a diminished sense of autonomy and initiative; they also lead to insecurity, low self-esteem, and poor self-confidence, as well as rage toward others and one's self. A child's emotional scars may not be as visible as his or her physical scars, but psychological scars may be less reversible than physical ones.

Over my years of infant and young child observation, I have seen on many an occasion a distraught mother of a young child who, abiding by our reasonable constrictions against child abuse, will glare or shows disdain at her three-or-four-year-old who is defying her expectation at a given moment. Close observation of the child's face suggests a painful psychological threat. As an infant observer, I assure the reader, such reactions are amply visible, but they do require tuning in to the child's reaction. I am speaking of moms especially because for children between ages two and five, they tend to be the limit setter more frequently than dads. To be sure, dads do similar things; many of them more harshly than moms.

My clinical data (verbalized by kids in psychotherapy) too, affirm that many young children, and even ones older than two-to-five-year-olds, wish their mother would hit them rather than give them a dirty look or say some of the hurtful things too many moms (and dads) say. The idea of "the evil eye" has long existed, so has "the look that kills." Our understanding of its chilling effect, especially when it comes from one's mother, does not require education. Or consider the feelings of the child whose mother explodes, "You brat, you'll be the death of me." The epitaphs run wild and are highly injurious.

Note that kids two to five can tolerate mom's anger; but they have much trouble with mother's hostility, hate, or rage. As I explained in chapter 5, anger does not cross the line: "I can't tolerate this; this is more than I can take." Crossing that line leads to so much unpleasure (psychic pain) that it generates hostility, and if it becomes more intense or happens too frequently, will lead to hate and rage. Children can handle mom's anger (as I have defined it) because they can sense that mom is registering a complaint, but mom's expression of hostility carries with it the wish to hurt, to rid herself of that which is causing mom too much unpleasure (psychic pain). It is also in this sense that I tell parents that their being firm with their child should be distinguished from their being hostile. One can be angry and one can be firm without being hostile. Crossing the line "This is more than can take" generates hostility in all of us.

So, children can take mom's or dad's angry look; that's bearable. In fact, Jane could no doubt see her mother's angry look. I saw it. At the moment it did not stop Jane's teasing mom. What would mother have done next? Jane was intensifying the challenge to mom.

I learned much from seeing such interactions among mother-child pairs whose relationships, according to current mental health attachment measures[9] were quite good. Is all physical punitive contact abuse? What is? What is not? Was Jane's mother's action child abuse? Was it sadistic? Did she derive pleasure from striking her daughter? Was Jane's mother's aim to bully, tease, mock, or humiliate her? That was not my impression. She wanted her feisty three-year-old daughter to stop disregarding her expression of distress and comply. I think that the concept "child abuse" is at risk of losing its specified and valuable meaning if we call all physical punitive contact child abuse, a meaning that can guide us to clearly declare what is harmful and what is not.

Elementary School Years (5 to 12 years)

From five to eight years of age, the child's abilities to think and express himself verbally continue to develop. So does his beginning to evaluate where he stands compared with others in school; this self-evaluation even begins in the peer group. He or she is developing a sense of right and wrong, of rules and regulations in all aspects of her or his behavior and interactions with others as these apply to the self and to others. This is a high point when rather common and innocent lying and cheating in good kids can be dealt with constructively.

With these, the child's ability to judge his or her own actions and those of others is developing and she or he can now really begin to cognitively (intellectually) grasp what her or his parents' and teachers' expectations are and why they stand for them. For the five-to-eight-year-old, explanations for and discussions of principles behind expectations begin to be appreciated and meaningful things to think about. Developing the ability to comply is now increasingly based in both cognitive and emotional understanding the whys and wherefores of expectations. While parents' efforts have already been activated during the preceding years toward this end, especially during the two-to-five-years period, this five-to-eight-years era is about the best time to work on achieving compliance. Limit setting, its instructional aspect, is routine.

The ability to work begins during this era. This is why throughout cultures over the centuries, children this age are sent into the fields, to school, and are expected to start helping at home. While some ability to work starts earlier in life, once on track in elementary school the ability to work becomes necessary.

> One three-year-old girl, sitting at breakfast with her family, was busily coloring on paper with her grandmother interacting with her at her side. She looked up at those around her and declared: "Grandma is helping me with my homework." Little doubt, she was identifying with her high-school brother who at the time had declared that he needed to and managed to do some of his homework while visiting his family out of town. In this, the three-year-old revealed that she was internalizing the notion that she too, will soon have to learn to work.

The self now, between five and eight years, takes a large step in further developing his or her becoming a learner and a doer. She wants to be shown what to do and try to learn to do it herself. Many challenges loom.

The early school years begin to demand of kids that they come to school on time, sit in their seats, follow instructions, as well as restrain their movements and behaviors.

Compliance with others than mother and father, while already expected in preschool, now becomes a daily, more taxing challenge.

Most kids learn to meet these challenges satisfactorily—if by virtue of their relationships with their parents they have already learned to comply with their parents' expectations.

When they have not, the challenge of complying in school will generally be more difficult. Limit-setting efforts by teachers will increase with those kids who resist demands for compliance with school expectations.

Children whose parents are engaged in their child's school experience, by asking their kids, and listening with interest to what they say about their school day, by checking the work their child brings home—what they've done in school and what homework they have—by going to parent-teacher conferences, will feel supported and encouraged to engage in their school work. This really is when learning to work begins; the child brain and cognitive (intelligence) functions are developing sufficiently to make this possible.

Where school compliance is good, and when the child's school efforts are duly acknowledged and complimented by the parents, the child's self-esteem is boosted, which encourages the child to continue in his efforts to do well. Where school compliance is poor, parents' efforts to encourage it will be best achieved by guidance—explanations of the importance of complying with teachers' expectations that ultimately will benefit the child—and by setting limits. As I said in chapter 8, having been in school for about seven hours, most second and third graders, if not also first graders, will have some homework to do. "I was in school all day, and now more work to do." Yes, and when kids don't comply with the teacher's demand, it becomes the parents' responsibility to get their child to comply with the teacher's expectations.

In addition, all kinds of additional daily events will require encouragement and even limits such as getting up in time and doing all the things needed to get ready for and be in school on time, being at dinner with the family, getting ready for bed in due time, and more.

Limit setting for the five-to eight-year-old will become most centered around:

1. Peer-related activities both at home (between siblings) and outside (e.g., learning to play by rules);
2. Breaking rules surreptitiously, that is, cheating and lying. It's not just bad kids who lie, most kids do;
3. School-affiliated responsibilities, book bag preparation, and homework;
4. Home affiliated responsibilities, such as beginning to help with chores, keeping one's own or shared room in reasonable condition;
5. Self-care responsibilities, health and hygiene, etc. These challenges to the child's developing sense of self are large. That sense of self must increasingly be secured, and limit setting must aim at facilitating this critical development and not undermine it. Sibling conflict resolution will continue to be required; the same principles apply as were suggested for the two-to-five-year-olds.

What to Do?

The same basic model of setting limits constructively works well. Parents know their child well and knowing the type of limit setting that seems to work best with their child will be used. Because the demands of everyday life continue to demand much effort from them, and many frustrations and disappointments occur to all five-to-eight-year-olds (and at all ages), irritability, anger, even hostility will be part of every child's experience. The fortunate ones will most express this at home, the safest place on earth to lose one's cool and temper. Those who don't feel secure enough at home to risk being angry there will have to find other places to let loose. If this is done in school, optimal school functioning and learning may suffer; if it's done in the community, the cost to friendship, respect by neighbors, and peer approval (which is difficult to achieve well) will no doubt be negative.

Punishment is quite likely to be required. Compliance with parental expectations commonly is not achieved by five years of age; much is yet to be developed cognitively, emotionally, and adaptively to further establish the sought-after degree of meeting the parents' expectations. Limit setting will be required and set, and with all normal enough five-to-eight-year-olds, limits will at times fail. The withdrawal of privileges, always the punishment of choice, can work well. Time-outs are not as likely to be onerous to the six-year-old as they were earlier, and therefore are not likely to be as effective. Withdrawing TV programs, or computer privileges, especially computer-learning games devised for those young ones who just take to computers like fish to water, will work better.

Physical punishment should now be totally avoided. Even a swat on any part of the body can cause more problems than it can solve. Privilege withdrawal now means even more to the child than it did before; therefore, it is from here on the punishment of choice. Insults, shaming, humiliating, hurtful statements, all should be avoided; all of which comes down to: avoid emotional abuse! If the parent is about to give his or her kid the evil eye, the parent needs to call a time-out (like is done in sports) and come back to the problem with the five-to-eight-year-old (and older kid) when somewhat cooled down and in better control.

Some loving, well-behaved kids seem to become more or less expectation-resistant during this five-to eight-year era. They may resist complying with expectations because of difficulties that have shown themselves to a degree from very early on in life, but were not yet leading to worrisome challenges for parents. Some kids are more insistent on wanting to do things their own way; it is more difficult for them to tame their own resistance than it is for others.

Kids with greater or lesser stubborn streaks (usually due to a greater inborn tendency for obsessive-compulsive ways of coping with challenges) will present greater challenges in learning to comply with expectations.

In some, it may become evident now that they have some up-to-now not recognized learning dysfunction, perhaps even some degree of dyslexia. They are likely to resist doing homework, perhaps even dislike going to school. When such resistances persist, given that they may ultimately affect the child's learning capability and interest, consultation with school psychologists or child psychiatrists can be enormously helpful and guiding in optimizing that child's development. Not complying with doing homework and not liking to go to school may not be due to being a kid who just wants to play; it may hide some underlying problem that causes the child to feel bad about himself and that needs professional attention.

Some energetic, constantly in-motion kids will now show evidence of being unable to sit still in school, or to not be able to pay attention over a span of time. Teachers are likely to be the first to tell parents that their child seems to have such a problem. Again, consultation with aforementioned professionals can clear the picture and lead to their prescribing some helpful programs for handling these difficulties or, where needed recommend specific forms of treatment. As a general principle, it behooves parents to seek consultation with professionals when they are troubled by their children's too persistent noncompliance with their expectations. Generally, where they can be beneficial, the sooner such interventions take place, the more likely it is that changes for the better can be initiated. Most kids want to please their parents and be loved and respected by them. It is well that parents ask themselves, "Is something going on that needs attention I'm not specifically educated to understand?" Mental health professionals and child development experts have learned more about how to optimize a child's physical and psychological development during the twentieth century than we had known during the entire history of civilization. Being a good parent does not make one an expert in how to optimize one's child's psychological and emotional development.

From 8 to 12 years of age, all that has been set in motion between 5 to 8 years of age continues. School demands continue with demands increasingly commensurate with the child's further developing cognitive and adaptive capabilities. So, too, are home chores now added for which the youngster is age-adequately developed that will commonly require encouragement and even some limit setting; most kids this age can facilitate mom and dad's homemaking responsibilities—there's always more than enough for everyone to pitch in. Homework is critical, and for many kids whose sense of autonomy and self-discipline has not developed optimally, parents staying on top of their performance can keep them going and continuing to grow.

Limit setting to further enhance the child's self-discipline where it is weak is much needed in order to prepare the child adequately for further education. The same general limit setting measures apply as they did for the five-to eight-years period.

Punishment of choice is privilege withdrawal. The privileges we give our kids are more and more cherished by them. TV, computer games, and for some of our Internet whizzes, Internet contacts, chats, Facebook, and the like are high priority privileges. Withdrawing these stings but does no harm; withdraw them when needed. Again, withdraw privileges that are not essential for your 8-to-12-year-old's wellbeing. For instance, with a child who has some difficulty making friends, don't take away his privilege of asking a friend over after school. For those of us who are fortunate enough, kids should never be punished by being sent to bed without having had dinner.

Physical punishment and emotional abuse should be avoided.

Adolescence (12 to 18 Years)

Psychological models of adolescence have considered it in terms of either two or three stages. Mental health professionals recognize the large and critical stage it is during which humans evolve from the child into the young adult. In my own work,[10] I have suggested that adolescence be considered as extending from 12 to 21 or so years. While the 18-to-21-year period transitions into young adulthood for many who go on to college, some developmentalists hold that the protective conditions of college prolong the experience of being an adolescent that may then, for many of them, carry over into those years. Let me also mention that the period from 10 to 12 years has also been, quite reasonably, considered to be "preadolescence."[11] I have included these years in the 8-to-12-years period just discussed.

Given the large challenge their child's adolescence brings with it for parents, it may serve parents well to have a psychological development grasp of the challenges their teenager faces during this era. Erik Erikson, a preeminent psychoanalyst proposed[12]—and it has stood the test of time—that in the course of the child's development, adolescence is the developmental period during which the young person's "identity" becomes definitively structured in her or his mind (psyche). While self-identity will continue to develop over the years, this is the period when one's self-identity first consolidates. A metamorphosis of the self takes place that is especially influenced by the following dramatic developmental tasks[13] of adolescence:

1. There is an acceleration of the process of becoming an individual able to govern all aspects of oneself in one's world including beginning to consider the direction one's life will take; essentially thinking about "Who am I? Whom do I want to become?"
2. There is a gradual reduction in the family of origin's being at the center of the adolescent's universe, with a progressive turning toward the peer

world, given that this is the universe where during the rest of life the self's personal life interactions will most take place, including eventually finding a mate with whom to take on the biological mandate to "preserve the species" and establish a new generation to continue community life.

3. There is further detailing and specification of one's gender-self and of one's aggressive-self. One's ultimate gender determination gradually establishes and stabilizes during adolescence; so does the sense of oneself as someone with a defined aggression profiles—including both nondestructive and hostility-laden aggression. Both the gender and aggressive aspects of self create a good deal of anxiety, and both strongly codetermine the self's character and personality.
4. There is a striking evolution of one's adaptive capabilities, including one's defining body growth, size, form, features, attributes, etc., which contribute much to one's self-image and personality.
5. There is a dramatic evolving of one's cognitive and emotional capabilities that serve the mastery of the enormous volume of school learning and socialization expected by peers, family, and society (see third paragraph below).
6. There is a continuing defining of one's enlarging skills and talents, such as in sports, art, music, dance, theater, etc., which in essence are creative ways of using one's energies, what in psychology we call "sublimation." These sublimations, when further developed in adolescence become pathways for creatively channeling psychological energies that may when not harnessed lead teenagers into trouble. It's well known that when teenagers are involved in sports or the arts, they tend to not only get into less trouble, but that it also enhances their positive self development.
7. Critical as well is that with the process of more and more becoming an individual, shifting the center of one's universe from the family to the peer group, leads to the family's values and mores being tested against those of the selected peer group and with this, there may be some revisions of one's mores and values; that is, some revisions in one's conscience. Here again, the better the family relations have been over the years, the less the revisions of conscience and conduct; the poorer the relationships at home, the greater the influence of the peer group over these revisions.

These adolescent developmental tasks, these remarkable changes that make our children soon-to-be-adults, magnificent as they are still leave the need for parental guidance and help. In a recent piece, journalist Elizabeth Cooney[14] reported on findings on the adolescent brain, which she garnered from an interview with Dr. Frances Jensen, a neurologist at Harvard Medical School and Children's Hospital Boston. Cooney writes that Dr. Jensen points out

"We all know what the frontal lobe does: . . . It's insight, judgment, inhibition, self-awareness, cause and effect, acknowledgment of cause and effect. And big surprise: [Its development is] not done in [the] teen years. Hence [teens'] impulsiveness, their unpredictable behavior, their lack of ability to acknowledge cause and effect, despite the fact they are getting 800s on the SATs and can be cognitively highly functional and memorize at a much more impressive rate that we as adults do later." So, as all parents know, adolescents at times absolutely need to be told to abide by our guidelines, mores, and wishes. And then, no bargaining. In families where teens and their parents have a good, secure relationship, children will heed parents' wishes 80 percent of the time—that's not a B; that's an A+ for parenting. Where the relationship is troubled from early childhood and onward, parents' wishes will not go far.

Limit setting now occurs everywhere, at home, in school, in the peer group, in individual peer relations, in society. And limit setting continues to be needed, but so is the protection of the integrity of the adolescent's developing self. And, adolescents will now become more than ever protective of their dramatically developing self. Their progressively growing emotional and physical power and aggression will be well mobilized in the service of this self-protection.

What to Do?

This answer does not warrant the same answer for all of adolescence. We have to consider what to do in terms of the phase of adolescence we are talking about.

Above all, parents must *respect* the adolescent's developing sense of self. How, really, would the parent when an adolescent have wanted to be treated? That's the best guideline, if the parent really thinks of how he or she felt then. "My dad was right to be harsh and mean-spirited" is rationalizing how it felt to be an adolescent. Reasonable limits based on well-reasoned and explainable expectations, administered with loving firmness, will usually eventually work well with the adolescent.

During the 12-to-15-year period the need for limit setting takes a very challenging turn. First of all, the challenges of school, homework, home chores, health self-care, and hygiene often demand encouragement if not outright limit setting. With regard to school and homework, where kids have developed a good degree of self-discipline, showing interest in the state of their activities and due encouragement are not only very supportive but also tend to diminish the need for limit setting. "How did the homework go?" "How's school?" "How did your project go over?" etc., demonstrate your interest. Of course, the parents' interest has to be genuine to be meaningful and encouraging to the developing student-worker.

As self-discipline expands and further stabilizes, an interesting phenomenon occurs in some very bright kids when they enter the middle-to-high-school years. Being very bright, they have breezed through elementary school with only moderate exertion. They seem to expect, not altogether wrongly, that learning will continue to be achievable with moderate effort. Now a test comes back, not with the expected A, but with a C. The C wounds the kid's healthy narcissism and she rationalizes, "Oh, that was a fluke." Mom and dad don't get upset. "Hey, you just have to study more; you're in seventh (or eighth, or ninth) grade now." Then the next test comes back, not with an A, but again with a C. Now the wound is deeper and doesn't yield as well to rationalization. Now mom is worried and dad is furious. Now mom, and maybe dad, too, give her a bit of a lecture. And then yet the the third time, the expected A turns out to be a C. Mom is furious: "Take away all of her computer time and her iphone."

Dad talks to a work friend whose daughter went through a similar experience. The friend explains to him that this is an opportunity for her to learn that being smart is great, but it isn't enough to be successful in life; one also has to apply one's intelligence to the challenge at hand—in her case, the challenge of learning increasingly more difficult materials by studying. Intelligence is no longer enough to learn complex problem-solving strategies like algebra, for instance, or to sort out the dynamics of two countries in conflict. Now, rather than yelling and taking away privileges, mom and dad have a heart-to-heart talk with their daughter and explain to her what dad learned from his friend. This was actually not strange to dad given that he went through a similar experience at her age. The 12-to-15-year-old who has relied more on her intelligence than on applying that intelligence with self-discipline now has to be encouraged to further develop his self-discipline: "You have to study long enough and well enough to really learn this more complicated material." This 12-to-15-year-old really had not yet learned that she has to learn to work. Now, the problem is an opportunity to help the daughter develop further and in a better, adaptive way.

With regard to home chores; resistance to helping is common. An eager-to-help-at-home 13-year-old is not often to be found in normal homes. Prodding is often needed. Where resistance is too frequent or high, limits will be needed.

Interestingly, self-care and hygiene problems are not uncommon in this age group. The reason is that the struggle with bodily changes that come with maturation and the development of their sexual body creates much anxiety in most kids. With these hormone-driven bodily changes comes heightened sexual interest and fantasies that at times, in normal kids, create much of the anxiety of this age period. This anxiety at times leads to defending against making these bodily changes attractive by over-eating, unconsciously driven to mask the bodily changes; or by, again unconsciously, making oneself smell bad by not washing or bathing, so as to keep interested others away. Limit setting with youngsters so affected is often needed. Focusing on hygiene is preferable then focusing on looking more attractive, which may be just what the 13-year-old who smells bad wants very much, but the anxiety it causes her leads her to avoid.

On the other hand, just as challenging if not more so are the kids who at this time, seeing the effect they have on their peers—generally peers of the other sex—are excited by this and search now for ways to deal with these changes in themselves. But the experience is new; the pressures have never been dealt with before. "Girls are saying and doing this; guys are saying and doing that; what should I do or should I not do?" These days, electronic media and channels of communication greatly facilitate activity between kids this age that they would not normally engage in directly, at least not immediately. Pictures on wireless phones are easily communicated. Texting flows like water. What gets written would not dare be said directly. Pressure coming from all sides among peers is unavoidable. Parents soon get hints that such activity is going by intercepting electronic messages or pictures. Many react in alarm at finding some of what is being shared between their kid and his or her peers. Limit setting is thrust into action, sometimes with alarm. Privilege withdrawal commonly is activated, particularly about the cell phone and the computer.

Among some 12-to-15-year-olds, alcohol and drugs may begin to be experimented with. Limit setting is again invoked. But peer pressure may make compliance with parents' expectations difficult and to enforce the limits set, privilege withdrawal is often then necessary.

What to Do?

The principles of limit setting spelled out before apply throughout the years. We put emphasis on parents' respecting their young adolescent's developing self, on their using loving firmness, and on their using reasonable measures. Limit setting now continues to predominantly be self-discipline consolidating.

By now, limit setting is well patterned. The 12-to-15-year-old knows only too well what mom and dad will do. They also quickly learn what particular teachers will do. Of course, they may feign innocence. Don't be fooled: 12-to-15-year-olds can predict.

Now even a bit more than before, let the adolescent argue your reason for the limit; let him talk and you listen. If the reasoning is pretty well done, say so. If you agree with it, you may elect to change your mind about the limit. If you don't agree with it, or if you do but still see more merit in the limit, tell him his reasoning is good, but it doesn't weigh as much as your reason for the limit, and hold to it.

But as we all know that where the history of battles of wills has been hard and long, and relationships are overburdened with ambivalence, setting limits may become a most troubling task. The development of compliance and of self-discipline may be less optimal than could be based on needing to reject parents' expectations. Professional help may be what could set good development back on track and could possibly improve parent-child relationships.

Punishment is in the form of privilege withdrawal. But exercise care to not withhold where the child's well-being will benefit. For instance, grounding can be used—but not if the 12-to-15-year-old's well-being depends on it, such as "You can't go to John's house" to a kid who has difficulty socializing. TV withdrawal is now feeble with the 12-to-15-year-old. No computer use for an evening or cell phone withdrawal for a day works. We value a heart-to-heart talk with the adolescent after such episodes have cooled a bit.

Physical punishment is highly problematic and potentially too destructive. Punishments that carry with them shaming, depreciation, and humiliation of young adolescents—emotional abuse—will mobilize much hostility and hate and may eventually lead to delinquency and even crime.

From 15 to 18 years of age, the same challenges listed for the 12-to-15-year-olds continue. But to these, the further challenge now lies in how and when parents set limits with their mid-to-late adolescent. From about 15 to 18, and then into the 18-to-21-or-so age group, as the offspring is well on his or her way to making his or her peer group the center of his or her social life, a greater or lesser degree of distancing himself or herself from his or her family of origin and abiding by the emerging mores of the peer group prevail. This challenges the parents to modulate their demand for compliance from their teenager with in-home mores.

As I said in chapter 7, where relationships with family have been good over the years, the peer group selection will most likely not impose a dramatic change in already-acquired life mores. The demands of the selected peer group are not likely to be incompatible with those of the family. While there will be challenges for both adolescent and parents, they will most likely be modest.

Where parent-child relationships have been burdened with conflict, be it that parents are unduly demanding and controlling, have used too constraining limit-setting and discipline, kids have been oppositional and too defiant, or any other strain factors have existed between parents and child, parental limits may now trigger more or less rigorous adolescent resistance if not rebellion.

Where parent-child relationships have been outright hostile and parents have been abusive, parental limits will just not work; the shift to the peer group will be welcome and drastically diminish compliance with parental demands.

What to Do?

Limit setting with the 15-to-18-year-old will still occasionally be needed, certainly so in those whose self-discipline continues to need fostering and encouragement. This will also occasionally be required for getting the teenager to let parents know where he or she is after school and on weekends and who she or he is with. The truth is not always easily brought forth.

Developing stronger self-discipline with regard to studying is highly self- and life-protective. Encouragement always facilitates teen's efforts. Where self-discipline is weak, this era of development is crucial for parents to make their best efforts possible to encourage self-discipline in their kids. If such has not be sufficiently secured beforehand, parents might consider outside tutorial help if they cannot themselves tutor their teenager without getting into yet more battles of wills.

Enormously challenging for parents and teenagers at this age are the issues of sex, smoking, alcohol, and street drugs. These are best addressed with the teenager in the spirit of helping her or him find ways to navigate her or his way through substantial peer pressures. Parents using shaming, humiliation, or insulting strategies destroy more than they build. They cause resentment and they generate hostility and hate. In many teenagers, these strategies will trigger a negative backlash against the parents and what they stand for, including their mores and expectations. In some teens, they will trigger rebellion.

Where limits fail, punishment should be instituted. Giving up on the teen is likely to push him or her farther away from family values.

Punishment is in the form of privilege withdrawal. But as always, exercise care to not withhold where the child's well-being will benefit. Grounding can be used effectively. Allowance withholding where allowance has become ritual can be effective. In older ones, disallowing the use of the car can weigh fairly heavily.

Physical punishment now is outright destructive to all concerned; it can be deadly. See chapter 3 for details of research over the past century for the effects of abuse on kids, especially adolescents.

NOTES

1. For instance: S. I. Greenspan & J. Salmon, *The Challenging Child: Understanding, Raising, and Enjoying the Five "Difficult" Types of Children* (1996), and S. Turecki & L. Tonner, *The Difficult Child: Expanded and Revised Edition* (2000).

2. H. Parens, E. Scattergood, R. C. Hernit, & S. Duff, Parenting: Love and Much More. Thirty-nine one-half hour programs produced by CBS for Broadcast on WCAU TV, Channel 10, Philadelphia. First aired June–July, 1979. Program #9: "Am I Crazy If I Talk To My Baby?"

3. Some quite healthy kids with an obsessive-compulsive disposition, or the ones "with a mind of their own," will not be able to accommodate as easily to mother's or father's expectations of behavior. These kids will require greater patience and compromise on the part of the parents to eventually be able to abide by their expectations.

4. We must distinguish between "high-energy" and "hyperactivity" in children. High-energy or high-activity level is a normal variation inborn in disposition in kids. High-energy kids are well regulated, energetic, but they are readily controllable. In contrast, hyperactivity is an energy level that is high, but it is also impulsive, more or less hyperreactive due to a modest, built-in, brain hyperreactivity over which the child has weak or no control. Fortunately, such kids tend to respond well to specific medications that tend to decrease the brain hyperreactivity and with that increase the child's ability to better control his reactivity, concentrate better, and all together, slow down. The problem is that these medications, at the time of this writing, are not recommended for children under six years.

5. E. H. Erikson (1959, 75).

6. H. Parens & L. J. Saul, *Dependence in Man* (New York: International Universities Press, 1971), chapter 5.

7. H. Parens, Malignant prejudice: Guidelines toward its prevention, in *The Future of Prejudice,* ed. H. Parens, A. Mahfouz, S. W. Twemlow, & D. E. Scharff (Lanham, MD: Jason Aronson, 2007), 278.

8. See especially H. Parens, S. Scattergood, A. Duff, & W. Singletary, *Parenting for Emotional Growth (PEG)*, which includes *PEG: The Textbook; PEG: A Curriculum for Students in Grades K thru 12,* as well as H. Parens & C. Rose-Itkoff *PEG: The Workshops Series.* All these PEG works are contained in H. Parens (2010). CD: Parenting for Emotional Growth (see http://jeffline.jefferson.edu/peg/).

9. Based on psychoanalytic and attachment models of early childhood development. Spitz, *The First Year of Life;* Mahler, *The Psychological Birth of the Human Infant;* Stern, *The Interpersonal World of the Infant;* Bowlby, *Attachment;* and Ainsworth, *Patterns of Attachment.*

10. In the set of materials we just produced into a CD entitled *Parenting for Emotional Growth* (H. Parens, 2010). Parenting for Emotional Growth (PEG) consists of (1) *PEG: The Textbook* (2) *PEG: A Curriculum for Students in Grades K thru 12* by H. Parens, E. Scattergood, A. Duff, & W. S. Singletary (1997) (3) *PEG: The Workshops Series* by H. Parens & C. Rose-Itkoff (1997).

11. M. Harley (1971). Some reflections on identity problems in Prepuberty. In *Separation-Individuation: Essays in Honor of Margaret Mahler*, ed J. D. McDevitt & C. F. Settlage (New York: International Universities Press) 385–403.

12. E. H. Erikson, Identity and the life cycle. *Psychological Issues* 1:1–170.

13. Psychoanalytic child development theory holds that each phase of psychological-emotional development brings with it challenges or "tasks" the child has to achieve. I have here listed those that adolescents have to achieve.

14. Cooney wrote this article for the *Globe*, which via the Internet was distributed to its members by the Regional Council of Child and Adolescent Psychiatry of the Greater Philadelphia Region. Cooney can be reached at ecooney@globe.com.

Chapter 9

Teaching the Child to Express Hostility in Reasonable and Acceptable Ways

"You're not allowed to hit me!" Two-year-old Jane's mother half shouted at her. "If you're mad at me, tell me. But it's not OK to hit me!" Jane smirked, but soon seemed subdued and looked like she felt scolded.

> When 16-year-old Mike's mother told him he could not make a phone call just as the family was about to sit down for dinner, he stormed "What the *&%$ is this? You're not at the table yet!" Showing feelings of being offended, his mother said, "Don't talk to me like that! I know you're mad, but you can find a better way to let me know that than by acting like some foulmouthed kid."

The generation and mobilization of hostility (HD) in children being unavoidable, even in the best of child rearing, all children, whatever the age, have to be helped to find reasonable and acceptable ways to express these feelings. When hostility is generated in us there is a built-in tendency to discharge it. Given its inherent pressure, we have to do something with it: we discharge it outwardly or more commonly than parents think, kids discharge it toward themselves.

That which is not discharged is retained within us.

Hostility does not evaporate.

When HD is not appropriately and constructively dealt with by the child, it accumulates and becomes part of the child's personality. This aspect of personality continues into adolescence and beyond. As such it then leads to behaviors that create all kinds of problems and can color painfully all aspects of the individual's life.

It falls to parents to help their children from early life on learn how to cope with hostile feelings. It's built-in that as the child's caregivers, parents will have to do so. Parents know only too well that, as their caregivers, our children unavoidably become very angry with us and feel hostility toward us. Unpleasant as it is, however, this is an opportunity to help them learn to express these feelings in ways acceptable to us and to the community in which we live. The approach I have found that works in my clinical work is to help the child or adolescent recognize that he feels angry or hostile, and we try to discover what emotional pain is causing his anger or hostility at a given time. We then consider what he can do with and about it. Most helpful, I have found, is to find ways to talk about it. The younger the child learns that when she feels anger there is some psychic pain causing it, the easier it is for the child to find ways to deal with it constructively.

Often, the child under two will try not to hit although control over the reactive impulse to do so is then unreliable. I infer this from the fact that commonly when a one-year-old has hit someone, the infant reacts with anxiety as if he expects something painful to happen. He may have already seen that when he hits he gets an unpleasant reaction from his mother, those around, or the one he hit. There is a universal fear of retaliation when one hits another, unless the other is seen as much weaker than the one who hits. This is easily seen in adolescents—even if the individual puts on a brave face—and continues into adulthood. To be sure, acting tough often hides being afraid.

From two to six years of age the child's efforts will be increasingly effective and self-discipline will increase based on conditioned learning, especially due to: "Mother always gets upset with me when I hit." In many families, though regrettably not in all, "Mother gets upset with me when I'm being mean." Later in this chapter, we'll talk about "being mean" that is when we talk about teasing and taunting, which begins to appear in some kids from about 12 months of age.

Note that I make a distinction between hitting and being mean. Let me elaborate here why I make the distinction between hitting or wanting to hit and being mean. In English, as in other languages, we have an array of words that in one way or another describe and define the various ways we discharge aggression. In chapter 5, I detailed why I find it useful to consider the different major trends that make up this complex thing, human aggression, which in a variety of ways serves us in adaptation and survival. One trend I say, is nondestructive aggression, which, without destroying anything directly serves adaptation and the achievement of our goals. Another trend is nonaffective destructiveness, which is destructive but is not driven by hostility; that is, we destroy living things, animal and plant, to feed ourselves, not because we hate them, in fact we love some of the things we destroy; we destroy them, but not out of ill-will. And the third trend, hostile destructiveness gets generated in us physiologically, in the face of a threat to our well-being, which is what feeling pain alerts us to. If we allow that which causes us pain to go to extreme it would destroy us. This too then, hostile destructiveness is in the service of self-preservation.

This last trend, hostile destructiveness, I said in chapter 5 is generated in us by the experience of excessive psychic pain (unpleasure). Parenthetically, one can argue that hunger, which drives nonaffective destructiveness, also causes us pain. But (1) it is not instigated by some outside force, and (2) it is essentially physical pain, not psychic (emotional, psychological) pain. The same can be said for the pain of gastrointestinal spasm or muscle spasms, etc. However, even though physical pain may not of itself cause psychic pain, some conditions surrounding the experience of the physical pain may bring with them some psychic pain. For instance, a young child may feel that mother should be able to stop his physical pain, but she doesn't. Or someone may feel that her physical pain was caused by someone else's carelessness and this may cause some psychic pain. To be sure, if the physical pain is intentionally caused by someone else, it will also be experienced as psychic pain. Also, some physical distress, such as difficulty breathing will not cause pain but it may be experienced as a threat to life, in which case it will cause psychic pain and may then generate hostility in the individual. But what most causes each of us psychic pain is when it is caused by someone outside of ourselves; and especially when that pain is perceived to be caused intentionally.

Also, as I emphasized in chapter 5, hostile destructiveness (HD) has the distinctive feature that the intensity to which it is generated correlates with the intensity of the psychic pain experienced. Given that the intensity of the psychic pain we experience mounts over a wide range, from very low-level to very high-level intensity psychic pain, so will the intensity of the HD generated vary accordingly.

When we consider the intensity of the HD generated, this is when we get into using different words to describe what is felt. Elsewhere[1] I have examined the spectrum of manifestations of HD starting with annoyance, then irritability, and then anger. These I consider to be generated by mild to moderate psychic pain. Up to this point, annoyance, irritability, and anger have only led to wanting the psychic pain to stop. In anger a warning may be given: "You better stop what you're doing to me." There is no wish to harm the person causing the psychic pain.

While I have put these lesser states of feeling the type of aggression in the trend of HD, it is when the psychic pain crosses the line of the individual's psychic pain tolerance, such as feeling, "This is too much, I can't stand it" that the HD generated brings with it a very significant dimension: wanting to inflict pain on the one who is causing us psychic pain. Until this line, really a threshold, is crossed, there is no intention to inflict pain on the other; you just want the other to stop what he's doing to you. When that line (threshold) is crossed is highly variable among individuals, and even within each of us depending on how we feel at a given time. In all of us, this threshold tends to be lower when we are hungry, tired, or sick, etc.

Once this threshold is crossed, as the level of psychic pain intensifies, the consequent HD feelings we experience tend to be expressed in terms of hostility, hate, and rage. There is yet more complexity in these terms that are useful for caregivers to be aware of. Hostility tends to reduce once the psychic pain caused us is stopped. Rage as I will detail in chapter 11, is a reflex-type reaction to very intense, unbearable psychic pain; rage too will tend to stop once the psychic pain stops. Hate, on the other hand, which the child can begin to experience from about 18 months of age on, is a state of feeling HD that has persistence and that continues whether or not the particular individual or condition to which one has attached hate is, in fact, actively then and there causing one psychic pain. When we hate someone, it's for the duration. And to undo hate, the relationship needs to be repaired—which requires much work. To undo a condition that causes us to hate, the condition needs to be neutralized.

Now we can talk about the difference between "wanting to hit" and "being mean." Wanting to hit is part of the primitive tendency to want to push away someone or something that is causing one pain. It is a tendency that is part of our self-protective reflexive reactions. It originates even before the infant is able to think. In chapter 8, we talked about the fact that while infants are able to have simple thoughts and ideas associated with what they experience prior to age two years, it is from about two years that cognitive processes begin to develop that will by seven years or so achieve the youthful level of being able to judge, to grasp consequences of one's actions.

The reflexive "wanting to hit" is not driven by enjoying causing someone pain. "Being mean," is enjoying causing someone pain. Later in this chapter, we'll talk about teasing and taunting, in which we see pleasure in causing someone distress, if not outright psychic pain. Enjoying causing someone psychic pain is where many highly troublesome interrelational and social ills have their beginnings. It is the essence of sadism, individual and collective. It drives not only teasing and taunting (see below in this chapter) but also eventually bullying, causing harm to others, and destroying property, and pushed to extremes contributes centrally to malignant prejudice, which pushed to its utmost limits, leads to murder and genocide.

Now let's return to when and what we can expect from our children.

From five or so on, the child will begin to really understand the reasons why not to hit. The distinction between wanting to hit and being mean will now begin to be understood. He should be made aware of the key sequence that emotional pain is what is making him angry and he ought to be expected to make the link that when he is hurt it makes him feel angry and hostile, and then he wants to hit. It is understandable that he would want to hit, but it's not a good way to let his feelings out. Once the child develops sufficient self-discipline in looking for what caused him pain and then finds constructive ways to deal it, the less will he be prone to lash out at others. And as he succeeds in finding constructive ways to express (i.e., to discharge his HD), the less will it accumulate in his psyche.

This ability to look for and understand the cause of his feeling hostility and increasingly to develop self-discipline over lashing out can begin to be expected by six to eight years of age although acquiring this self-discipline will vary from child to child depending on his or her inborn dispositions. Of course, one cannot expect a child who is temperamentally impulsive to easily develop the ability to control the discharge of his hostile feelings; parents will have to be patient and do much more work; it will take longer to help this child achieve sufficient impulse control. Also the child's reactivity type, whether the child is a slow-reactor or a quick-reactor[2] as well as her or his threshold of irritability, will make for variation in the child's ability to learn to control her or his discharge of hostility. And in addition, the child's life experiences—which by six years of age means: 6 x 365 x however many times a day he is maltreated for instance—are strongly determining of how much hostility he has already accumulated and how difficult the challenge will be for that child to develop reliable self-control. We find that in traumatized children, the challenge will be so large that their efforts to cope with their accumulated hostility is likely to range from total (defensive) inhibition to explosiveness.[3]

Increasingly then, from 8 to 12 and from 12 to 18 the self-discipline to not hit and not be mean, to the extent that each child achieves these, will be established. So will the understanding that emotional pain makes one angry and hostile and that this leads to one wanting to hit and if the hurt is caused by a mean-spirited person to also be mean in return.

In helping our kids not hit and not be mean to others, we will not only prevent the interrelational and social ills I mentioned before, but also we are opening up ways that will lessen the likelihood of their feeling unduly guilty and will make them less fearful of their own anger and hostility. Doing this will foster their assertiveness and healthy competitiveness and that will make them freer to learn and strive toward their personal goals.

RATIONALE

Many people believe that being angry or feeling hostile within the family is bad. Many parents ascribe anger and hostility to some evil tendency within the child. In both my clinical work and observational research, I invariably have found that hostility is reactive to life experiences that range from painful events to traumatizing experiences. My colleagues and I found no evidence that children are born with an evil tendency in them.

I hold that hostile feelings are mobilized by experiences of excessive unpleasure (emotional pain). This gives us a very different picture of what makes our kids angry and hostile. It means that any human being subjected to sufficient excessive unpleasure will become hostile. This is particularly so early in life. But it continues throughout childhood and adolescence.

When parents understand that when children are hostile it is because they are or have suffered excessive emotional pain, the parents will be less taken aback by their child or adolescent's hostility and more interested in helping their child, young or older, deal with the underlying cause of the psychic pain. And by focusing on the pain and its cause rather than the child's reactive hostility, parents will tend to reduce that hostility more readily.

When feelings of hostility are expressed, while unpleasant to witness and certainly to be subjected to, it gives parents repeated opportunities to progressively help their child understand his own feelings and what gave rise to them, and learn to mediate them more positively. Stepwise then, parents help their child learn to gain reasonable control over these troubling feelings. By doing so, parents protect their child against developing automatic trouble-producing reactions.

When such feelings are not allowed reasonable expression, the child internalizes them and fails to learn to deal with them in positively adaptive ways. It is therefore problematic when well-meaning parents disapprove of all signs of anger from their children, let alone hostility and hate, especially when they occur in the family. It is at home that these feelings are first experienced and expressed; and it is invaluable when it is at home that the child is helped to learn how to understand and deal with these in a growth-promoting way.

Unfortunately, in one way or another, many a child, young or older, is told that it is very bad to feel angry, let alone to feel hostile. In some cases the child is told she is evil, which of course, is painfully injurious to the child's healthy narcissism and developing sense of self. It often, in fact, leads to the child's believing there is something bad about her; her sense of self will likely be "I am bad," or "There's something wrong with me."

One adult told me that when she was an adolescent her father told her "Smart Jewish girls don't get angry." As an adolescent, what was she to do with that? Surely, there was something very unacceptable and wrong with her. Even as an adult, while she had by then long known that this statement was not based in good psychological, philosophical, religious, or simple everyday reasonable fact, she recognized that it had troubled her. The problem is that, even knowing that a given statement of disapproval expressed by a mother or father is false and unreasonable, the sting of disapproval the statement carries with it makes it difficult for the individual to ever totally dismiss.

Even though the statement was false, it hurt and it generated hostility toward her father. In addition, the father's declaration not only made the adolescent feel that feeling angry or hostile is a very bad thing, but also it may then have even made her doubt her own intelligence (including her self-confidence, self-regard, and self-appraisal)—which, however, her academic performance eventually redressed positively. This type of handling of a young or older child's anger and hostility is furthermore troubling given that on a number of occasions she saw her father, mother, and siblings also get angry. That, however, did not eradicate her feeling that there was something wrong with her. In time, this adolescent saw the falseness of her father's remark, which not only made her feel sad and angry with him, but also it lowered her esteem of him. The fact remains that while growing up, she felt that having angry and hostile feelings made her less of a person than she wished to be.

Here's another problem I have encountered more than once in the way many parents deal with their child's anger and hostility that is directed toward them. When very upset three-year-old Susan shouted at her mother, "I hate you," her baffled mother just reacted with, "Oh! I know you don't mean that." Well even though the meaning of the words Susan used were not yet fully reliable, she said what she felt. Interestingly, although a three-year-old's words may not carry the meaning we all have in mind, some words and things young children say are not hard science; they are not complicated. Some words they grasp easily. When we tell a two-year-old, "I love you," or "I'm angry with you," or "you're a bad boy," or many other commonly used phrases, the child grasps the meaning of the words by virtue of the emotional color with which he hears them said to him. I'll talk later about how to deal with that.

The point I want to make here is that a number of problems follow from three-year-old Susan's mother's intervention. Among other things, the child feels that she is not supposed to feel what she is feeling. The child is told to disavow, or that she cannot have, the feelings she knows she is experiencing. She overtly agrees with mother, but feels she is a little monster since she knows that she feels "hate." Generally even by three, a child will have a pretty good grasp of the progressive difference between saying, "I'm angry," or "I'm mad," or "I hate you." The child knows that "I hate" is much stronger than "I'm angry." But mother's saying "Oh! You don't mean that," leads to the child's doubting what she is experiencing. Her evaluation of what she feels is undermined, and this may lead to her feeling confusion about her own feelings. Because she may come to believe that what she is feeling is unacceptable, she may unconsciously set herself the task of denying the feelings she has, which is an undesirable way of coping with whatever feelings we have.

In clinical work, I have many times found that a person I am treating may not know what he or she is feeling. He or she doesn't feel good, but the person is uncertain what it is that feels bad about what he or she is feeling. This may apply to good feelings as well. It is a serious problem not knowing what one feels, and it robs the individual of finding ways to lessen feelings that are unpleasant and even painful. Equally serious, it may make uncertain one's feelings of love, or how to accept another person's expressions of love—even when these are directed toward oneself.

There is a further consequence of the parent's disallowing that the child hates his mother. Children themselves label feelings of anger and hate as signs of being bad. They do so sometimes even in the face of parents' telling them that these feelings are normal. Children are the first to judge that they are bad when they experience hostility toward the parent they love. This is because, as I have emphasized throughout this book, feelings of hostility toward those we love create within us a conflict due to ambivalence, which brings with it a profound reaction of disapproval of oneself by oneself. This conflict often leads to self-accusations and self-hate, which we all know as guilt. A child needs the opportunity to resolve these feelings of ambivalence that produce guilt, because they can lead to the development of too harsh a conscience—psychologically, a very costly problem in that a harsh conscience robs the self of well-being. So when a parent cannot tolerate the thought of the child's hating her, a thought difficult to hear to be sure, she denies the child the opportunity to deal with these feelings of hate constructively—a process in which the parent can have the most meaningful input.

This is an incomplete listing of the unfavorable consequences of not allowing a child to experience his feelings, whatever they are. When your child is angry with you, you have an opportunity to help the child deal with such feelings constructively.

It is important for parents to know that when feelings of hostility toward those we love are insufficiently "dealt with and metabolized," what in psychoanalysis we speak of as "working through," these feelings produces all kinds of emotional disturbance and misery in people. Feelings of hostility cannot be worked through unless (1) they can be acknowledged, (2) the factors that caused them examined, (3) the feelings given reasonable ways of expression and discharge, and (4) they are dealt with by the self and the parent (or therapist) in a growth-promoting way.

Over the past century, psychotherapists have found that the great interactive facilitator of working through troublesome feelings of hostility is to be given permission to verbalize them in the context of a meaningful, empathic[4] relationship. In the child, young, school age, and even in adolescence, the best relationships available to him are the ones with mother and father. The well cared for child naturally feels that they more than anyone will understand me and be sympathetic, and will be kindly disposed toward me. Siblings can also become meaningful facilitators of the working through of overloads of hostility, although they also often do become the victim of that hostility. My aim is to help mothers, fathers, and their children develop an emotional dialogue with one another in which anger, hostility, and hate can be talked about meaningfully in growth-promoting ways, which means in ways that reasonably, sympathetically, and responsibly reduce hostility.

INTERVENTIONAL STEPS

When it makes sense to the parent that the hostile feelings her child is experiencing are the product of some excessive unpleasure experience, she can frame her interventions in that context. To convey to the child that some hurt is causing the child's anger rather than some inner destructive or evil force at work in him, makes for an interaction of large beneficial consequence to the child's perceptions of himself, of his mother, and eventually of others, and to his well-being. It frames the child's experience in a positive quality of human relatedness.

Another thing this reaction will do is make it less threatening and noxious for the child to experience the hostile feelings he is having. Consider the atmosphere for a dialogue between yourself and your child, young and older, when you tell him he is being rotten again. Now compare that to telling your son caringly that you know something is hurting him, but you expect him to express his anger in reasonable ways. Can he talk with you about what's going on, you would like to know. With your teenager add, "if it's not too personal."

I have said many times that even the best of parenting cannot prevent numerous experiences of psychic pain, occasionally even excessive psychic pain. The generation and mobilization of hostility within family life is unavoidable. Let's take up again the example we talked about earlier: the unpleasant and at times difficult task of setting limits with one's beloved child.

In setting limits—even in the benign model we developed—the caring parent is the instigator of the unpleasure experienced by the child and, therefore, of the child's hostility. In our parenting project (chapter 1), we became aware of the important but distressing fact that the person the infant first feels angry with, and even first hates is the one to whom the infant is forming his or her foremost attachments, the infant's emotionally valued caregivers, the mother and father. Because other (substitute) caregivers are not as emotionally invested by the baby as are the parents, the frustrations or disappointments they cause the child do not produce as high a level of psychic pain.

As a result, kids tend to be less angry with them than with their own parents. Babies somehow know that those who most invest emotionally in them, their parents, are supposed to love and take care of them.

In general, the mother, the naturally best of caregivers, unavoidably becomes the first to frustrate her child. When, as we have seen increasingly in the last couple decades, the father is prominently engaged in caregiving to his infant, the same will apply to him. Therefore, because the parents are the first "frustrators" of their child, they become the first toward whom the child's feelings of anger, hostility, even rage, and later hate, become directed. Difficult as this is for parents, it is in fact, a very good thing. After all, who would put up with that? Who would be as committed to care and help a child learn to cope with his rage or hate, as is a loving parent? Who else is going to be as willing to put up with such bratty behavior?

> Thirteen-month-old Mary was absolutely adored by her mother and father, the only daughter and the youngest of several children they had. Mary was a quite alert, but rather calm infant until about six months of age when we began to see in her a striking upsurge in her activity level, which by 10 months was high. From six months on, Mary became a vigorous explorer of her environment.
>
> From about six months, the time of this upsurge of healthy nondestructive aggression, Mary's explorations and autonomy driven activities from time to time came into conflict with mother's efforts to keep her safe and sound. Battles of wills would now occur and by the time she approached 12 months of age, these battles began to heat up rather sharply. Mother, who was not a high-level activity person, occasionally had her hands full. A large battle of wills occurred when Mary was about 13 months of age.
>
> As nearly 13-month-old Mary's autonomy strivings intensified and began to organize, she at times wanted to go into the hall, extending her explorations to a cleaning cart that would occasionally be there at a given time during our child-parent observational sessions. Because of her concern about her daughter's interest in that cleaning cart, mother repeatedly told Mary she was not to explore it and when Mary did not comply, mother enforced her limit by picking Mary up and carrying her back into the observational setting. Mary's heretofore moderate objections gave way to loud vocal complaints, her body tensing, shaking, face reddening. Contorting her body to extricate herself from her mother's hold, she cried angrily, waved her left arm in a striking movement against her mother several times, kicked her, both from a distance but twice actually striking her mother with her arm. She once also struck herself.

> We saw clear evidence of her distress. For the first time, mother could not calm Mary as she had quite easily done so many times. Whether mother held Mary or tried to put her down, Mary's crying and manifest hostility continued. Whether she tried to explain, comfort, or distract, mother could not calm Mary. Mary physically rejected any efforts mother made to reduce her distress. Once her crying stopped, Mary looked angry and serious. She sat on mother's lap, erect, as if frozen at the edge of her knees, resisting mother's gentle efforts to bring her close and sharply complaining when mother tried to help her. After about 15 minutes in this state of immobilization, Mary's body tone gradually softened, she relaxed passively into her mother's body, thumb in mouth, and stayed there, awake, pensive, and downcast for 20 to 30 minutes more.[5]

One of the most salient points I make from this example is how troubling the conflict due to ambivalence, to be furious with someone one is attached to, is for all of us. Not yet knowing how to deal with it, Mary was immobilized; in fact she seemed paralyzed. We have to deal with our ambivalence. In order to not feel paralyzed by the anxiety ambivalence causes us the way it did to Mary, we use defense mechanisms. But, as I will show later in this chapter, while defense mechanisms do help us cope with anxiety and depression, they at times can lead to no end of problems. This is why we have to foster in our children the ability to talk about and express feelings they have that they experience as noxious and trouble-making.

But first, how does one deal with one's child experiencing what Mary did? First of all, once mother had determined that a limit was needed, she stuck to it. When Mary expressed her anger, then her mounting hostility at her mother to the degree that it got to that day, mother felt hurt and bewildered; this time it was a first with Mary. Mother asked what she should do. She felt embarrassed, because we were observing them, all of us, surprised at so strong a troubled reaction by this child with her mother whose relationship we all knew was so good. Of course, all parents are embarrassed when their child has a fit in public. I recommend to mothers or fathers to ignore the public reaction and just tend to their child's distress, not by giving in, nor by giving the child something to cry about, but by listening, holding to the limit, and offering to comfort.

Mother was stung by the feelings expressed by her baby, but mother did not stifle the child's expression of feelings. When a child cries and seems to curse at her mother (even before she has learned to curse with words), clearly expressing strong hostile feelings, the child is choosing the most normal pathway one can use: direct expression. This, given its clarity, actually facilitates the mother's dealing with her child's feelings of outrage and hostility.

Therefore, it is best not to prohibit the child's crying, protestations, and nonverbal "cursing"; the child is truthfully telling you what she is feeling.

Although pained and distressed to see her daughter so upset, and embarrassed even though she knew the group of mothers, kids, and staff would not criticize her—interestingly, there was no criticizing in our naturalistic group project (see chapter 1) —neither the mothers nor the staff criticized. We just talked about whatever went on and mother patiently waited. She thoughtfully tried ways of comforting Mary, but mother recognized that Mary did not accept mother's efforts to comfort; mother waited. She sensed that Mary was struggling with something large; she just waited. After a long period of observation, I proposed to the mothers that Mary's sitting upright on the edge of her mother's knees, avoiding being comforted; it was clear—none of the mothers disagreed. Mary was not ready to be comforted. Yes, she was still very angry with her mother. However, I proposed to them, Mary was struggling and needed time to figure out what to do. Mary, I suggested, was furious, but it was with the mother she values beyond question. Furious with the mother who meant so much to her, she did not yet seem to know what to do with this conflict of ambivalence. She was furious with her dear, dear mother.

Note that I am avoiding using the words "love" and "hate." This is because I am among those developmentalists who believe that the ability to love and hate requires sufficient brain development for the child to be able to link (1) the deeply felt affect (emotion) with (2) the idea of stably investing positive or negative feelings, and that (3) both love and hate are states of feeling that are enduring. "Liking" someone is not as deeply felt, nor does it necessarily last over time. Love and hate are more complex emotional states that last and have duration; they generally develop from about 18 months of age on.[6] So, 13-month-old Mary at the time of this conflict was furious with the mother to whom she was securely attached and whom she valued deeply and would soon develop the capability to love. Mary's secure attachment to her mother continued well into our 37-year follow-up study. But this day, 36 years before, Mary was very troubled by her conflicted feelings toward her mother. A mother could not have handled this crisis better than did Mary's mother.

When we think of helping our children verbalize their feelings of anger, hostility, and hate, we have to distinguish between words that hurt and words that insult. While we want to encourage our children to verbalize difficult feelings, we do not want them to go beyond certain reasonable bounds of what one can say to another person, particularly to one who is valued and loved.

We draw the distinction by saying that parents should not tolerate words that insult, but should allow words that may hurt without insulting. We have found that some parents find certain words intolerable, whereas others do not. Perhaps "intolerable" is a dimension we should add to words that insult.

Not only are we sensitive to certain words, but also we are sensitive to the tone in which words are expressed. The tone often carries the emotional quality or the affective coloring of the feelings expressed. In helping a child verbalize feelings of hostility and hate, a boundary must be drawn. Words and intonations that are insulting or intolerable should not be allowed.

For instance, a young child's outburst of "I hate you" at her mother, even in its most deeply felt intonations cannot be construed as an insult. A parent may find the words painful, yet they should not be disallowed. This example shows how difficult it is to state where to draw the line in allowing a child to verbalize feelings of hostility and hate. We each need to draw our own lines. But we have to bear in mind that it is necessary, in order to help our child, to find a range of expression that is permissible. Otherwise, there will be no verbal pathway to the resolution of hostility, and that will create otherwise preventable behavior problems.

When 16-year-old Mike stormed at his mother "What the *#&^% is this? You're not at the table yet," his mother was insulted. Yes, Mike just said words; he didn't throw anything, didn't break anything, he just said "*#&^%." But the word he used was not acceptable. His mother told him without insulting him that she experienced him then as a "foul-mouthed kid," which at that moment he was.

We all have our acceptable and unacceptable invectives. This author would have distinguished between one of his exasperated teenage sons calling him "a jerk" versus "a bastard" or "a son of a bitch." To be called a "jerk" by one's own son is a distasteful event. To be called a "bastard" or a "son of a bitch" is not acceptable to this parent.

In fact, we are talking about a far-reaching aspect of how to get along with someone one values and loves. How to fight and argue with those we love is a challenge to all of us. It certainly is a challenge to children. It is good when arguing (whether with loved ones or otherwise), to learn reasonable rules. For instance, even in boxing, there are rules: at all times, no blows below the belt. We might use that model in family fights, to draw the line between words that are hurtful and words that are out of bounds, inappropriate, insulting, and intolerable—below the belt.

Of course, parents get upset by their children's expressions of hostility toward them. When three-year-old Susan shouted at her mother "I hate you," mother was crushed. "Oh! I know you don't mean that." Well, Susan said it. And it's more helpful to assume that she meant it rather than in essence saying to her daughter, "You can't be feeling that way because I'm your mother." This, as I said, creates problems.

But consider this. I have said this to many parents. I have asked them: how often does your child say this to you? And when she says it, for how long do these enduring feelings of hate seem to be felt by your child? Commonly the young child's "I hate you" soon gives way to much kinder, more caring, enduring feelings. In most cases, once the feeling of hate is verbally expressed, it tends to lessen and then the feelings of love that were momentarily blanketed over—these much longer enduring love feelings—resurface. I ask the parent to consider "How much does she hate you? For how long does she hate you?" This much (I put my hands, palm to palm, and stretch them apart for about six inches)? And how much do you think she loves you (and I stretch my hands full arms length as wide as I can stretch)? The intensity and duration of the child's hate toward the parent is far less, by far, than how much the three-year-old child thinks mom (or dad) is great. I add that it's helpful for the parent to say this much to the child: "I know sometimes you get real mad at me; I get pretty angry with you sometimes too, you know. You're not an angel, and I'm not an angel. But I'm so glad that most of the time I know you really love me—and I sure love you!" (Use your own words.)

It's actually good that we get upset when a young child explodes with, "I hate you." If we did not get upset by it, it would mean that we are indifferent to our child's feelings of pain. However, some parents tell their child not to be angry, that it is bad to be angry, and—most unproductive of all—"I'll give you something to really be angry about." In general, a young child's exclamations of anger, as when 13-month-old Mary had "had it" with her highly emotionally invested mother, are desirable means of expressing what the child is feeling. It is helpful, of course, for the mother to recognize that the child is reacting to something mother is doing to her. Then the anger being directed toward mother cannot be surprising. It's not as though mother had not repeatedly interfered with Mary's strivings for autonomy.

Mary kicked her mother from a distance (without making contact) and twice actually struck her mother in the arm. Once she struck herself. Discharging hostile feelings by striking out physically is usually not a good way to express one's feelings. There are times, however, when a child's physically striking out is warranted, particularly when it is in response to being continually bullied or attacked by someone else. Some parents tell their child that when bullied by someone he should just walk away. This works sometimes—more or less—but many parents know that bullies are not likely to stop bullying until their child strikes back. There are variations to this thesis, but it is a commonly found phenomenon.

However, discharging feelings of anger by striking out physically at one's mother—I assume that a school-age child and certainly all but a few very troubled adolescents would no longer do that—produces a double jeopardy.

It is usually more difficult to reverse a physical act than a verbal statement. The exception is a mother's swat on her young child's clothed bottom (see chapter 8). Also, often, an act tends to be more hurtful, more unacceptable than angry words. Given the type of circumstance we are discussing now—Mary's having a fit in response to her mother's limit setting or Mike's curse directed at his mother—the old saying "sticks and stones can break my bones, but words will never harm me" tends to have some merit, but it is not always, nor altogether true, given that words that insult can in fact hurt more.

My overall impression is that children tend to feel more guilt when they physically strike out at their parents, than when they say, "I hate you." Given that there is a natural, almost reflexive, tendency in young children to hit when they feel angry, it is helpful for the parent to intervene and not let the child strike her or him. He should say what he feels and thinks, but he is not allowed to hit you. By the way, one can say to a less-than-two-year-old who does not yet use words to "*Say* what you feel and think, but don't hit." The child will get the message.

For the young child who persists in hitting mother, setting limits on that act becomes necessary. It is a worthwhile project; the limit setting strategies proposed in chapter 8 should be brought into play. When the limits do not work, the parent should go on to privilege withdrawal.

Doing to the child what the child is doing to the parent "in order to teach him a lesson," is not as desirable as withdrawing a privilege or, if comfortable with it, with a young child, administer a swat on the child's clothed bottom. For example, with a young child who bites, biting the child back is not a desirable way of teaching him not to bite. With a less than one-year-old, express hurt ("Ouch!"), set limits, and verbally scold. With a two- or 3-year-old, set limits and if he or she persists, go to a time-out. Beyond three years, it's uncommon for kids to bite.

Equally important, just as the mother should prohibit the child's striking at her, so should the mother prohibit and protectively disapprove of the child's striking herself, as Mary did. Parents will commonly find that children (even less than one year of age), when excessively angry, will not only lash out against others, but also against themselves. In very young children, this may occur as a result of both lack of control over reflexive reactions and insufficient differentiation between self and other—not knowing who is the self and who is the other—instigating the experience leading to rage.

Even in children just around one year of age, when there is an acute hostility overload, the child may restrict himself from directing his hostility toward mother or father. Even this young, as we saw in Mary, hostility toward those to whom the child is attached creates internal conflict. The alternative frequently used by young children is to direct the hostility away from the valued and needed parent and turn it toward himself or toward an innocent bystander by *displacement,* which I'll talk about shortly.

We find that children often tend to use the same reactions over and over. Thus the parent can recognize the pattern the child uses to deal with hostility overload. Parents will recognize it if their child tends to direct his hostility against himself as a selected way of dealing with hostility overload. As patterns of hostility expression and discharge are tried by the child, parents should endorse constructive ways the child uses.

> Three-year-old Phyllis seemed somehow to frequently get bruises, scratches, or cuts on her arms, legs, or face. We had noticed that she would fall or bump into chairs, even though she was not a clumsy child. We soon came to see that when she got upset with her younger sister and teased or hit her, and her mother would then scold her, Phyllis would scratch her own arm or bite her own hand. We inferred that she did this because she was unable to find reasonable ways to express her feelings of hostility and rage. When this was drawn to the mother's and Phyllis's attention, she began talking about her feelings in a matter of a few weeks. The physical attacks on herself began to decrease and eventually stopped.

Restrictions on lashing out against mother, as well as against the self, should take essentially the same form. First, one states the prohibition against doing just that. Second, one comments as to the reason for that prohibition, which is invariably in the form of, "I love you, and I don't want you to hurt me or to hurt yourself—and I don't want you to feel bad about what you do." Third, if this type of behavior has been going on for some time, point it out to the child, explain that you disapprove and expect the behavior to stop. Again, the child's lashing out against himself may require the setting of limits and where these fail, some benign form of punishment. And where the parents' efforts do not work, some professional help may be warranted—because self-hurting, self-defeating tendencies can have serious life-long implications.

Why Reduce Children's Need to Erect Defense Mechanisms to Cope with Their Feelings of Hostility?

Helping children find acceptable ways to verbalize and express their feelings of anger and hostility reduces their need to erect defense mechanisms to protect themselves against the anxiety these feelings create in them. Most parents don't need this encouragement, but it is in our children's best interest that we consider this task seriously. When a child is not helped with the expression and discharge of his hostility overload against mother or himself, the child does not feel protected against his own hate reactions and accumulating inner pressure to destroy. The child may then become afraid of what his own rage may lead him to do and even become afraid of this rage himself—like he has this destructive force in him that may even destroy him.

One of the largest challenges to the young child comes from her unavoidable experience-derived feelings of ambivalence, which at moments stir up in her the wish to destroy the mother she loves. Consider 13-month-old Mary's paralysis. What a remarkable illustration of the challenge to the child: What was she to do? How was she to deal with this eruptive force inside her? Yes, she'd been angry with her mother before, but this! She was mortified. Paralyzed. To be sure, it was the mounting of anger upon anger that intensified into rage. The indignation that her sense of self was being trashed by, of all people, her dear, dear mother. We were all awed by her bewildering dilemma. By the way, it was no picnic for her mother either.

Because her mother handled it so patiently, so empathically, so sympathetically, Mary was able to deal with it directly. And she was then eventually able to quiet her eruption and accept her mother's comforting. What would have been the consequences for Mary if her mother had just let Mary thrash around on the floor and maybe even called her a spoiled brat? The rage we saw would have stayed inside Mary—and who knows when and how it would eventually have been discharged.

Being afraid of one's own feelings, hostile or other troubling feelings, commonly leads to having to self-protectively erect defenses to not feel them. Then a child may simply repress them, or deny them, or inhibit the discharge of these feelings, blocking their reasonable expression and discharge. Without such defenses the child's emotional life might be frozen—as we saw only briefly, fortunately, in Mary. These defenses, and there are others in addition to those I mentioned, may however, lead to distortions of feelings including those of hate, which will then not be metabolized or resolved and will accumulate, as well, however, as those of love and affection, which may then negatively affect love relationships and eventually sexual gratification. Defenses erected to contain one's hostility may also lead to inhibitions in learning, and may eventually create school and work problems.

Here is an example of what I have found many times.

> A six-year-old boy is surprisingly quiet when with grown-ups, even with his own father. He tends not to talk to them, even at times when it is expected (as with a teacher in class). He tends to talk most easily with his mother. He does well with peers. He also is subject to temper tantrums that distress his parents greatly, and he is most enraged with his younger brother, who seems to be a source of much difficulty for him. Because at

> six years he has not yet learned to control his rage well enough and is in constant dread of its bursting forth, he has to set a big clamp on his feelings. This leads to inhibitions, which among other inhibitions includes not talking with grown-ups other than his mother.

Here is another type of event that needs a comment. I have at times seen a 16-month-old child bump into a chair because he was not looking where he was going. In response to the child's being upset by this, a mother may say "Bad chair." There are troubles with this type of problem solving. Clearly the chair did not walk up to the child and hit him. The accident occurred because the child was inattentive to where he was going. It is better to help the child's evolving sense of being someone who can initiate things, someone who is responsible for his own actions. "Look where you're going! Be careful," is far superior to "Bad chair."

The fact is that blaming an innocent thing or person for feeling hurt and then hostile enhances the use of troubling defense mechanisms in dealing with hostility overload. It also encourages the child to avoid dealing with situations realistically, which can only complicate the child's life. It is more to the child's advantage to learn to watch where he is going than to encourage him to believe that chairs magically move and hit you. Blaming chairs distorts facts, encourages frightening magical thinking—which all children experience, even into elementary-school years and later—and interferes with the child's developing healthy adaptive precaution and reasonable self-care.

But here's what makes this so important an issue: blaming an innocent object facilitates a highly problematic mechanism for dealing with one's hostility and hate—it's somebody else's or something else's fault. I didn't do it; he, or it, did it to me. This is a form of the defense mechanism we call *projection.* This kind of projection—of blaming someone else for something one feels or does is a close cousin to the defense mechanism *displacement.* Displacement is a mechanism whereby, when the child is confronted by hostility overload toward a person he loves and it stirs internal conflict, which can occur as early as the first year of life, may lead the child to displace the hostility onto something or someone else. Let us return to an event already mentioned.

> Twelve-month-old Jane was having a difficult time with her mother this morning. In the midst of one of their mild but then frequently occurring battles of wills, Jane picked up a small wooden block, raised her arm, and turned to her mother somewhat defiantly. Mother was looking at Jane quite sternly, and although she said nothing, her expression was clearly a statement of prohibition. Jane's arm came forward, and as it did so, she rotated her body slightly and threw the block at Mrs. G., who was sitting next to her mother.

We inferred from this that Jane's target was her beloved mother, but the prohibition from her mother and from within herself led Jane to displace her attack onto an innocent bystander, Mrs. G. We have extrapolated from such events that displacement is a self-protective coping mechanism implemented by all human beings to discharge hostility toward someone we love through discharging it against someone who is less important to us. This hostility discharge creates less conflict for us because that person is not as valued as the loved one.

I want to quote directly from what I wrote in chapter 3: "In our observational research, we saw a striking cluster of defenses young children erect when very angry with their mothers. (I should note that we saw the infants with their mothers; except on occasions, their fathers were not able to join us in our Tuesday and Friday observational meetings. Occasionally also, we saw some of our subjects' older siblings, as when there was no school on a given day.) For instance, already by 12 months of age we had seen much evidence of *displacement* (when angry with mother, Jane picked up a block and threw it not at her mother, but at the woman sitting next to her mother). By 18 months of age we saw clear evidence of *projection* (a strategy where the child projects her own hostility onto someone else: "I'm not angry at her, she's angry with me"), *rationalization* ("I'm angry with her because she was mean when she told me to brush my teeth"), and *denial* ("I didn't do that; it was an accident"). Then, especially organizing of prejudice, starting from five to six years on, we saw behaviors from which we could infer reality-distorting defenses, including *reductionism* ("All Blacks want to do is rob you"), *caricaturing* ("All Jews have hooks for noses"), *depreciation* ("All Spics are lazy and don't deserve to be paid like Whites"), and a recently minted *vilification* (All Muslims are terrorists"), defenses that play a key role in the organization of what I call *malignant prejudice.*

In the use of all these defenses, someone other than the person toward whom the rage and hate was initially experienced has become the recipient of that rage and hate. And this can happen even many years after the noxious experiences took place and seem to be forgotten. But both psychoanalysis and neuroscience now inform us that experiences of intense psychic pain get registered in the brain from very early on in life and continue to reverberate in us indefinitely, unless they are metabolized or revised either by reparatory life experiences or intensive psychotherapies (see chapters 2, 3, and 7).

Like limit setting, learning how to control one's anger and hostility and to discharge it in socially acceptable ways requires time and repeated efforts on the part of the parent. Helping kids express their hostility in acceptable ways continues well into the elementary-school years and at times into adolescence. As I emphasized in chapter 8, in adolescence our efforts to get compliance, to set limits, and now to help our kids establish acceptable ways to discharge hostility takes special care. When an adolescent needs help in improving his way of discharging hostility, the effectiveness of the parents' efforts are highly determined by the adolescent's past history in interaction and relatedness with these parents. Perhaps more so than before, the history of secure, good relatedness will now make helping our adolescent gain further control over how to discharge hostility constructively both less necessary and more feasible. By contrast where there has been much negativity, especially where there has been abuse and neglect, helping teenagers discharge high loads of hostility in socially acceptable ways will most likely be problematic, if not outright ineffective.

With kids, both during their school-age years and adolescence, whose relationships are quite positively secure, but in whom personality traits make not only limit setting and compliance rather difficult to achieve without some struggle, negotiation, and compromise, but also now further developing their skills in controlling a fair load of hostility they experience, things are more complicated. Some kids with obsessive traits, or some burdened with self-disappointment due to some learning difficulty or some other inborn challenging trait, may have more difficulty dealing with their hostility and require more effort on the parents' part to help them continue to make efforts to discharge these difficult feelings in reasonable ways. It continues to be challenging to parents to help such kids when they go into adolescence, but the parents' efforts need to be continued. With some of these kids, a "tough love" approach may be very helpful. In this approach, limits are set with firmness (not hostility), even in the face of much distress felt by both adolescent and parent, and punishment must be reasonably but clearly measured and limited to privilege withdrawal. Side by side with this then, helping the teenager continue to improve his ability to express his hostility in acceptable ways is paramount, because much hostility will get stirred up by the "tough" approach. Physical punishment with adolescents is not part of tough love; it's abuse and it's very risky.

What complicates the parents' efforts to further help their adolescents discharge their hostility in ways parents believe to be acceptable is that the parents standards of what is acceptable increasingly carries less weight in adolescence due to the shift of the center of their universe from the parents (the family) to the peer group. The consolidation of self-identity has to include mores of hostility discharge that are acceptable to, and have to straddle the standards acceptable to, both the family and the peer group. Again, where relationships are good, this may not be difficult to achieve; where relationships are not, the likelihood is large that what's acceptable to the peer group may not be to the family, and what is acceptable to the family will likely not be acceptable to the peer group. By the way, with teenagers whose challenging behavior comes from having been traumatized or neglected, tough love strategies work only with a limited number of them. That prevention is worth a pound of cure is an underestimation; it's the difference between a fruitful, gratifying life and a life of trouble and misery.

It is well to bear in mind that there are ways of discharging one's hostility in graduated doses and in ways that are tolerable to both the self and the target of one's anger. Verbalization of one's hostility in a positively meaningful relationship allows for the lessening of its accumulation in the psyche and prevents its coloring the personality. It also facilitates the development of internal controls over how one discharges hostility and hate, a process that develops gradually, with much help from parents. As with limit setting, teaching children to verbalize hostility often requires repetition to gradually effect a working through of feelings of pain (unpleasure) and mobilized hostility.

The parents' efforts to develop, maintain, and enhance a positive dialogue with their child—which can be put into play even when dealing with angry feelings and hostility—not only provides a vehicle for the working through of painful experiences, hostility, and hate, but also secures the vehicle for healthy development in the child, including the formation of good relationships and heightened well-being.

We should also toss into this promise the idea that if parents want their child to talk to them when they become adolescents—something that is not guaranteed in all families—they must talk and listen to their child and encourage their child to talk about feelings and experiences from infancy on.

DEALING WITH TEASING AND TAUNTING

As I reported in chapter 5, we saw behavior at about 12 months of age that took us by surprise. I am referring to what I catalogued as aggressive behavior that seems to suggest pleasure-related destructiveness. As I said, we had not seen this type of aggression before that time. Let me remind the reader of the three examples I recorded in chapter 5.

The first example is the one that took place between 11-month-olds, Jane and Tammy.

> Jane was exploring her environment in her usual way. She came to Tammy, who was also just going about her explorations, pacifier in her mouth as was usual for her at this time. Jane paused a moment standing in front of Tammy, both looked at each other, when Jane just reached for and plucked Tammy's pacifier from her mouth. Jane's mother reacted immediately, getting up and returning the pacifier to Tammy while

> telling Jane not to do that. Jane didn't seem particularly troubled by her quite reasonable and loving mother's reaction. Jane walked away, looking around. Then she circled back to Tammy and looking at her, reached for Tammy's pacifier and again pulled it from her mouth. Jane now seemed intent on doing this. Tammy got upset. Jane's mother's tone was more urgent and firm this time. Jane walked away seemingly not too dismayed about all this. In fact, she had a bit of a smirk on her face. After a few moments, there she was again, in front of Tammy and again, pulled the pacifier from her mouth. This time Jane smiled as she did this; Tammy now started to cry.

I was very puzzled by this behavior. Here rather than experiencing psychic pain, this 11-month-old was causing another child psychic pain.

Here's another of the examples of this type of behavior:

> Two-and-a-half-year-old Susan seemed rather restless one morning. As she went from one toy to another, she noted with interest a toy one-and-a half-year-old Tommy was exploring. With a half smile on her face, she reached for that toy and pulled it from Tommy's hand. Her mother was looking elsewhere and did not see this. Within moments, Susan—again smiling—grabbed the next toy Tommy picked up. Again, she watched Tommy's reaction with pleasure and some satisfaction. Tommy fussed. He picked up yet another toy, and in a moment, Susan grabbed it. Her smile now left no doubt that she was getting pleasure out of being nasty to Tommy. Now Tommy was heard, and Susan's mother, now tuned in to what was going on, intervened. No one would argue: this was intentional. It was *taunting.*

The third example here was more complex, but helped us see and understand what could have been at the base of both 11-month-old Jane's and two-and-a-half-years old Susan's behaviors.

> When Candy was about 18 months old, she and her twin sister were exploring among the other children as we carried out our usual observations (during the project I described in the introduction). For no reason visible to us, two-and-a-half-year-old Donnie approached Candy, suddenly thrust his arm around her neck and grabbed her head—in the wrestling move called "a half-Nelson." We were all startled—the mothers, the observers, and certainly, Candy. Mothers intervened quickly. Candy did not retaliate against Donnie. She moped; and she disrupted her sister's play with some toys. Her mother calmed her sympathetically.

> At our next group session three days later, Candy, her sister, and her mother came as usual. Candy seemed subdued. Some 20 minutes later, I saw Candy's face come to attention as she focused across the Unit's Day Room where we met. Donnie, his younger sister (one of our research subjects) and their mother had just walked in. Quite directly, Candy walked up to Donnie and without a sound, raised her fist and struck him in the arm. With this she smiled softly, a bit like Mona Lisa. Donnie was startled, but interestingly did not strike back. Candy's mother readied to get up but saw that the event was over. It made clear sense to me; it might have to Candy's mother as well. In fact, I commented to the mothers that it seemed as though Candy had been planning how to let Donnie know that she was very angry with him for what he had done to her three days before. I wondered if Donnie's reaction of doing nothing might have suggested that Donnie too understood that this was retribution for what he had then done to her three days before.

To be sure, parents need to intervene and help their child know that teasing and taunting creates problems. Most parents agree that this is not acceptable behavior, needs to be interrupted and, even with less than two-year-olds, a firm enough mini-lecture is called for. Talking about it again later, when things have quieted down is highly desirable too. Teasing and taunting in early childhood that is not dealt with by parents can lead to a pattern of abuse of others that can create painful problems for others, but also for the child herself. In fact, teasing and taunting is problematic for both the teased and the teaser.

The teaser needs help in that teasing and taunting can create problems of socialization that may lead peers to reject the teaser. Already at 11 months, Jane needed fairly firm limits by her mother, given Jane's rather hefty disposition. Jane was not teased by her mother, but she may have been teased by her father or one or more of her older siblings. It did seem that her behavior just came up spontaneously, as part of her exploring her universe, including people in it and especially kids her own age.

It was not clear to us what Jane experienced as pleasurable when she saw Tammy upset. I wondered if she derived pleasure from making something happen; she caused a change in her universe. Did she have a drive to be nasty? Some would believe this. I don't. She certainly already had had run-ins with her mother in which we saw Jane get angry with her. She may also have had such experiences with her father. No doubt she did as well with her siblings. Was she taking her anger toward her mother, father, or siblings out on Tammy? My inclination is to assume that all of these might have contributed to her teasing Tammy: her need to have an impact on her universe, causing others annoyance and psychic pain as she felt was done to her, being pushed by her already accumulating anger to displace her accumulating hostility by being nasty to another.

Susan's actions toward Tommy are easier to understand. He was her unwanted baby brother. No one consulted her about having another baby in the family to share her parents with. She liked being the only princess in the house. Now her privileged position had been eliminated. By whom? Like every firstborn, Susan didn't blame her parents—who of course did all this planning to have another baby—instead, she displaced upon her brother her resentment about being displaced from cherished priority status to common plebian all because of that brat.

The dynamics of Candy's behavior were clear: she had been attacked. Given the pain she experienced, it registered firmly in her young mind. Days later she acted to get back—quite mildly I should say—for what Donnie had done to her. This gave her satisfaction, even pleasure.

Parents should address teasing and taunting by their child because this may evolve into her becoming a sadistic individual, one who derives pleasure from being mean to others. Then, no doubt her relationships with loved ones, peers, and others will suffer. In addition, the teaser may in fact evolve during childhood into a bully or later in life into someone easily drawn to harmful behavior toward others as occurs in acts of malignant prejudice (see above and chapter 3).

With the young child, limits are the first order of things. But with that, talking to the child is essential. With preschool kids and school-age ones, parents need to take the time to get the child to try to explain why he teases. And to follow this up with telling the child, young or older, that complaints he has toward others are better dealt with by talking with the other where possible than by teasing and taunting.

We have to bear in mind that there is a rather direct line between kids feeling maltreated whether at home or in school and their later teasing and even bullying others. Several of the defense mechanisms I just talked about bring this about.

The child who is teased needs help too. Depending on his or her age, the teased child may at first need to be protected and progressively helped to self-protectively stand up for himself or herself. This is a well-worth project that will serve the child for many years to come. Some young children protect themselves automatically with confidence; they act to stop the aggressor. Others, like Tammy, are stunned, may become frightened and end up feeling helpless; they turn for help to the caregiver. Whatever way the teased child reacts, when needed the parent should comfort, then the parent should to help the child, whatever age, by discussing ways to deal with a teaser or a bully;

the school-age child and adolescent will surely be confronted by one at one time or another.

Some school-age children and even adolescents will not tell their parents they are being teased, often due to the shame they feel about having allowed themselves to be intimidated and humiliated by a bully. Such a child or teenager is then likely to be upset and this may express itself at home. Trying to get the youngster to say what is upsetting him might well bring this out.

A parent ridiculing his or her teased kid, of whatever age, is extremely hurtful and generates hostility toward the ridiculing parent. Helping the teased child should put a priority on talking about and offering suggestions to the child—this applies at times even to teenagers—as to how to deal with a teaser or a bully. Unfortunately, dealing with a bully may be more difficult than anyone wishes. Although the teased kid might try to talk to this bully, this often fails to achieve a positive end. If the bullying becomes physical, this is one time when one may need to advise one's kid to hit back. Talking rarely helps when a bully goes physical. For young school-age kids, it's wise to suggest they tell the teacher about it, but for the older youngster and teenager this is likely to cause more embarrassment than help.

NOTES

1. H. Parens, Rage toward self and other in early childhood, in *Rage, Power and Aggression,* ed. S. P. Roose & R. Glick (New Haven: Yale University Press, 1993) 123–147.

2. Reactivity type is to be distinguished from impulsivity, the latter being due to a weakness in the organization and regulation of discharging feelings, which makes it much more difficult to learn to control them.

3. See (in chapter 11) the case of Richie who was well nurtured until six months of age, when a painful change in his teen mother's life soon led to his being sadly neglected and painfully abused, which severely arrested his up-to-then normal development. Richie's history demonstrated painfully how he turned from a loving, beautiful little boy to a shriveled, failing-to-thrive, raging child. H. Parens, Cruelty begins at home, *Child Abuse and Neglect* 11 (1987):331–338.

4. In psychotherapeutic work, it is critical that the therapist be empathic or is capable of empathy. By this we mean that the therapist must be able to not only listen, but also to emotionally perceive, grasp, and understand what the patient is feeling and trying to convey. It is being able to feel what the other is feeling; not to feel the same way, but to grasp that the other has these feelings. The therapist must resonate with the patient's feelings not just his or her words. Such empathic relatedness is not just reserved for the therapist; it is a highly desirable capability in any relationship, intimate or not, but it is especially so in the parent-child relationship. Indeed, it is an

essential requirement for growth-promoting parenting (H. Parens, E. Scattergood, A. Duff, & W. Singletary, *Parenting for Emotional Growth (PEG): The Textbook* and *PEG: A Curriculum for Students in Grades K Thru 12* [1997]).

5. H. Parens, *The Development of Aggression in Early Childhood* (Lanham, MD: Jason Aronson, 2008) 204–205.

6. J. B. McDevitt, The emergence of hostile aggression and its defensive and adaptive modifications during the separation-individuation process, *J. Amer. Psa. Assn.* 31:5(1983):273–300 and H. Parens et al., *Parenting for Emotional Growth (PEG): The Textbook* and *PEG: A Curriculum for Students in Grades K Thru 12* (1997).

Chapter 10

How to Handle Temper Tantrums and Rage Reactions in Growth-Promoting Ways

I will describe two young children, David who had temper tantrums and Richie who experienced rage reactions. There are differences between the two types of reactions that bring with them the need to understand them and deal with them somewhat differently.[1]

Thirty-eight-month-old David's temper tantrum. David was born with a low threshold of irritability and a tendency to quick reactivity with difficulty in organizing intense feeling states and in calming. He is an intelligent, lovable kid, who by virtue of his inborn dispositions, however, quickly gets upset and very angry, which in turn, cause much distress to both his parents. From about one year of age on, his hostile destructive (HD) outbursts began to organize into temper tantrums.

By 38 months, David's outbursts gave the impression that at moments of disappointment or frustration his efforts to contain the distress and HD mounting within him were suddenly overpowered. This particular morning David seemed on edge when his mother rolled him and his 11-month-old sister in a stroller into the observation setting. Mother, who was weary but because she now understood her son's inborn vulnerability could also be very sympathetic toward him, did not immediately respond to his pressured need to get out of the stroller. He squirmed vigorously, made efforts to get out himself, conveying intolerance for his inability to get on his feet and do what he seemed just driven to do. Once she was able to, mother helped him out of the stroller, while trying to calm him as she complemented his impatient efforts to get out.

Phew! He could now move where he wished. He darted to the fruit on the table; smiling, he signaled to his mother that he had noticed it there.

He went to the toys, briefly interacted with two peers there, and busily manipulated toys, making them move. During this time mother had gotten to his sister, a much calmer and easier child, and helped her out of the stroller. Ten minutes had passed when David brought an apple to his mother. It was not clear if he wanted her permission to eat it or simply to inform her that he was going to do so. Mother did not want him to have it because he had complained of stomach pain, and she told him that she feared it might upset his stomach more.

He erupted. Virtually at once his face showed intense pain and hostility, crying, blustering nonverbal vocalizations, he dropped to the floor, kicking and flailing at his mother who had just taken the apple from him. Mother looked pale, embarrassed, and moderately bewildered—she [and we] had been through this with him before—as she tried sympathetically to calm him, telling him why she had taken the apple from him now. His kicking and flailing made her pull away slightly, but as he calmed a bit, she came closer and continued her effort to explain and calm him down. Within 30 seconds he let her hold him, and she, now seated in a soft chair, continued her efforts. Both child and mother looked pale, drained, and tensely in pain still—both, it seemed, trying to contain David's still palpable potential for eruption.

About one minute into the calming phase, as another child picked up the wooden car with which David had been playing before the tantrum he erupted again, though not as harshly. As David, enraged, complained and demanded the return of the toy, he picked up a block and threw it toward, and nearly hit, not the child who was playing with the car, but another group mother who was totally uninvolved in the event. David, further frustrated by the second child's resistance in returning the toy, in quick sequence grabbed his sister's bottle that was at hand, threw it at her, picked up another block and threw it at me [the parenting group instructor], nearly falling off the chair in doing so. He looked at me anxiously, more surprised than enraged as I told him I was sorry he was feeling so bad but that I did not want him to throw things at me or to fall off the chair. I wished he could talk to his mommy or me about the things that were making him so upset. Simultaneously, his mother, scolding softly, was telling him not to hit his sister and that Dr. Parens had not done anything to him, and made good efforts again to calm him, telling him he could not throw things at people. With his mother's help, the second child returned the car to David, and David became calm as his mother continued to talk to him. Both David and his mother looked exhausted and pained.

As he recovered gradually, David began to annoy his sister by taking the toy with which she was playing, looking at his mother as he did so, smiling provocatively. The teasing continued and intensified into taunting. Mother now became angry with him. At the moment when he was on the verge of going too far, David abruptly changed his activity, asking his mother to take out his letter cards and play with him at identifying the letters of the alphabet. David and his mother continued to look emotionally drained.[2]

I have selected Richie, a child who was severely traumatized, to describe rage reactions because his reactions were clear and give us a sad opportunity to compare a rage reaction with a temper tantrum. Richie's rage reactions were quite harsh and explosive, commensurate with the degree to which he was traumatized. Like with tantrums, rage reactions have a wide range of intensity, frequency, and degree of difficulty. Fortunately, not all kids who have rage reactions have them because they have been traumatized to the degree that Richie was. Generally, the less the child feels miserable as a result of excessively painful experiences due to environmental (foremost, caregivers') actions, the more moderate the rage reactions. I want to emphasize that kids who have rage reactions, as well as tantrums, need thoughtful parental help—difficult as it is for parents to deal with them.

To make clear why Richie's rage reactions were so harsh, I will give more details as to how I postulate Richie got to be the way he was when we saw him.

Fourteen-month-old Richie's rage reactions. When we first saw Richie he was 14 months old. He was depressed, hyper-vigilant, with a painfully distrustful look and very sad eyes. He was subdued and his movements were sluggish. He looked no more than eight months of age. Although he probably experienced some stranger anxiety in our setting, his initial response to us was to withdraw. Richie was brought to our group by Mrs. V. because she was deeply shocked by what had happened to Richie (whom she had known since his birth), by what had become of him, and by how difficult he now was to care for.

Given the child we saw, it is important to note that Richie had an excellent Apgar[3] evaluation at birth and was in very good physical health and in quite good mental health (ascertained both by history and by a series of photographs of him) until six-and-a-half months of age. At this time, Richie's teenage father gave his 17-year-old mother the alternative of moving away from her home with him or he would leave her. Bewildered, she moved with him into a rented room. Within two weeks, the young father abandoned them.

Probably acutely depressed and immobilized, perhaps hoping her boyfriend would return, Richie's mother stayed in that room with her baby, rather than returning home. Becoming more and more depressed, Richie's teenage mother could not tolerate his complaining, whining, and not eating. Bear in mind that Richie had been very well cared for by his young mother and those around her while she was in the protected setting of her home.

Increasingly bewildered and finding her baby's crying and refusal to eat unbearable, mother began to put him in the hall when she could not get him to stop crying. According to Mrs. V., who had known Richie before, Richie had changed dramatically at nine months of age and became withdrawn. We assumed from her descriptions that he became "anaclitically depressed."[4] At nine-and-a-half months of age, Richie was brought to the emergency room at our hospital due to a clothing-iron burn on his back. Mother said that during a fight with Richie's father, the iron fell and burned Richie. Seeing mother and child in their respective emotional states, emergency room staff assumed child abuse and Richie was placed in city custody. He remained there until just before he was 14 months at which time, grandmother took him into custody. Now very difficult to care for, through the intervention of Mrs. V., Richie's grandmother brought him to get some help in our observation-educational setting. Here are a few condensed excerpts from our data recordings.[5]

At one (year) - two (months) - 25(days), Richie continued to be depressed and emotionally and motorically sluggish. His exploratory activity was minimal except for his hypervigilance. He occasionally smiled, bounced on his knees, several times seemingly spontaneously, and he threw toys harshly in just any direction, the pressure of his aggressiveness eliciting immediate limit setting (Parens 1987, 332). Interestingly, even though his grandmother was there, he turned to Mrs. V. for comforting.

At one year, three months, one day of age, affect was unstable, depression dominated. But he also beamed, for the first time, when two-and-a-half-year-old Doris engaged him to play ball with her. She rolled a 3-inch rubber ball to him, and he brusquely rolled it back to her. She rolled it to him again, and again he returned it her. In the spirit of play, Doris hid the ball between her legs. He appeared confused and suddenly unbearably frustrated, he cried, seated on the floor he just contorted his body harshly and fell back banging his head on the floor in the process, all to Doris' pained dismay. Mrs. V. intervened. Soon thereafter he went into a rage reaction when he could not have a toy he wanted (332).

At one year, three months, eight days of age his depression was softer, he seemed less morose, smiled more at people. Exploratory activity expanded and he reached out to several project children. He used toys more constructively. Nonetheless, in exploring the toy cart he continued to throw toys out harshly one by one, which elicited the need to contain him. We felt that the load of HD he was experiencing "invaded" his physical activity, that it became too harsh and destructive (332). Relatedness with others was improving. He now began to waken during the night screaming. Grandmother could comfort him within minutes. We assumed he was now having nightmares.

Twelve weeks later, at one year, six months, seven days of age, he was walking without support, wobbly but upright. He had sudden bursts of explosiveness, suddenly throwing toys sometimes in a wide trajectory that would alarm the mothers and bring immediate intervention.

At 1 year, 7 months, 23 days of age, we recorded that his affect was much improved. Sudden, too aggressive outbursts with toys continue. But we have not seen him attack people or babies whom he now approaches with interest. He then seems low-keyed.

At 1 year, 8 months, 23 days of age, we noted enormous strides in development: improved affect stabilizing, control of aggression, coping functioning at a more advanced level, more positive relatedness to others (333). At this time as he approached the toy cart we saw no explosive toy throwing. Rather, he folded his hands on his chest as if to control himself and at times shook his head "No" at such moments. He then continued to have about three nightmares per night. He now said things that made people laugh. Grandmother and Mrs. V. said that it brought back memories of how he was responsive and entertaining at four to five months of age.

The most dramatic of Richie's rage reactions was his reaction to Doris' playfully hiding the ball from him. His reaction was explosive, his entire body contorted, he lost his balance banging his head on the floor seemingly unaware that it might hurt him. In fact, he did not seem to react to having banged his head. I wondered if, given that his entire young being was in agony, harshly banging his head didn't register with him. Richie's rage reaction overran any self-care. Fortunately the floor was carpeted, but nonetheless, he really banged his head hard. His rage reaction was so sudden it took us all by surprise. While the staff and I knew he was a tortured young child, his reaction to lovely Doris' behavior was jarring. By contrast, when a child has a tantrum, you can see it coming.

As we proceed to consider what these "crisis-behaviors" are—temper tantrums and rage reactions—and how to intervene constructively in helping our children who suffer from them, two terms stand out as we aim toward optimizing the development and well-being of our children. These terms are (1) *prevention* and (2) *damage-repair*. With regard to these "crisis-behaviors," *prevention* requires knowing what causes them and what can be done to lessen the likelihood that they occur; lessening the frequency of their occurrence is a start. Some cannot be prevented, but, critically some can—this especially applies to those category three rage reactions that result from child abuse and neglect.

Damage-repair requires knowing what can be done to reduce the pain and repair the damage caused the child, the caregiver, and the relationship between them.

Close observation of children like David and Richie revealed that temper tantrums and rage reactions differ in several ways. Both temper tantrums and rage reactions are behavioral reactions to experiences of intense psychic pain, which generate in the child high-level hostile destructiveness (HD). Just looking at these behavioral reactions, we see that they are not all the same and that while there are common basic ways to handle them in growth-promoting ways, at the same time it is helpful to understand what drives them and why they are happening. In fact, observation of what seems to provoke them and of their characteristics—all of which are important to parents' knowing how to most optimally handle these behaviors—lead me to cluster them as follows.

There are temper tantrums. As I shall explain, tantrums tend to occur from two to about seven years of age.

There are rage reactions. These vary widely in their dynamics—what factors give rise to them and what factors make them look as they do.

The Strucure of Temper Tantrums Is Complex; the Structure of Rage Reactions Is Not

We'll look at this structure more closely later, but for now let me say that a full temper tantrum has two dimensions, or we could say it has two waves. (1) As I try to illustrate in figure 10.1, the first dimension is the entire tantrum period, which I represent as a more or less long wave-like event that has a beginning, mounts rapidly, reaches a peak or climax, then gradually more or less slowly wanes and dies down. The second dimension consists of tantrum outbursts, which I represent as smaller, episodic waves that ride on this overarching full tantrum wave. (2) Each of these episodic outbursts has a similar basic wave-like structure: a beginning or climbing limb, followed by a crest and then, a down or descending limb (see figure 10.2, below).

A rage reaction has a simpler structure; it generally is an outburst; it tends to start suddenly and to stop when the kid runs out of steam or someone puts an end to it—either by giving the child what he wants or often by threatening him. It does not tend to give the parent a warning, since it may not have a discernible beginning, which can alert the parent of its coming. We were all shocked by Richie's sudden explosion. To be sure, if one is determined to get a rage reaction from a child like Richie, one can predict that at some moment, the explosion will occur.[6]

Time of Emergence in Development

A second difference is this. Rage reactions are a reflex-like reaction. In fact, this reflexive reaction is built-in in the infant's biological tendency to react to experiences of intense pain with a an appropriate intense affective reaction, generally energetic crying we may suppose, as some affect theorists have told us, to get help from the environment. As a reflex, it's a simple though intense response that occurs without being driven by thought. In essence, a rage reaction is a life-preservative reaction to a life-threatening event. I would guess that seven-month-old Richie might have experienced his mother not tending to him as she had up to then as a threat to his life. Suddenly the nurturing mother was lost and he was helpless to get what he needed to survive. Thus, as a life preservative reflexive event, a rage reaction can occur from the first days of being out of the birth canal.

By contrast, a tantrum does not tend to occur until there is a significant degree of development of the child's emerging conscious sense of self. The psychological organization and experiencing of one's sense of self as an entity, does not occur until about the middle of the second year of life. Some research findings help us identify this development. Margaret Mahler[7] and her colleagues describe how the infant begins to experience himself as separate from the mother, as beginning to conceptualize himself as a separate entity, from about 18 to 24 months of age on. Of course, common to all scientific endeavors, not all researchers agree on this. In my research experience and way of thinking about it, it holds up well. Also, Rene Spitz[8] reports the observation that in general, a child will begin to assert himself on life events by declaring "No!" when he does not want to comply with his mother's or father's expectation. In this he is asserting his sense of autonomy and of self. "I" don't want to do this or that.

As I discussed in chapter 8, this sense of self grows out of and becomes highly invested with healthy narcissism, the sense of being a valued individual. But this is just the beginning of this conscious, developing self-valuation. The 18- to 24-month-old will generally joyfully ride this wave of self-valuation but will then experience with some distress not getting what he wants. The more he wants what he wants, the more challenging he finds accepting not being able to get what he wants. Many children in fact, will find this so distressing, so psychically pain-inducing that some may have a tantrum. Not getting what he or she wants is not experienced as life threatening, but it sure feels lousy, even very lousy.

Early-Life Temperament and Experiences Play Their Part

Now, why do some children, when they cannot get their way from about 18 to 24 months of age on develop tantrums and some do not? This in large measure will depend on the child's rather rapidly developing early-life temperament.[9] It will depend on the child's (1) threshold of irritability (low, moderate, or high); (2) threshold for pain tolerance (low, moderate, or high); (3) reactivity type (whether quick, moderate, or slow); and (4) history of tantrums, which by "kindling"[10] facilitates their occurrence. A child who temperamentally has a low threshold of irritability and is a quick reactor, and has a history of tantrums is likely to have full tantrums. Not all children who have tantrums, however, have full tantrums. Some children known to have full tantrums may at times have only partial tantrums, such as a tantrum that starts explosively, or some that end abruptly after one outburst. These partial tantrums may be difficult to distinguish from rage reactions.

To these early-life temperament dispositions (1) a low threshold of irritability, (2) a low pain threshold, and (3) a quick reactivity pattern add an underlying obsessive-compulsive disposition (a child who has to have things a certain way because he or she seems to not be able to deal with events that do not correspond with his or her expectations) and the chance of his or her having temper tantrums multiplies. The point I want to assert here is that children who have tantrums do not suffer from neonatal dysfunctions or from maltreatment at the hands of their caregivers; rather it's their inborn dispositions that lead them to develop temper tantrums rather than rage reactions. Thirty-eight-month-old David was quite healthy at birth and he was not an emotionally or physically neglected or abused child. In fact, his parents were very good to and with him.

In contrast to what drives temper tantrums, rage reactions tend to arise from three quite different intense-pain inducing experiences/conditions. (1) From physical system immaturities or defects present at birth that, for example cause colic, painful gastrointestinal reflux, allergies reactivities, or the like, or from irritability of the central nervous system that comes from anatomical and physiological consequence of having been exposed to an addicted mother's intrauterine environment—be it due to alcohol or drugs. (2) There are those that occur in normal toddlers who have a high-energy endowment—which shows itself in their determination and stubbornness to do what they feel driven to do—when they encounter their parent's limit setting. And (3) there are those rage reactions that come from more or less intense conditions of neglect or abuse at the hands of primary caregivers (parents).

While infants' birth defects influence the child's temperament, these kids' category one rage reactions differ from the tantrums quite normal kids develop from about 18 to 24 months of age. The rage reaction of a child with colic is induced directly by intense physical pain; once the pain stops, the rage stops. The pain this child experiences arises from within the child's own compromised physical condition, and when the pain is intense it will trigger a reflexive rage reaction. The human environment's efforts to comfort the baby, especially the parent's efforts, are not lost on the baby. Even from the first weeks of life, efforts to soothe and calm become part of the experience that gets internalized and inscribed in the midbrain—in the amygdala and hippocampus where early experiences are registered and recorded. This category of rage reaction is dominantly triggered by a physical-biological event that arises from within the child.

Category two rage reactions, the easiest to deal with, are those that occur when a healthy, vigorous toddler, well endowed with a high level of nondestructive aggression (see chapter 5) encounters the parent's need to set limits (see chapter 9). The child's high-energy driven thrust to autonomy, which is fostered by her or his healthy narcissism (see chapter 8), makes the child determined to explore her or his environment. But it is when this determined one- to three-year-old explorer is prevented from her or his goal by a duly attentive, well-meaning and equally determined parent who is now setting limits on the toddler's reaching that goal, that the toddler may erupt into a rage reaction—much as 13-month-old Mary did (see below for the example of Mary's crisis with her mother). How the parent-child dyad handles this type of crisis, depending on the history of this type of experience, its intensity and frequency, the type of child-parent interaction that then occurs, will, for good or bad, get recorded in the midbrain. Over time, it too will contribute to the child's character formation and ways of coping. Note that these rage reactions, like temper tantrums are much determined by the child's inborn disposition, in this case that of being a high-energy, high-activity kid.

By contrast, category three rage reaction, like that of Richie's, comes primarily from what the child perceives as extremely hurtful actions inflicted on him by his own caregiver(s); it is a experience of intense physical and emotional pain directly inflicted on him by his own home environment. This too is not lost on the child since it too becomes registered and inscribed in the midbrain where intense experiences are recorded that shape personality moods and traits. As with Richie, these rage reactions come more from experiential events rather than primarily from inborn defects or temperamental dispositions. In fact, Richie was quite healthy at birth and had a very good inborn temperament disposition. Even as an infant of five to six months he was calm and pleasant, interacted warmly, smiled delightfully, and could put on really cute faces. But then, when, as was with Richie, children are more or less harshly emotionally or physically neglected, or they suffer from caregiver or environmental abuses, the psychic pain these experiences cause leads to their generating and accumulate increasingly large loads of hostile destructiveness (HD) (see chapter 5). Many children so maltreated, burdened with large loads of HD, will develop tendencies to react in a myriad of hostile destructive ways. They will act destructively toward others, themselves, and anything and everything in their environment (see chapter 2). When they experience an intensely painful event, they may explode in a rage reaction. If pushed far enough, they can go on a rampage. Generally, the rage reaction will be variable in duration and in whatever destruction it may bring with it. Children who have tantrums do not tend to destroy; children who have category one and two rage reactions also do not tend to destroy. But children who rage, as did category 3 rage reactor Richie, are likely to. Because his young mother suffered from painful neglect and abandonment by her youthful and irresponsible mate, Richie was a severely neglected and painfully abused young child. Richie had category three rage reactions.

The Development of Temper Tantrums and Rage Reactions

There is yet another way in which temper tantrums differ from category one and three rage reactions. Given that tantrums result for the most part from inborn temperamental vulnerabilities, these may be modified not only by the way parents handle their children's tantrums, but also by the progressive developments in the child that bring with them increased control over his or her temperamental dispositions and behavior. This can also be said for category two rage reactors whose inborn high energy and high-level activity progressively become more governable by the child. In both tantrum and category two rage reactors, increase control over behavior occurs along both psychobiological and emotional tracks of the child's developing self. Along the psychobiological track, (1) anatomical (both specific brain areas maturation and the development of interconnectivity between brain areas) as well as physiological (biochemical) brain developments evolve remarkably from two to seven years of age. These brain developments bring with them the dramatic development of cognition that makes possible numerous thinking functions including the ability to perceive differences, to perceive and evaluate one's behavior and that of others, and to reason [see chapter 8]. Along the emotional track, not only does cognitive development bring the ability to evaluate and reason, but also the perception of the child's own affective (emotional) state and that of his or her caregivers, in addition to which the ability to judge, to assign value of good or bad on his own and the caregiver's experience, weigh in to influence the child's behavior. To the degree that the child who has tantrums or category two rage reactions is not maltreated by his parents (caregivers), to that degree he will tend to trust them and therewith want to identify with and please his parents and comply with their expectations. These developments probably account for the finding that temper tantrums tend to occur especially in the early years of life and to progressively diminish to about seven years of age, by which time the child is better able by reflective, evaluative, and reasoning strategies, to govern his reactions to psychically painful experiences.

Children with category one rage reactions—caused by intense pain due to bodily dysfunctions—with soothing and comforting care along with maturation of these dysfunctional body systems and medical treatments to correct dysfunctions and lessen pain experiences, these children's rage reactions lessen over time and often can be brought under control within the first year of life. Colic for instance, tends to spontaneously stop at about six months of age. Here too, good parenting handling facilitates trust of the parents and with it, facilitates compliance with their expectations.

Category two rage reactions are likely to stop in the early years, generally by three years of age, assuming good-enough parental handling. The inborn dispositions in these kids are quite healthy; they have normal thresholds of irritability and of pain. It is rather the high energy of their thrust to autonomy that creates the challenge and the pain for the child and the parent. The frustration of high-energy level autonomy in kids with a normal threshold of pain does not cause the level of pain that kids with low thresholds of pain and irritability experience because the low pain threshold child does not have the resilience to tolerate, attenuate, and deal with pain when it is felt.

Category three rage reactions by contrast, because they are driven by intense-psychic-pain-generated, high-level hostile destructiveness toward caregivers and by mistrust of them, are not as readily controllable by average-expectable developments that can be put to service to reduce spontaneous reactivities of inborn temperamental dispositions. Unlike the child who tantrums, the raging child tends to mistrust those with whom he has relationships, which reduces this child's ability to accept and adhere to the wishes of those that populate his or her world. The wish to comply with the caregiver is far less predictable in the child who is being or has been traumatized by his or her caregiver than in the child who is in fact well cared for by them—a point I repeatedly make in this book.

Below we'll talk about when and how parents can intervene in helping the child deal with his or her tantrum or rage reaction.

RATIONALE

To be sure, temper tantrums and rage reactions in children are enormously worrisome and painful for parents. But it is important to recognize that not only are they also enormously troubling and painful for children, but also both tantrums and rage reactions tend to be traumatic[11] for children. Here are a few reasons.

Because they are unleashed by intense psychic pain, a tantrum and a rage reaction are driven by high-level hostility. While high-level hostile destructiveness (HD) is experienced in both the conditions and dynamics that drive the discharge of their HD differ significantly. In the child who tantrums, the activation of HD is due to his or her inborn intolerances of everyday life events and demands. In the child with category one rages, the activation of high-level hostility commonly is caused by an inborn dysfunction that causes much pain. The category two rage reactors experiences intense pain at not being able to do what she or he feels strongly pushed to do. In category three rage reactors it is caused by a history of traumatization by the caregiver(s). This makes the dynamics that caused the experience of intense psychic pain in David, that in a child who has colic, that in a child like Mary, and that experienced by Richie dramatically different. And over time, each child, well before he or she becomes an adolescent, recognizes and grasps the dynamics of his or her specific experiences and will cope with each accordingly. Very different strategies will be put into action by each child as he or she develops. In each of these, the way the parents react to and deal with the child's challenging behavior critically determines the strategies for coping that the child or teenager will use.

Also important is that only part of the hostility in both tantrums and rage reactions is discharged in the child's crying, thrashing, and hostile behaviors. But given the child's recognition that the caregiver who is at the receiving end of and shares in the child's experience is very troubled by the child's behavior, in addition to the intense psychic pain that gave rise to the tantrum or rage reaction in the first place, the child, especially the young child, now experiences yet additional psychic pain due to his fear that his parents will stop loving him and may abandon him. David did give the impression of worrying that his mother might pull away from him and while testing the degree to which he could act on his hostility, he came to wisely protect against the danger of mother turning away from him again by deciding to invite her to engage in a constructive activity he knew she prized, learning the letters of the alphabet. Depending on the caregiver's response, the young child with an inborn bodily dysfunction will experience fear of abandonment according to the negativity with which the caregiver cares for him or her; so will the child who excessively challenges her or his parents' expectations. On the other hand, due to his traumatized psyche, Richie seemed oblivious to this danger while he was raging, but once the rage subsided, he probably did. Fortunately, most kids' rage reactions do not occur under conditions as drastic as were Richie's. Of course, children who are neglected or abused will feel rejected by their parents, but even these youngsters will dread abandonment—even if they put on a good show of not caring.

In general, even with good parental caregiving, more of the high-level hostility generated by the experience that leads to the tantrum or rage reaction will be retained in the child's psyche than will be discharged. Therefore, parents' efforts in helping their children deal constructively with temper tantrums and rages can bring enormous dividends. The child who has temper tantrums ought to be helped as soon as a tantrum begins to emerge. The child who has rage reactions needs help immediately as well.

Also of concern, a temper tantrum is an intense and massive emotional reaction during which, at intervals, the child loses touch with reality, experiences a loss of boundaries between himself and his caregiver, and experiences an inner sense of disorganization and helplessness. All of these component elements of the tantrum in and of themselves cumulatively activate anxiety, which by its nature causes further psychic pain (see chapter 12). This state of experiencing occurs even in two- to three-year-old children. Indeed, it is more likely to occur the younger the child, because differentiation of self and others,[12] testing of what is really happening, and higher levels of cognition and psychic organization are less developed.

In addition, the traumatic effect of a tantrum or a rage reaction does not just stay with the child during its actual occurrence, but is reexperienced repeatedly as the child relives the event in his or her mind and attempts to master the bewildering state he or she then experienced. In fact, clinical evidence reveals that experiences such as having temper tantrums are retained in the psyche for years after, where they maintain an undermining influence on well-being. The strength of this influence depends on the intensity, frequency, and duration of these tantrums over time. We have had the opportunity in working clinically with adults to learn about the unfavorable and long-lasting consequences of having experienced temper tantrums during childhood, especially when they continued from the first years of life through early elementary-school years.

In the child whose rage reactions are reactive to intense pain coming from some inborn dysfunction, or quite less so, the high-energy child determined to do what she wants, the caregiver's handling of these is strongly determining of the degree to which the child will perceive himself or herself as defective and causing of trouble for his or her mother or father, of causing trouble to others. To that degree the child may or may not fear abandonment.

And, as we now know (see chapter 2), those who experience difficult trauma-derived rage reactions during childhood tend to continue to have them in adolescence and into adulthood, often with dire consequences to themselves and society. This child will to a greater or lesser degree also experience that he or she is not wanted, not lovable, and a burden to others. It is likely that the youngster will protect himself or herself against such feelings by believing that others are rotten and that the world is rotten.

Again, I want to underscore that my aim is not to alarm parents. Rather, it is to encourage parents not to take tantrums or rage reactions lightly—which most do not do anyway. And at the same time, while these reactions are difficult to experience and to deal with, I recommend that parents not let tantrums or rage reactions intimidate them. In addition, I recommend that parents try to not let their child's behavior embarrass them—at times a difficult challenge. While sometimes parents are responsible for their child's tantrum—such as when a limit set is not really necessary—but most of the time parents are not. The child cannot be held responsible for being burdened by his temperamental inborn givens. Infrequently only do children have tantrums just to get their way.

And let's face it, a child's tantrums can be a singular factor in making a parent dislike, resent, and distance herself or himself from her or his own child. Consequences to the parent are also very painful.

To what degree the rage reactions impact the parent-child relationship depends on their causative factor. In the category one rage reactor the intense pain comes to be recognized by the child as coming from some inner physical torment and not from a caregiver. For instance, the child with colic will register the source of the pain as coming from inside, but as I said before, will then also register and record in the midbrain the environment's efforts to soothe and comfort him or her.

This is quite different from what we saw in Richie whose rage reactions occurred because of the trauma he experienced as a result of his teen mother's failure to meet his vital basic needs, physical and emotional. Beyond the earliest years, most rage reactions are caused by the child's having been or being maltreated by his or her own caregivers. And it is most likely, given what we have learned over the last eight or so decades that these caregivers were themselves maltreated, whether by neglect or abuse by their own families during their own childhood, which may have continued even into their adolescence. Category three rage reactions go even further than tantrums in estranging and even rupturing parent-child relationships.

I want to repeat here that harsh, overly strict child rearing is often experienced, and often in fact is, abusive and traumatizing, and generates high levels of hostile destructiveness in children (see chapter 8).

For these reasons, temper tantrums and rage reactions ought to be dealt with as soon as they emerge and better still, these reactions ought to be avoided where possible without making oneself hostage to a child's fits of temper.

We must bear in mind that dealing with tantrums and rage reactions early in the child's life may not only reduces the cumulative pain and the HD these generate within the child, but also that this will reduce the "kindling" effect that comes with frequent tantrums and rage reactions; that is, the more frequent the tantrums and rage reactions, the more progressively they are facilitated and activated by lesser experiences of frustration and disappointment. We therefore want to pay special attention to them from the time they begin.

INTERVENTIONAL STEPS

Because temper tantrums and the three categories of rage reactions are driven by different causative factors, each requires a different approach to dealing with them. Most children who have these reactions will usually have one of these categories of reaction. Some may have both tantrums and one or the other rage reactions. Most parents have a pretty good idea which of these reactions their child tends to have.

Let's first consider intervening with temper tantrums, then we'll address intervening with rage reactions.

Temper Tantrums

I indicated before that temper tantrums have structure, which can guide us as to when, and how to intervene to help the child. Children, like 38-month-old David, are frequent temper-tantrum reactors. Others will have temper tantrums very infrequently, and when they do occur, they occur gradually and are easy enough to deal with.

In some children, the temper tantrum may occur explosively, with little warning. However brief the warning time may be, though, there are always signs of an imminent tantrum. We were not surprised when David's tantrum erupted, because he had been cranky for an extended period of time and his tendency to tantrum was known. His mood seemed to suggest a storm brewing. Most parents have a good sense of when their child may seem on the way to having a tantrum. One of the problems is that the signs that point to the child's becoming vulnerable to a tantrum elicit a range or reactions in parents from worry and distress to challenge and even provocation: "Go ahead, have a tantrum and see what you'll get." Just hoping that the child won't, or challenging the child to have a tantrum, does not help the child cope with it in a constructive way.

It behooves the parent to learn the particular signs her child gives off before the point of eruption so as to, in fact, help constructively. It is helpful to bear in mind that most children[13] are very troubled by their tantrums; they don't want to have them. As I said earlier, I have found that they feel bewildered, drained, in jeopardy and in pain, and feel shame after a tantrum.

Temper tantrums have a structure, even in children whose temper tantrums seem to emerge suddenly. For the most part, one can see the following structure in them. A temper tantrum has a beginning, mounts, reaches a peak or climax, then gradually wanes, and dies down. This major curve (see figure 10.1) is typical of all tantrums.

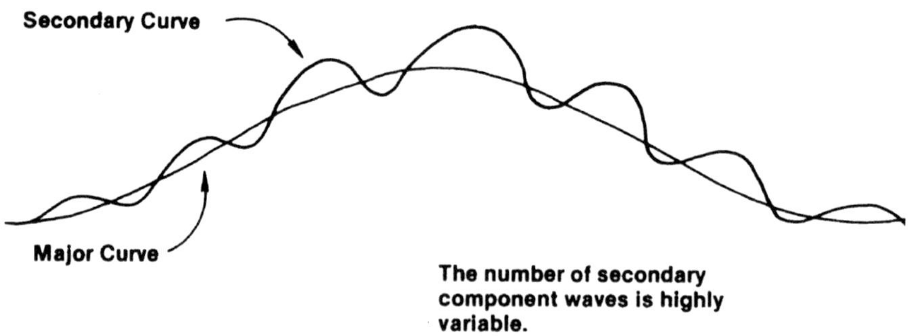

Figure 10.1

A full tantrum usually mounts gradually, reaches a peak, and runs out in exhaustion. This is its major curve. But when fully developed it is not a continuous outburst. It consists of episodic bursts of bewildering rage and despair. These episodes can be said to constitute a secondary curve riding on that of the total tantrum experience.

If we consider 38-month-old David, we could see by the way he struggled irritably to get out of this stroller that this morning he would have greater difficulty than usual in coping reasonably, age-appropriately with frustration and disappointment. Dysphoria (feeling uncomfortable or irritable), in kids who tantrum or rage, is like the angry-gray clouds that forewarn us that a storm may break out at any moment. This is a pretantrum (or prerage) state. This is a very good time to talk to one's child in order to try to reduce the feelings of discomfort or strain he is experiencing: "Hey, David, what's the matter? Calm down, Sweetie. Slow down a bit." If David is able and willing to say what's going on, this may reduce his tension and discomfort, lowering the likelihood that a storm may break out. Talking to the child ought to be in order to calm him down, to reduce the tension, which is best done with a tone sympathetic to his distress. Threats such as, "Listen, you better calm down before something bad happens" only increase the child's tension by further burdening him with fear. Unfortunately some parents do turn to threats to control the child's behavior. While David's mother was sympathetic with David, she did not intervene preventively. She admitted painfully that she didn't really know how to help David (which is why she came to our parenting group).

Looking at the overall event, David had two distinct tantrum episodes—when mother took the apple away and when he found another boy was playing with the car he had just let go—and he seemed on the point of having a third one, when he very wisely shifted his behavior in a positive direction. At a moment when he might have created more problems for himself, his mother and sister, he changed the course of his behavior and asked his mother to play the learning letters game to which she agreed (no doubt greatly relieved). This was an exceedingly good sign of David's efforts to control himself, stop the potentially oncoming tantrum episode, and to comply with his mother's expectation—indeed, making it part of his own self-expectation.

Thinking of David's behavior diagrammatically, one can see that superimposed on the major curve of his overall temper tantrum is a secondary dimension (or curve) constituted of tantrum episodes—of which he had two—which, may become more or less intense as they ride the major tantrum curve (see figure 10.1).

Let's look at the structure of one of these tantrum episodes. Each of the episodes consisted of a climbing (up) limb, a crest, and a down limb (see figure 10.2).

Each episodic burst in the tantrum has a climbing limb, a crest, and a down limb. The child's ability to perceive external stimuli is lowered during the climbing limb and he is then usually difficult to reach emotionally. Efforts to calm then will be frustrated. Calming and helping the child pull himself together are better achieved during the down limb.

Analyzing the first episode closely, I got the impression that during the climbing (up) limb—which in David was steep so that his first episode erupted—the HD discharge mounts in intensity and David then tended to be inaccessible to his mother's interventions. The reason is that once the climbing limb is set in motion, the child's ability to pay attention to external stimuli

COMPONENT WAVE OF SECOND CURVE

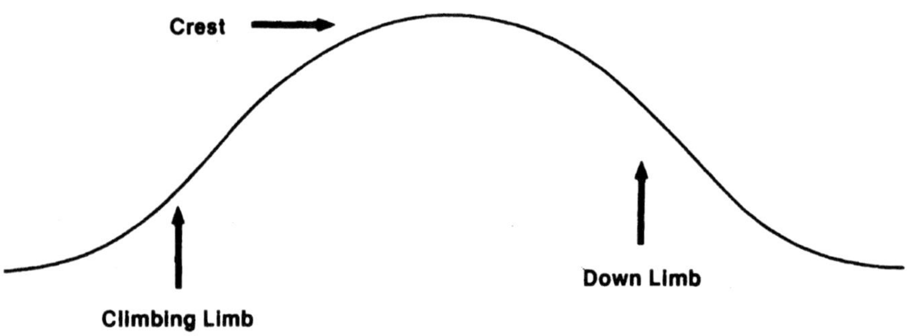

Figure 10.2

seems to be overwhelmed by the mounting discharge of hostile destructiveness rushing out of him.

This kind of overwhelming of adaptive/coping functions by the discharge of a flood of HD happens as well in some rage reactions. For example, Mary, whom I describe below, in her category two rage reaction, experienced such a state too. And this happens as well in rampaging category three rage reactions, when we say, "He went into a blind rage." Fortunately, this state in a tantrum is better characterized by "flailing" than by "destruction." As I said earlier, a child who tantrums does not tend to destroy, given that the tantruming child does not experience the despair or the mistrust of those in his environment as do category three rage reactors.

During the crest, there was some leveling off of David's HD discharge that allowed him to be better aware of his mother's efforts and he was able to be responsive to what was going on in and around him.

It was, however, during the down limb that David was most able to hear and perceive his mother's efforts to calm and comfort him, because, we assume, the internal overtake of HD discharge he was experiencing lessened.

While once the climbing limb is set in motion it's too late to intervene helpfully; it is best for the parent to prevent the flailing child from hurting herself, hurting another (usually the mother), or accidentally breaking things by thrashing about. Generally, during this interval of time, it is best to allow the child to thrash on the floor and protect him from harm. It is usually not necessary to take hold of a child who is thrashing about during a tantrum because it is uncommon that he then intends to destroy.

During tantrums, it is important that the parent be near and be available to the child, especially for children four years of age or less. This is because feeling abandoned—of which the child will become aware as soon as the crest of the tantrum begins its down climb—while in the throes of feeling disorganized, helpless, and bewildered by the intense HD discharge, is highly likely to be further traumatizing.

In the course of treating a young woman analytically, she recalled again and again one traumatic event that has stayed with her: when she was seven years old, her mother walked out of a store when she had a tantrum, leaving her momentarily behind. When she came out of her state of disorganization to find that her mother was gone, she was petrified. Much despair and hostility was attached to the fact that her mother had abandoned her in that state of helplessness.

For this reason, I believe that putting the child in a room by herself when she is having a tantrum may be harmful. The threat of being abandoned—based on, "I deserve it, because I was very, very, bad"—is then superimposed on the trauma of the tantrum. To be abandoned at that time is to be abandoned when the child feels terrible about who she is and feels helpless.

However, there is a time when such a separation may be warranted: when the parent fears losing control of herself and physically abusing the child. We recommend that the parent then tell the child why she is leaving. When the child is sent to his room, the child is most likely to feel it is because he is unbearable. It is important to be brave and honest with the child and tell him that the reason mother is putting him in his room is because she herself fears losing control. "You're driving me up a wall, and I can't help you right now. In fact, I am afraid I am going to hurt you. For that reason, I am going to go to my room for a while. You go to your room for a while, too." You should let a child know when she is driving you up a wall, even if it upsets him—which it will—or even if he may not be able to hear what you are saying.

Under these conditions, it is imperative that the parent talk to the child after the tantrum has subsided. She should say she regrets having had to put the child in his room, and the reason she did so is that she was so upset by what was going on that she feared she might do something she would later feel very bad about. We would furthermore add that a parent could then make it a task for the child and for herself to make every effort to try to control feeling so angry. All parents get angry because we all suffer experiences that produce excessive unpleasure in us. As parents, we need to learn to develop sufficient controls over our hostility when it is mobilized.

The parent can be most actively helpful during the down limb of the tantrum episode. At this time the child is more responsive, can better perceive what is happening outside of herself, and will be more receptive to the parent's efforts to reduce the child's distress. When the mother feels the child's tantrum episode is in its down climb, offering sympathetically to comfort the child, talking to the child about the pain she is experiencing, repeating again that the child can't have her way, and encouraging the child to get a hold of herself often succeeds in making the child regain control over her behavior. The parent's sympathetic tone is crucial because it helps the child feel that in spite of his troublesome behavior, he is still cared for and loved. The child may not accept mother's efforts to help right then, but such efforts are warranted because they reassure the child that mother values him and this facilitates the child's accepting mother's expectations. Such efforts eventually lessen traumatization and help the child develop a positive self-image over and above feeling bad about his behavior.

Recall our discussion of limit setting regarding the fact that many a distressed child will turn to mother and plead for comforting through signs of wanting or asking to be held, or by leaning into the mother's body. This is a highly favorable signal for the resolution of the tantrum, and it is favorable for the parent to respond to the child's wanting to be held and while doing so, to continue with her or his growth-promoting intervention. I say with a sense of urgency because to not respond to the child's plea for comfort is a missed opportunity to resolve the parent-child conflict and simultaneously to enhance the child's compliance with parents' expectations.

As all mothers know, children will not always appeal for comforting during the down limb of their tantrum episode. Even when the infant does not appeal for comforting, the mother or father would be well advised to offer it then. Sure, when angry with the parent a child may reject the parent's offer of comforting. I encourage parents not to take this rejection too painfully. The child's rejection then simply means that the anger felt is more intense than the need for comfort.

David's tantrum (the first episode) was triggered by mother's setting limits on his eating the apple he showed her. Mother felt she had a good reason for setting this limit—she was protecting her son who had complained of abdominal pain. She tried to explain this to him, but her explanation did not quiet his wish to eat it and his tantrum was unleashed. Mother was upset, embarrassed, and herself bewildered by her son's behavior; she'd been through this with him many times. It was probably helpful that once the tantrum episode was beginning to lessen in intensity (in its down limb), David was able to let mother pick him up and let her repeat her limit and its reason. While calming him, sympathetically she said something like, "I know it's hard to not be able to have what we want. But you can't have the apple because it could hurt your stomach more." He listened quietly. If he argued with her that his stomach wouldn't hurt, she might have simply gently held the line and told him she didn't want to take the chance. The child's arguing quietly is welcome. Mother ought to just keep the tone sympathetic and hold the line.

During the second tantrum episode when David wanted to reclaim the car now held by the other child, had mother not been still so upset, and had the other mother not returned the car to him, David's mother could then have tried to calm him by reasoning with him that he had stopped playing with it and it was the other child's turn. She then could also have added something like, "I wouldn't let him take what you're playing with, and I can't let you take what he's playing with. It's hard, but you have to wait your turn again."

Now if the child rejects his or her mother's efforts to calm him or her, it should not make the parent give up on her effort to comfort the child. The fact that the infant is rejecting the mother's comforting or the mother's now-benevolent admonition should not be taken as a sign that the mother's effort is not working. We all know the positive impact such a gesture has on us when we are angry with someone. Before we are ready to respond in a conciliatory way, we may well be aware of the other person's efforts to be conciliatory. Most often such efforts are appreciated by us even if we are not yet ready to reciprocate in kind. So, too, the infant hears the mother's efforts, and even if he is not ready to reciprocate in kind, the child is soothed and comforted by them.

Let us add a few notes about dealing with a tantrum. It's helpful when a parent does not get too angry with the child having a tantrum. Knowing that the child is experiencing acute pain and excessive unpleasure, and feels terribly helpless, ineffectual, disorganized, and often threatened, can help a parent not become too angry with the child. There are times when being faced with their child's difficult-to-handle reaction, parents believe the child is trying to manipulate them and is a spoiled brat. The fact is that if children want to manipulate their parents, they may have a fit that is much closer to a mini-rage reaction. That is not a tantrum—which leads the child to feel much pain, misery, and loss of control.

Turning to rage reactions, let me say that, much of what I have said and recommended for dealing with temper tantrums also can apply to rage reactions.

Rage Reactions

To facilitate the handling of rage reactions in kids and adolescents I have tried to clarify the fact that different conditions can drive these difficult reactions. Let's look at the three categories I propose.

Category 1 Rage Reactions: Pain-Causing Physical Dysfunctions

An infant who has colic suffers from abdominal spasms that occur in clusters and cause much pain. Holding an infant who has colic, the parent will easily register the baby's torturing experience. Many an infant like this will have infantile rage episodes. Each episode will be directly related to the physical pain as it is felt. Once the pain alleviates, the rage reaction will run itself out depending mostly on the way the caregiver is interacting with the child.

If the mother of the colicky infant has already had a baby who was a well-developed and healthy baby, she will know that something is wrong with the colicky newborn. This mother or father, too, will know that she was able to handle her first (or more) child(ren) well enough and that she is a mother capable of caring well enough for a baby. It is another matter when a mother's first baby is one who has colic.

First infants who are colicky present a large challenge to the first-time mother. Because a first-time mother has never taken care of an infant 24/7, even if she has "baby-sat" when she was younger, will struggle with the dilemma. "Is it me, or is it the baby?" Initially the first-time mother will recognize that there is something troubling the baby and she will try her best to calm, comfort, and feed her baby. Unless she knows that colic is a biological problem that challenges even the best childcare, she will soon feel incompetent, empathically experience a great deal of pain herself, and get angry—with the baby and with herself.

And then, when her mother comes over and much to her mixed pleasure and distress, her mother seems to be able to make the baby calm down and feel better, she will be convinced that she is a failure as a mother. Due to her own distress at feeling inadequate as a mother, disappointed in herself and humiliated, she fails to recognize that her mother is not necessarily a genius-mom who can fix everything. All the young mother needs to do is to remember what her mom was like when she was a child. There are no "genius-moms," or "genius-dads" for that matter. But her mom does have more experience at feeding and caring for a baby. And, perhaps more important, her mom has not been struggling with this colicky baby five times a day for weeks now, or even months (most colic stops at about six months). So, grandmother is not tense when she picks up the baby to try to calm and feed him, she doesn't expect that she will fail at it; often in fact, having seen such infants, grandmother tries her best and does not despair the moment the baby fusses. Even when the baby fusses, grandmother continues to calmly, soothingly comfort the baby, managing to get enough food into his stomach to reduce the intensity of the hunger and maybe even the stomach spasms. Commonly, this is how the event unfolds, variations of it depending on the cast of characters, especially mother and her mother.

Colicky infants, or infants with other pain-inducing dysfunctions, will challenge any first-time mother and father. Not surprisingly, such infants who are difficult to calm are the ones who most need to be calmed and comforted. And this is the large challenge to the young first-time parent who has such a baby: How do I calm my baby who is making me a wreck? Mom has two people to calm: first herself, and then to do her best to calm her highly distressed baby. It's like they tell us on airplanes, "If the level of oxygen drops in the cabin, a mask will drop from above your head. Put the mask on yourself first, so that you can take care of your child(ren)." To calm the baby—in fact to do anything for and with the child—mom (or dad) has to first tame her (or his) own frustration-induced angry reaction toward the child, and try to calm herself (or himself). This principle, by the way, applies to many caregiving situations where the child is doing something that upsets the parent, which is easier said than done. Yes, but aiming for this often brings much benefit to both child and parent.

Then, doing two functions at the same time: calming-soothing and, gently-patiently feeding, the parent ought to just do the best she or he can. In addition, it is well for the parent to bear in mind that the infant is not really on a path to aggravate the parent whose help the baby needs badly. Nor is it that the baby is a bad, rotten baby; the baby is hurting.

Once the baby has gotten enough food, continuing to hold the calmed baby rather than immediately putting the baby in the crib will prolong the calming and health-promoting experience. This will inscribe itself in the baby's midbrain: that the holding parent will try and try, and eventually will be able to help, comfort, and calm the baby. This midbrain inscription will be reinforced when the same holding and comforting experience occurs. And eventually, the infant will be able to remember that the parent is a comforting, soothing, helpful parent and that most of the time, this can be gotten from the parent when needed. This then becomes internalized and helps the child eventually do for himself, and later for others, what the calming and comforting parent has done for him many times. This continuing to hold the baby for a while after the feeding experience is equivalent to later, when the child is of the age when he or she can talk. Talking with the child about an event that did not go well at first, but by talking about it together and discussing constructive actions by the child and parent turned out well.

With this type of child, it is highly advantageous when both mother and father can develop the skill of sympathetically calming and comforting the very pain-troubled baby. Parents' taking turns when the baby gets challenging can be enormously helpful to all—and tends to foster good relatedness between parents as well as between child and parents.

Category 2 Rage Reactions: Healthy Narcissism and the Caregiving Environment

Two most common causes of category two rage reactions are

1. When the young child finds the pain unbearable that mom or dad is failing to meet the baby's needs within the limit of his tolerance for delay of

gratification. The pain he feels is experienced by the child as an injury to his healthy narcissism.
2. When the child's thrust to autonomy—driven by his healthy narcissism—runs up against the responsibly protective/socializing parent's limit setting. In both instances, the child's temperamental givens play a part. Let's look at each in turn.

Low Tolerance for Delay of Gratification

A child with a low tolerance for delay of gratification will experience pain much more quickly than one with a higher tolerance for it. The first child will be much less patient than the latter.

Let's take the example of a six-week-old infant having signaled (by fussing and crying) that he needs to be fed. Delays are at times unavoidable whether the baby is breast-fed or bottle-fed. However, Today, mother just could not get there quickly. By the time she got to her infant, his crying had escalated rapidly into an infantile rage.

Commonly, a mother finds that when she attempts to put the nipple in the mouth of her infant screaming from hunger-pain, her attempts will not immediately succeed if the infant is reacting in rage. Mothers of such babies know that the emotional storm will delay the child's ability to feel and respond to the presentation of the nipple. Often a mother will gently rub the nipple on the six-week-old's lips, sensing that the child's attention has to be brought to the nipple—that is, the nipple has to be brought to the baby's mouth in order for the baby to quiet his rage reaction and make the feeding process possible. What is happening is that under conditions of the rage reaction, the infant cannot perceive that the environment is now making it possible for feeding to occur. It is as if the environment is tuned out, and can be tuned in only when the rage reaction has sufficiently toned down. The rage reaction makes the infant blind and insensitive to the possibility of gratifying the need that started the rage in the first place.

High-Energy Thrust to Autonomy

A child with a high-energy thrust to autonomy (the push to do what he seems driven from within to do [see chapter 8]) will experience limit setting much more painfully and much more quickly than one with a low-energy thrust to autonomy.

Let's go back to 13-month-old Mary, that wonderful little girl who had been progressively running into more and more difficulty with her beloved mother due to mother's limit setting (chapter 9). As I said, mother had told Mary a number of times that she was not allowed into the hall when the cleaning cart was there because there were things on it that could hurt her. But driven by her high-energy internal engine, Mary persisted and this time when mother got to Mary and picked her up, Mary exploded. I described how while mother carried her into our day-room, Mary cried angrily, waved her left arm in a striking movement against her mother several times, and kicked at her. Twice she actually struck her mother with her arm, and once she also struck herself.

After this explosion, 13-month-old Mary was terribly distressed. For the first time that we knew of, mother could not comfort her. She cried angrily, would not let mother try to make things easier for her; she just would not accept whatever mother tried to do. It was critical that mother was so accepting of Mary's distress and did not get angry with her.

Mary was somber and serious. She sat upright at the edge of her mother's knees. Only gradually her body tone softened and she relaxed passively into her mother's body, thumb in mouth, where she remained, awake for 20–30 minutes.

With regard to Mary's rage reaction, I read several things into what we saw. Mother's efforts to comfort Mary were rejected. Mother was sensitively responsive to Mary's rejections, but she seemed sympathetic to her daughter's distress and did not react by rejecting her child. Mother made several efforts to comfort and perhaps distract Mary from her large internal feeling of distress. But Mary protested her mother's continuing efforts to comfort. Mother seemed not to take offense at this. On the contrary, mother let Mary gradually settle in her lap, collapse against her body, and let her stay there sort of passively holding her in her lap.

However, Mother's passively holding her infant was a superbly active intervention. She afforded Mary the opportunity to make further efforts to get hold of herself, and to quiet her rage toward mother, and calm herself down. In a home setting, if a child were to have that kind of reaction, a mother might not find it reasonable to just sit there and hold her enraged and distressed child for a period of 20 to 30 minutes. Nonetheless, we were impressed by the beneficial effect of Mary's being held by her mother, and by her mother's emotional and physical availability to Mary while Mary was doing the internal work of getting over her rage reaction.

It is sometimes difficult for a mother, who always has too much to do, to recognize the enormous value and benefit of sitting for 20 to 30 minutes with an infant who is overcoming a rage reaction or a temper tantrum. But in fact, it is timesaving, emotionally protective, well-being securing, and more, for a mother to spend that kind of time in that kind of effort under conditions of a rage reaction or a tantrum experience.

This, by the way, was the only time in the years that followed that Mary had a rage reaction toward her mother. From then on, while Mary with her hefty thrust to autonomy did not take easily to limits, and she would get angry with her mother, but she did negotiate the problem of running up against her parents' limit setting increasingly reasonably.

With a child who is beginning to talk well-enough, talking sympathetically about such events when things have calmed down, and even at times when things are going fine between child and parent, can be enormously valuable in helping the child understand the reasons for her parents' expectations of her. To talk about such an event in a scolding or threatening way makes things more difficult. The family philosophy of limit setting, the why, how, and when of it should be brought into play (see chapter 9).

Category 3 Rage Reactions: A Byproduct of Child Neglect and Abuse

Fourteen-month-old Richie was a severely neglected and abused infant. Sadly, he is not the worst example of what some children, of all ages, are subjected to (see chapter 3).

Several critical factors distinguish category 3 rage reactions from the other two categories of rage reactions and from temper tantrums. Category 3 rage reactions occur

1. In the context of not trusting the environment and the people in it;
2. They will tend to occur from earliest childhood through adolescence and even into adulthood.

The consequences of the conditions that lead to category three rage reactions are enormous.

Here are a few.

In terms of not trusting the environment and the people in it, given that the development of "basic trust" or on the other hand, of "basic mistrust"[14] in relationships occurs in the child's first year of life and in the context of the child's relationships to his or her parents, neglect and abuse that start very early in life and at home tend to determine the individual's trust in other human beings. The die is cast in the abused or neglected child that humans can't be trusted. This means that parents will be very ineffective as persons who can convince the child that it is in his best interest to control his rage reactions. And furthermore, any efforts later made by humans, even well-meaning ones, to comfort the traumatized child and adolescent will not be trusted and therefore, at best be difficult, if not ineffective. This contributes to the difficulty encountered by helping professionals of all kinds, doctors and therapists, foster families, school teachers, police officers, and programs when they try to help individuals painfully traumatized by their own parents.

In addition, traumatization at home in contrast to the other factors that lead to rage reactions, leads to not just the intense-pain experience being recorded in the midbrain, but the entire event that brings about the pain—the parent-child interaction be it of omission or commission, the entire experience constellation gets set down in the brain as a predictable condition of life. The experience-constellation then becomes expected when any element of it is felt. The earlier in life the conditions of traumatization at home occur, the deeper its imprinting in the individual's brain, and the longer it will remain part of the home-traumatized individual's life. Thus, unlike the other rage and tantrum producing vulnerabilities, which have a more limited life-time duration, category three rage reactions may continue from early childhood well into adulthood.

A potentially serious problem arises in some children who have often felt harshly rejected by their parents, be it by neglect or abuse. Having frequently felt painfully rejected by those the child counts on for love and protection, these kids come to dread being hurt when they experience needs for closeness, comforting, and love, and they will not make these needs known. They may even hide such needs from themselves; they "don't need love." In fact, even unconsciously feeling the need for expressions of love, soothing, and comforting, makes them feel weak and vulnerable. But the high-level energy of feeling very angry and enraged gives them a sense of feeling strong. Given that needing love and approval makes them feel vulnerable, and feeling destructive makes them feel strong, they will avoid emotional closeness and when they feel vulnerable, they may turn to violence to feel better. To be sure, they will avoid expressions of the need for love or help from their own parents, which will render their parents' efforts to deal with their child or teenager's rage reactions ineffective. Sufficient intimidation may at times look like parents are getting obedience from them, but it is likely that this obedience will easily be corrupted by enticing opportunities for destructiveness.

Also, both distinctions of category three rage reactions contribute significantly to the fact that in trying to prevent individuals convicted of crimes from repeating crimes by means of punishments such as jailing—which in general is experienced as painful, except when it is seen as preventing homelessness and starvation—tends to not prevent recidivism and that rehabilitation and treatment programs may achieve a better result (see chapter 3). But treatment and rehabilitation are not easily achieved when the degree of traumatization started early in life and was intense. To help a child like Richie, a number of strategies would have to be implemented.

I regret that we did not have the opportunity to continue our work with Richie, who for reasons not clear to me, was not brought back to us after the summer break of our program. We would have strongly recommended a combination of several treatment strategies, including parenting education for his foster caregiver as well as caregiver-child therapy. And in addition, probably as times passed, we would have added individual intensive psychotherapy for Richie. No child highlights more clearly than Richie how dramatically prevention of his neglect and abuse could have spared him the suffering we witnessed in him and in his behavior.

NOTES

1. Thirty-eight-month-old David was not one of our research subjects. (I describe the research project in chapter 1.) We saw him, however, in the same setting after the project ended. Fourteen-month-old Richie, on the other hand, was seen in the same setting well into the latter part of the project era; he was brought in by one of the project mothers who felt seriously concerned about him.

2. H. Parens, Rage toward self and others in early childhood. In: *Rage, Power and Aggression,* Eds. S. P. Roose & R. Glick, 123–147. (New Haven: Yale University Press, 1993). Event description condensed from pp 124–125.

3. The Apgar evaluation has now been done for decades by a qualified medical professional very soon after birth to determine the state of maturation of the newborn and the level of intactness and functioning of all its vital systems.

4. R. Spitz, Anaclitic depression: an inquiry into the genesis of psychiatric conditions in early childhood. *Psychoanalytic Study of the Child* (1946), 2:313–342. Spitz, a strong psychoanalytic infant researcher, described the reactions of infants who, when separated from their mothers at about six or so months of age for more than three months, suffered from this infantile depression, a very serious condition. As have others, I have found that very young children can experience such depressions even when the mother is at home but by virtue of her own depression or other emotional state cannot be sufficiently emotionally available to her baby.

5. H. Parens, Cruelty Begins at Home. *Child Abuse and Neglect* (1987), 11:331–338.

6. In a recent (2010) Spanish film, *The Secret in their Eyes,* an attractive woman lawyer, acting like a detective, in an attempt to prove the male suspect capable of the brutal rape and murder of a young woman, prods the suspect with denigrating, emasculating remarks about his body and sexual prowess—in essence saying "there is no way in the world this little runt could have committed such a sexual crime"—which, while he tolerates her mounting insults, eventuate in the suspects flying into a rage and attacking her. By assaulting her, he documents his ability to commit the crime in question.

7. M. S. Mahler, F. Pine, & A. Bergman, *The Psychological Birth of the Human Infant.* (New York: Basic Books, 1975).

8. R. Spitz, *The First Year of Life.* (New York: International Universities Press, 1965).

9. The child's temperament is determined by his or her brain's neurobiological characteristics as these are shaped by the child's unique progressive life experiences. For instance, early life experiences that overly challenge the young child's inborn ability to cope, such as frequent or intense experiences of distress or pain, are likely to lower inborn thresholds and intensify reactivities in neurobiological givens.

10. "The kindling phenomenon" is a process found in the study of seizures disorders. Graham Goddard first reported the phenomenon of kindling in the late sixties (G. V. Goddard, Development of epileptic seizures through brain stimulation at low intensity. *Nature,* [1967] 214: 1,020–1,021) (homepages.nyu.edu/~eh597/kindle.htm). Researchers have found that seizures induced experimentally in research animals could be triggered by progressively lower voltages of electric brain stimulation; this occurred without producing pathological changes in the animal's brain. While I am stepping outside of its original application as a mechanism that facilitates the production of seizures, as a phenomenon, "kindling" adheres to the overarching "conditioning" principle, which has been firmly proven, that the reaction to a stimulus can be facilitated by experience. As I see it, as a principle, facilitation can be generalized to occur in and be at the basis of all learning. Speaking a bit loosely, one might say that this is why "practice makes perfect" and that "kindling," as a principle, has elucidated and been applied to many physical and psychological processes.

11. Any event that overwhelms the child's adaptive capabilities has the potential for being traumatic.

12. By "differentiation of self and other," I am referring to the assumption to which I subscribe—which derives from Margaret S. Mahler's theory of separation-individuation (M. S. Mahler, F. Pine, & A. Bergman, *The Birth of the Human Infant* [1975])—that during the first three years of life the infant differentiates or evolves into perceiving himself, as a "self," as an entity, distinct and separate from his mother and father.

13. Some children who have felt rejected by their parents, be it by neglect or abuse, and who dread being hurt when they experience needs for closeness, comforting, and love, will feel strong when they are angry, even when they are enraged. They then, are not troubled by their rage reactions. This is not usually the case with kids who have tantrums.

14. E. H. Erikson, Identity and the life cycle. *Psychological Issues* 1:120

Chapter 11

Helping the Child Cope with Painful Emotional Feelings

Bearing in mind the basic hostile destructiveness (HD) formula that "excessive unpleasure (psychic pain) generates hostility," it helps parents to know that from the first months of life children are able to experience feelings that bring them a great deal of emotional pain. The old idea that newborns and little babies don't really feel pain and if they do they'll forget about it anyway is totally false. We now know that pain experiences are registered in the midbrain and are retained for years to come; in fact, they may be indelible. And, it is well established now that by the middle of the first year of life, children are capable of experiencing anxiety, as well as feeling painfully ungratified and abandoned. Many people, parents included, are surprised to learn that infants from five or so months of life can experience depression—some, very severe depression.

While *anxiety* is the feeling of helplessness in the face of an inner, undefined danger, *depression* is the reaction experienced after that event has occurred. The threat of danger has materialized, and now there are feelings of helplessness, hopelessness, and giving up. Since depression is painful, when it is intense, it too generates hostility. This is especially evident in that when children recover from depression, one of the first signs of recovery may be that they become angry, or even overtly hostile and destructive (see below, the case of Richie).

Because such emotional reactions can be very painful and can leave their mark for a long time, we want to consider how parents can intervene in ways that can mitigate such experiences and thereby, in the long run, lessen the generation and mobilization of hostility in their child. It is highly advantageous for children when parents, who may try to prevent them from unduly experiencing anxiety, help them cope constructively with anxiety when they feel it, and help their children work through an anxiety reaction that has occurred. Similarly, they should do the same for feelings of depression.

Although there are other emotional reactions that create pain—envy, jealousy, fear, and shame—I shall not deal directly with them. When parents understand that psychic pain experience is evident at birth, and they are able to deal with their children experiencing anxiety and depression, they will be able to figure out ways of dealing constructively with other painful emotional reactions that their children experience.

Overall, parents must gradually, from as early in life as needed, develop an emotional dialogue with their children about all painful feelings. First, let's talk about dealing with anxiety and then about dealing with depression.

COPING WITH ANXIETY

Mrs. J. was puzzled. She is a very perceptive and tuned-in mother. She had told her three-year-old son, Kenny that she would be out shopping while he was taking his nap, grandma was there, and she'd be back soon. When she came back, Kenny was at the window and on seeing her, gave her a beaming smile. He seemed clearly happy to see her. But when she walked into the house carrying bags, he was scowling and outright angry with her. He was mad at her being out, but she had told him she would be.

We told her it had been very helpful that she told him she was going, and that she would be back. But, even though she prepared him for it, this did not prevent his experiencing separation anxiety of sufficient intensity that it generated hostility in him. On seeing her, he was greatly relieved and happy. And then, secure that mother had come home, the anger from the anxiety he had experienced came to the surface. Because he felt safe enough with mother, he could let her know just exactly how he was feeling.

From weeks after birth on, humans experience anxiety when they feel helpless in the face of what they experience as a danger. Since when it is intense, it is very painful and generates hostility, it is important for parents to know what anxiety looks like in their child, what it sounds like, and seems to feel like. Also it is useful to know what kinds of experiences commonly cause anxiety in children.

Under five years of age, the most common events or conditions that trigger anxiety are: separations from parents, the appearance of strangers, the fear of losing one's parents' love, the fear of bodily harm, and the dread of losing one's autonomy and sense of self. We will also talk briefly about events and conditions that cause anxiety in children older than five and in adolescents. Because the child or adolescent feels helpless and vulnerable, it helps the child or teenager to know that he is not alone in attempting to deal with what is causing his or her helplessness. Parents should make efforts to comfort and calm their child or adolescent during and after anxiety reactions. When possible, as did Kenny's mother, it is advantageous to prepare the child for the event or condition that is known to cause anxiety, even if it does not succeed in preventing its happening. This effort should include talking about and dealing with both the child's (or adolescent's) anxiety and the hostility that his anxiety generated or mobilized.

Rationale

At one time or another, we all experience anxiety; it's universal. It becomes clearly evident in children from about the middle of their first year of life on, although some children as young as four months show evidence of it.

Children vary in their vulnerability to experiencing anxiety; we all have a temperament-based threshold for it. Some children's threshold is very low. They may react with anxiety to a loud noise. Some kids' threshold is high. It takes much more to get their imagination going that something bad is about to happen. Anxiety needs to be dealt with constructively. It should not be dealt with by shaming or forcing a child into an anxiety-producing situation.

Because it is psychically painful, anxiety generates hostility. While the anxiety will be manifest, the hostility it generates may not manifest in behavior; it may be inhibited or defended against from very early on it life, it may be turned against the self, or, it may become evident in the form of irritability and moodiness. Sometimes, as with Kenny, it may be expressed directly. Even when the anxiety has abated, it may produce an after reaction of anger—and even rage.

Whatever the level of anxiety, the anxiety itself and the hostility it generates will dissipate if the anxiety is worked through. When anxiety reactions are worked through, the event or condition that has triggered anxiety may become less likely to continue to produce anxiety. When anxiety is not worked through, the hostility that it has generated will be discharged in one way or another or it will accumulate in the psyche.

In its extreme form, anxiety appears as a panic reaction; it will then undoubtedly generate substantial hostility. It is important to recognize that panic reactions can lead to all kinds of problems including inaction due to the need to avoid panic-producing situations, or even psychic paralysis.

Interventional Steps

Recognizing Anxiety in Children and Adolescents

First, it is important for parents to try to identify what anxiety looks like, sounds like, and feels like in their child. If they can do so with their young child, they will be able to do so when that child becomes an adolescent. To be able to recognize anxiety in one's child, the parent will have to empathize with what the child is feeling. With anxiety, depression, and all painful feelings, trying to recognize whether or not one feels "this can't be happening to my child," and to empathize with what the child is feeling is of utmost importance.

In the mental health field, anxiety is said to be "a feeling of impending doom." It is likely that most parents would recognize anxiety in its extreme form—a panic state. If you have any doubt about what you're seeing, simply imagine that you're feeling like the sky is about to fall in on you. What do you feel like? What do you look like? What sound do you make? Similar sounds and appearance will be evident in the child.

For milder states of anxiety, the infant may look apprehensive, frightened, or bewildered. Age will influence the sounds the child may make. For example, the older child may verbalize fear and apprehension. Prior to language capability, the parent will have to rely on preverbal sounds such as crying, whimpering, and exclamations of apprehension and fear. In terms of bodily communication, very commonly a young child (from four months of age on) will cling when near the parent—and cling with a pressure that may feel quite uncomfortable to the parent.

Remember the two principal ways in which one's empathy can be sharpened. The first is to listen to the child, look at the child, and then imagine and try to feel what the child may be feeling. Ask yourself how you would be feeling if you looked as the child does, and sounded and felt like the child seems to feel. In other words, put yourself in your child's shoes and ask yourself what that would feel like to you.

The second way is the converse. Start by asking yourself what you would look like, sound like, and feel like if you were experiencing helplessness in the face of some really scary danger, or how you would feel if you were in a panic state. Then check to see if that is how your child appears to you. Whichever way works best for you, use it.

It is impossible to prevent the occurrence of anxiety. In fact, it may not even be desirable to do so (see discussion later in this chapter). Given human imagination, it is not possible to prevent anxiety, whatever the parents' efforts. However, once one recognizes anxiety in one's child, help him or her deal with it; try to prevent its gathering momentum and increasing in intensity. Ignoring the child's anxiety may increase it since it will heighten the child's feeling of helplessness. Above all, shaming the child such as telling him to "stop being a baby," may stop him from showing feelings of anxiety, but the anxiety will continue and the parent's humiliating the child will intensify his HD.

Developmental Aspects of Experiencing Anxiety

In order to reduce the likelihood of an anxiety reaction, and to understand what might be causing it so as to deal with it reasonably, it is useful to know what kinds of experiences commonly cause anxiety in children.

Mental health professionals have proposed that anxiety reactions are normal at given developmental periods. These reactions have been organized by psychoanalytic researchers–clinicians as consisting of a series of emotionally perceived dangers that emerge sequentially during the course of normal development. Let us underscore that these are *normal* reactions.

My clinical and research-supported mental health orientation[1] affirms the by now well-established series of anxiety reactions that normally occur in children.

The first clear evidence of anxiety in infancy emerges at about five or so months of age. Anxiety then occurs during the process of the child's developing an attachment to his prime caregiver, his mother. This attachment is a biological imperative; the infant comes into the world primed by instinctive mechanisms to attach. When fathers are involved in the care of infants, an equivalent attachment to him organizes as well. The process of attachment brings with it two distinct anxiety reactions: separation anxiety and stranger anxiety. Separation anxiety is quite common in infants; for instance, a less than 16-month-old, may cry, reach out for, and cling to mother when she is about to leave for work. The distress is clearly tied up with separation from the mother and the anxiety this stirs up. I discuss this extensively in chapter 12.

The second common source of anxiety is the fear of losing the love of one's parents. This anxiety tends especially to occur from the end of the first year of life through the second year. This anxiety also tends to remain with human beings to some degree, for an indefinite period of time.

The third major source of anxiety is that associated with fear of bodily harm and fear of losing vital body parts, especially the genitals. This fear may emerge in the latter half of the second year, in some children. It usually occurs at about two-and-a-half years of age and runs an acute course through the fifth or sixth year of life, after which the manifest anxiety tends to subside.

Again, like the other sources of anxiety, it may remain with an individual, to a more or less intense degree, for a longer or shorter period of time.

These major sources of anxiety are commonly evident in the behavior of children under five years. For instance, two-and-a-half-year-old Robbie's pants were not zippered. Mother, seeing this fact, called him to her and quite casually and gently began to reach for the zipper and pull it up. Robbie sharply pulled away from his mother, with a look of distress on his face. It is not uncommon for boys of this age to show evidence of acute anxiety in the face of what they misconstrue to be a danger to their penis.

From about two to three years of age, the source of anxiety may be difficult to discern from the child's behavior and may even be unknown to the child. For instance, a three-year-old who has trouble going to bed may be afraid of the dark or of going to sleep. It may not be clear whether the child is coping with feelings of separation, feelings of being unloved by mother, or feelings of being punished for having hostile feelings or transgressive thoughts. The four-year-old's fear that a big black bear is going to come and get him most likely pertains to some Oedipal conflict and rivalry with his father, or with castration anxiety (more about this in chapter 12). However, the child will not be aware of its source.

Other distressing behaviors—such as phobias, nightmares, sleep difficulties—all bring with them a significant degree of anxiety, without clearly revealing what the underlying sources might be.

In addition to anxiety arising out of some undetermined inner conflict, young children also often react to some environmental events with sharp fear. By triggering the child's imagination in trying to comprehend the disturbing event, anxiety may be triggered by what dire explanation the child imagines. This often event then stirs anxiety and may cause a great deal of psychic pain. For instance, two- and three-year-olds are known to experience reactions of fear and distress from loud noises, sirens, barking dogs, motorcycles, and fights between parents. These fear-anxiety reactions can be significantly helped by the way parents deal with them.

All of these early childhood experiences create a situation in which the child feels more or less helpless and vulnerable. Therefore, one critical way of helping a child is to show him and help him feel he is not alone in attempting to deal with what he perceives as a potential danger. A parent acting in the child's behalf can go a long way to lessening the child's anxiety, and so does the child's feeling that he is loved, or else why would the parent make such an effort to help him cope with danger.

For instance, a four-year-old boy is awakened from a frightening dream in which a big bear is chasing him. Mother (or father) may not understand what the dream is about—and if she (or he) does, interpretation by parents is replete with hazards and great care has to be exercised. But even without addressing the meaning of the dream, the child may be comforted by the parent's gently saying, "That was a scary dream. You're having some scary thoughts. Mommy and I are here to help, anytime. And, there are no bears here." Side by side with this reassurance, again, the parent's expression of love by comforting helps to decrease the child's anxiety.

It is important for parents to learn to distinguish anxiety and fear from orneriness, which is well described by the phrase, "I want what I want when I want it!" Both require a response from the parent. However, the responses should be different. Anxiety-induced or fear-induced crying requires talking about what is upsetting the child, reassurance, and comforting. Orneriness requires empathic and reasonable limit setting. Even though parents may not always be right, parents who really believe they are doing the best they can, should trust their judgment as to what they think the young child may be feeling. Even if not totally certain about it, it is important that parents trust their reading of their child's emotional reactions and the feelings their child arouse within them.

Much of what I have said so far about the young child also applies to elementary-school-age children and adolescents, although age-appropriate modifications are required. So, let us continue the series of anxiety sources through these years, as well.

The fourth major source of anxiety is intimately linked with the fear of losing the parent's love, which tends to continue throughout life. This source of anxiety though comes from what the child has progressively internalized of his parents' mores and beliefs of what is right and wrong. In a sense these reflect the parents' conscience. Internalized, these now become a major contributor to the child's conscience. What the child now fears in addition to fearing losing his parents' approval is the fear of disapproval by his own conscience. This already is at play from about three to six years when the child's conscience develops to the degree that it then begins to have some governance over the child's thoughts and behaviors. That governance, essentially one dictated by the child's own approval and disapproval of his thoughts and actions can be quite harsh. At that point in development, transgressive, and what the child perceives as undesirable fantasies, wishes, and acts lead to his experiencing strong feelings of guilt. We all know how much we want to avoid feelings of guilt. Increasingly then, during the period from about 6 to 10 years of age, and continuing thereafter, the threat of disapproval by our recently developing and consolidating conscience is an uppermost source of anxiety.

The fifth set of major sources of anxiety emerges during puberty. Foremost is the fear of being governed by the powerful pressure of one's pubescent sexuality. The fear of losing control over their sexual impulses and behaviors creates an enormous challenge to adolescents. Where anxiety about this is intense, efforts may be made by adolescents, female and male—incredible as this may seem— to make themselves unattractive. Unconsciously driven by this anxiety, some teenagers refuse to wash in order to smell bad as a deterrent to being found attractive. Side by side with the sexuality-driven anxiety, teens may also, as a result of their enlarging body, experience anxiety due to their much more powerful capability to act on their aggression. When a father is overly hostile to his 15-year-old son, that son perceives his wish to react with equal hostility toward his father as highly threatening, because of his increasingly more powerful body. The fantasy of killing his father may become alarming; it is a major source of anxiety during adolescence.

There are other sources of anxiety that occur in the course of development—the dread of losing one's autonomy and sense of self, or the adolescent's dread of disapproval by his peers. Each requires parental patience and efforts to understand them. Anxiety is painful, and although it is often not resolvable by parents, they can lessen its impact on their child and adolescent by the way they help them deal with it.

Dealing with an Anxiety Reaction

Let's talk about dealing with an anxiety reaction. Assume that you have a 16-month-old child and are about to leave for work or for an appointment. Your child is crying, tremulous, in despair, and may be clinging to you. You know this reaction is produced by the fact that you are about to leave. You are now feeling very upset, even to the point of canceling your appointment or not going to work because of the guilt you are feeling and because you are being torn apart by your infant's reaction.

If it is necessary for you to go, then tell your child such. Yes, you speak to a 16-month-old. You tell a 16-month-old (or even younger child) where you have to go and why you have to go. You tell your child that you will be back, and when—using indicators that a child may understand. "Before you go to sleep, mommy will be back," or "Before we eat again, mommy will be back."

You also tell the child that the substitute caregiver will take good care of him while you are away, and that you are ready to leave. Efforts to comfort while you are talking are useful, although they may not be as effective as you would like. In fact, it is likely that your child may not calm down before you go, and you may feel all your efforts are fruitless.

Years of work with mothers and their infants make it quite clear to me that even though a parent's efforts to comfort the child and calm the child's anxiety may not bring immediate results, in the long run such efforts do build a base of security, trust, and feeling cared for within the child. This trust decreases the level of anxiety and unpleasure experienced at times of separation and leads to a lessening of the generation of hostility.

There are going to be times when your child experiences anxiety that you cannot alleviate. Efforts to alleviate that anxiety ought to be made anyway, because by doing so you convey your wish, your hope to help the baby and ultimately your efforts convey your message, even when they do not immediately alleviate the experience of distress. The best that can be aimed for in helping a child who is anxious is conveying the sense that you want to help and trying to lessen that feeling of anxiety as best you can.

The second step in working on relieving, stopping, or alleviating anxiety is to work through the anxiety reaction when it is in the process of waning or has stopped. For instance, let's come back to the mother who has to go to work, leaving her 16-month-old boy in distress.

You have left your infant crying. You were distressed and feeling terribly guilty. All in all, it was a very difficult episode. Now you are coming back home, and you are not quite comfortable about encountering your child. You walk in the house, and immediately on seeing you, he reacts with a big smile and eagerly extends his arms toward you. Greatly relieved, you rush to your baby, pick him up, and give him a big hug. A moment later, the child hits you. Or, he begins to fuss and, in one way or another, to aggravate you like three-year-old Kenny did.

We infer the following from this: the child is greatly relieved to see you, blissfully happy at the sight of you. But then the memory of his recent pain comes to the foreground, and he is angry with you. Although you are probably tired, you now have the task of facing an angry 16-month-old. Yes, the rascal is angry with you. That's all you needed.

The fact is your infant's welcoming reaction—both the manifest love feelings and the angry feelings—is the product of the infant's attaching to and valuing you. The separation anxiety was highly painful to the child, and it produced excessive psychic pain and generated hostility. Since you were the instigator of that pain, the hostility is directed toward you.

Rather than a most unfortunate added burden to your day, this unpleasant encounter in fact is a valuable child-rearing opportunity in a number of ways. First of all, it is an opportunity to help the child learn about the realities of life. Second, it is an opportunity to help him learn about human relationships; namely, that people who love each other can get angry with each other without undermining the love in the relationship. In addition, this is an opportunity to talk to the child about what upset him, why you had to behave as you did, your understanding of how he feels, and your feeling upset by the fact that he felt so hurt; also discuss that although you can understand his being angry with you, that does not mean you will allow him to hit you, and so forth. It is an opportunity to talk about what caused the child to be upset and angry in the context of which the parent can be reassuring and comforting. This is an opportunity to repair the hurt caused by the anxiety and undo the hostility it generated.

We can apply what happened in this event and the child's reactions to it to the various events and conditions that quite normally cause anxiety reactions in kids younger than six years of age—and with age-expectable difference to kids older than six.

When parents have learned what makes their kids anxious, how they manifest anxiety, and have helped them with being anxious, kids find ways of letting their parents know when they're anxious. For instance:

It's spring and seventh grade, nearly-13-year-old Barbara has done fairly well in school, but is now getting worried about this new challenge—final exams. Yes, they do that in her school. She has been doing her homework, but she's not sure she really has done enough of it. She's not hungry at dinner. That's unusual. Seeing that Barbara looks upset, mom asks her what's going on.Oh, she's just not hungry. Both mom and dad know Barbara pretty well. "Barb, looks like something's going on. What is it?" "Finals," mom says. Barbara had expressed concern about them, so both mom and dad got it. "Oh, well, did you do what you need to do to be ready? Did you study enough? You still have this evening," said dad. "I think I'm OK, but I'm not sure," Barbara said. And so mom and dad talked about how exams do this to people. They too had worries about exams and said that the best thing to do is to study—and just do the best you can when the time comes. Dad added a couple thoughts about taking a deep breath now and then and trying to think of relaxing. Mom added that reading questions twice helped her a lot.

And in short order, Barbara found her appetite and was able to eat. The conversation even lightened up a bit. Her parents were there for her and her anxiety slackened some.

Here is an anxiety-producing event that happened to a 17-year-old, John. It's the kind of example that happens frequently in which, how the situation is handled by the caregiver can reduce anxiety and with it the HD it generates or can in fact, intensify both.

John was learning to drive a car, being instructed by an outfit known in his community. Things were going quite well and he was looking to take his driver's test in a week. He was doing well so his instructor took him for a lesson during high-traffic time. Coming to a well-traveled intersection at the bottom of a steep two-lane street leading onto a three-lane bridge crossed by the rather popular two-lane street he was on, he was due to take a left turn onto the bridge. It was a tight turn and everyone seemed to be pushing to make the light. He suddenly froze. "Go ahead," said his trainer. He didn't.

He felt humiliated. Sweating, he waited for the light to change. He didn't look at his instructor. When the light changed he hesitated and had to wait again. Now he felt even worse. He mumbled something. His instructor, being a reasonable man who knew what he was doing, said: "John, it's for this that I got you to take this way home. Now, just relax, take a couple deep breaths. When the light turns, just edge into the intersection and when the on-coming car holds back—which will signal you that he'll let you turn first—then go. Relax." Later, John explained to his parents that that's what did it, " . . . just the way Bob told me to relax and take my turn carefully, but without too much hesitation because then the on-coming car won't know what I'm going to do and he's not going to wait for me to decide." John was very appreciative to Bob; so were John's parents.

Bob had seen this before. He knew that some even very bright teenagers will get acutely anxious at such moments in learning to drive. He didn't embarrass John, he didn't tease him; he took John's anxiety seriously and kindly. He reassured, encouraged caution and action, and seemed to convey confidence that John could do this. Imagine what John might have experienced if Bob had shown impatience or had ridiculed him. Experiences such as these are what gives kids confidence that they can do something that at first scares them. They facilitate the kid's own tendency to push himself to do things that are challenging.

I want to stress the importance of allowing the child or teenager to express being worried or scared; he or she shouldn't have to hide it out of fear of being ridiculed. Allowing the child, younger or older, to go over the experience and talk it through lessens that experience's potential to generate further HD.

COPING WITH DEPRESSION

We first saw Richie when he was 14 months old. As I said (see chapter 10 where I report on Richie), at 14 months he looked about eight months old. His face looked awfully sad and pained, his eyes were dull, and he seemed to look through me. He was subdued, sitting on the floor where his foster mother had put him near her, even though there were other children milling around and toys scattered on the floor. He didn't engage visually or in action with any of them, kids or toys. Rather, he looked wary of all us.

We learned that prior to six months of age, he had been cheerful, even charming, gratifyingly interactive, and developing very well physically and emotionally. A serious family problem developed: his young mother and he were abandoned. Mother became very upset, withdrew emotionally from him, and it was assumed that she abused Richie physically. He was placed in a shelter for about seven months, and then he was taken into foster care.

For this chapter, here is the point I want to make. When Richie began to recover and became less depressed, he became physically explosive and destructive. He would throw toys in a seemingly disorganized way, as if unaware that a thrown toy could hurt someone or break something. He would have sharp rage reactions at even very slight frustrations, as in play with lovely three-year-old Doris who seemed to be trying to make him feel better. When young children recover from depression, one of the first signs of recovery may be that they become angry, perhaps even overtly hostile and destructive.

A number of factors contribute to one's becoming depressed. Some among us are endowed with genetic factors that predispose us to react with depression more readily than others. Certain types of depression bring inordinate pain and produce enormous problems. In addition to one's being born with a genetic predisposition to certain types of depression, human experience brings traumas into our lives that in and of themselves produces depression. Mental health professionals believe it is essential that we human beings all learn to cope with feelings of anxiety and depression because depression is unavoidable. But, both predispositions and life events and conditions influence the intensity, frequency, and duration of the depression we experience.

As I said earlier, anxiety is the feeling of helplessness in the face of a perceived, even if undefined danger; it is an often indefinable feeling of impending doom. Depression has been described as the reaction we may have after that event has occurred. For instance, the 16-month-old child experiences separation anxiety due to a feeling of helplessness in anticipation of the mother not being there. Depression is the reaction of loss he feels when, after a period of time, mother does not return. The threat of danger has materialized, and there are feelings of helplessness, hopelessness, and of giving up.

Unlike the causes of anxiety (see above), the causes of depression are not attached to a developmental schedule. But it is imperative that parents know—and many do not—that children are capable of suffering from depressive feelings from even the early months of life on. By six months, infants are capable of looking intensely sad, and within months are capable of a full-blown, serious depressive reaction.

Whatever the genetic predisposition in any given child, excessive feelings of deprivation due to insufficient attention (neglect), excessive feelings of rejection (abuse), all tend to lead any one of us into depression—infant, child, adolescent, or adult. Once a child becomes sufficiently attached to his mother and father, usually by five to six months of age, the loss of that parent, unless satisfactorily substituted for, will lead to depression. Where a child is not sufficiently attached to his parent at six months, such a depressive reaction will not occur. But this is no consolation, because a five-to-six-month-old's not having formed a specific attachment to his mother brings effects that are known to be more dire than depression. Many adults (parents included of course) are surprised when I tell them that for many decades now, clinical work and research[2] have documented the fact that infants can and do experience depressive feelings from the middle of the first year of life on. Prior to that age, as Spitz[3] reported in 1945, excessive deprivations and insufficient attachments usually do not lead to depressive feelings, but will lead to withdrawal, failure to grow and thrive, and even death.

In addition, mental health professionals have long linked depression with the defense of directing excessive feelings of hostility away from valued others toward the self. This is often due to the fact that when young children experience hostile destructive feelings toward their caregivers, children tend to fear abandonment; this they dread more than the pain caused by depression.

A complication sets in that needs to be acknowledged here. Yes, depression is significantly painful and as a result it will usually produce hostility. But it will not do so when the hate felt toward caregivers produces guilt, which then leads the child to turn the hate against the self, which then, in turn, leads to depression. In this case the self-hate is experienced as punishment "for having bad feelings toward the parents one also loves," which will alleviate the guilt—it's a form of suffering in atonement. The pain of depression will then be welcomed and may then not further mobilize hostility within the child.

Also, when depression follows feeling ashamed of something one has done, this depression too will not generate hostility—except possibly toward oneself—because oneself is the one who did the thing that caused one this shame. This is to be distinguished from being shamed by someone else, which, because this pain is caused by another, does generate hostility in us.

Parents want to intervene in trying to reduce their child's feelings of guilt and shame, which is best done by talking about what is making the child feel guilty or ashamed, but when the guilt is due to the child's experiencing hostile feelings toward his parents, or feeling shame due to having done something he is too embarrassed to tell his parents, this is not easily achieved. This is where professional intervention may be needed—more on this later.

Rationale

Depression can be exceedingly painful. Considering, its consequences when it emerges and its impact on personality formation and development, efforts to deal with it are highly warranted.

Our aim here is to help parents prevent undue depression and help them help their children cope with unavoidable depressions and then help parents know the value of helping their children work through experiences of depression after they have occurred. Toward this end, it is important for parents to know what depression looks like in their child or adolescent and to acknowledge it when it is there. Next it helps to try to figure out what could be causing the child's or adolescent's feelings of depression. The loss of a loved one, a severe disappointment, persisting deprivation of basic emotional needs, or the child's or teenager's feeling that he is bad or doing unacceptable things, these are common sources of depressive feelings. If at all possible, it helps to lessen and even try to undo the cause of the conditions that caused the depression. Where circumstances causing a depression cannot be undone, making efforts to comfort and be available to one's child or teenager are invariably helpful—even when these efforts are not immediately effective. Such efforts include empathic nurturing where indicated, as well as talking about and dealing with both the child's or adolescent's depression and the hostility this depression has generated or mobilized.

A further note of clarification is needed. Clinically, the resolution of depression always shows an associated discharge of what seems to be depression-bound hostility. In fact, the opportunity to express and discharge that hostility in ways tolerable to the self is assumed to be essential for recovery from depression in children—as well as in adults. How that depression-bound hostility is permitted expression and how it is discharged are important to the success of working through the depression. For instance, we know that a child recovering from depression will commonly become hostile and difficult to handle, which may cause caregivers to reject the child and not allow the needed expression of pent-up rage and hate. This in turn will unquestioningly interfere with the child's recovery from depression.

Interventional Steps

Recognizing Depression in Children and Adolescents

What does depression in children look like? The principal features of depression or depressive feelings are the same in children (even very young children) as they are in adults. Consider feeling hopeless. What would that look like? Consider that a painfully sad thing has happened to you. It does not have to be as traumatic as what happened to Richie. Let yourself feel you have just lost someone you value greatly, or that you are severely disappointed in an expectation and there is no hope that the expectation will ever be fulfilled. That is depression.

The infant will look sad, and his facial expression will be flat. When you let yourself feel what the infant's face elicits in you, you will feel sad and may have a sense of hopeless. Children traumatized as was Richie who are depressed (even infants as young as eight or nine months of age) will tend to withdraw, be inactive, move slowly, and respond to another person's approach with little experience of pleasure. Some infants will even withdraw into sleep.

Describing them simply, depressed children, even infants who crawl or walk will tend to move slowly and sluggishly. Richie, at 14 months, just sat where he was put down when we first saw him. The child may refuse to eat, tend not to demand food, and perhaps not even feel hungry, and will respond to efforts to feed him with sluggishness. A three-year-old or a seven-year-old experiencing these feelings is not at all difficult to identify; just apply the same features to them. Some children will be able to say they feel sad, and may get irritated if you push them to cheer up.

A teenager may mask these feelings, may avoid interaction, be overly quiet, stay in her or his room much of the time, or not want to go outside even on a beautiful day. If she can talk about how she feels she may say things that a parent will probably find worrisome to hear—unless the parent makes the mistake of dismissing what the teenager says.

We learned a number of years ago, especially in studying a three-year-old whose father died, that adults have much difficulty in seeing the various expressions of pain that children show. From this three-year-old and a number of other children, I have learned that a major obstacle to an adult's recognizing depression in children comes from the adult's needing to deny the child's painful feelings. This is especially so with younger ones, and even more so with infants. How can a baby be depressed? Well, they can—and too many are. It is just too difficult for many of us to acknowledge that children can suffer so. This fact, of itself, makes it difficult for adults to help depressed children.

Let me add a note here: it is not only parents who have difficulty recognizing when a young child is depressed. For example, a number of years ago, in preparation for a professional presentation and discussion, several child psychiatrists reviewed a video presentation prepared by one of our well-regarded colleagues, the aim of which was to illustrate how difficult it is for children to acknowledge and deal with the death of a parent. The tape showed a three-year-old's nursery-school activities soon following the death of her mother by cancer. In several close reviews of this tape, we found five instances in which the child made reference to hospitals, illness, as well as her mother, each of which was stifled by the well-meaning nursery-school teacher. She told the child that they were not talking about that at this time.

What we inferred to be the child's efforts to talk about her mother's illness, hospitalizations, and eventual death were not just disregarded, they were obstructed. This occurred in a nursery that was part of a psychiatric clinic and research center. Our intention is not to criticize. It is, rather, to point out what we learned from it: helping a depressed child deal with his feelings, thoughts, and fantasies is extremely difficult for adults, even for teachers and possibly for some psychotherapists.

It is quite clear that without opening oneself to empathically experiencing a young child's pain, anxiety, or depression, one cannot hope to help the child cope with it constructively.

The first step then is to know what depression looks like and to acknowledge it when it is there.

Dealing with a Reaction of Depression

The next step is to try to sort out what could be causing the child's feeling of depression. The loss of a loved one, a severe disappointment, a persisting deprivation of basic emotional needs for attention, feeling being valued and loved, feeling recognized as a self, or the child's own feeling that he is bad, all of these to a varying degree may precipitate depressive feelings. Without listing all the possibilities, in a three-to-six-year-old, a move to a new place, the loss of a dear little friend, and the loss of a favorite caregiver (other than a parent) can also produce feelings of depression.

In a 6-to-12-year-old, the loss of a parent or sibling, of a beloved grandparent or other family member to whom the child is attached, significant family problems, a move from a really liked neighborhood and school to one not liked, poor performance in school, rejection by a very special friend (not common at this age) may lead to feelings of depression. In a 12-to-18-+-year-old, the same as for the 6-to-12-year-old, plus rejection by someone the teenager has a crush on—parents should know that "love" in adolescence can be serious and bring with it deeply experienced feelings of joy or pain. Shakespeare was a great psychologist; he knew that only in adolescence can love be such that a 14-year-old Juliet and a 17-year-old Romeo would choose to die rather than be deprived of the other. Minimizing and, worse, ridiculing adolescent love can be very costly to the adolescent—and the family.

It's not bizarre that some parents of a young child, not aware of its potential hurtful consequences, might want to take a vacation without the child. Fortunately, most parents don't feel that way. But some do, sometimes for good reasons, as for instance, things not going well between the young couple, they think that perhaps a break away from the child (or the children) may give them a chance to restructure their relationship for the better.

Here is a not so uncommon instance. Parents of a four-year-old who had troubling symptoms told me that a couple years back they had been troubled by the fact that when Tommy was two years old, after they came back from a two-week vacation they took without him, he reacted as if he did not know them. I learned that when he had been about one, his parents had gone away without him for one week and a responsible caregiver had stayed with him. They did not recall how he reacted on their return. But after their vacation when he was two, for a day or so he seemed not to recognize them. After working psychoanalytically with four-year-old Tommy for some time, I came to understand that he had found the separation from his parents so painful—he felt that his parents had abandoned him because he was bad—that, unconsciously, to stop his pain he suppressed the image of his parents. In the course of our work it was not clear whether he had felt sad or hopeless when his parents were gone, but there was much evidence of his hostile feelings toward them. In his play-therapy he often played out a fantasy of a witch who was mean and threatening to children and who would invariably, herself, meet harsh treatment by one type of force or another. In psychodynamic therapies we assume that such fantasies in a child's play—a very productive way of working clinically with children—arise in the child's imagination from his experiences in actual relationships, most commonly within his family.

When one knows the cause of the depression, if it can be undone, it is wise to do so.

If it cannot be undone, it is highly to the child's advantage that her depression be dealt with. For instance, if a young child, especially an infant is showing signs of sadness because mother has now been in the hospital for two days due to surgery, it would be helpful to telephone the mother and have the infant hear her voice. Better still, if you can work it out with your doctor and the hospital—and we encourage parents to make such demands—take the child to see the mother in the hospital. A young child who shows feelings of sadness because mother has gone to the hospital will most likely recover from those feelings when the mother returns home—if the separation has not been too long, say a few days, and the child is helped to work through the depressive reaction based on her feelings of loss.

Some parents are afraid to call, because the young child will be upset on hearing mother's voice. True, the child will be upset because mother's not home. But he'll be less upset than by thinking that she's gone forever, dead. Furthermore, the fact is that the child already is upset, whether he shows it or not. In fact, the longer the absence and the silence, the more intense and entrenched the upset feelings become. The less the distress is vocalized, the more it becomes embedded in the psyche. Therefore, although unpleasant, it is better to call than not call.

Young children who are left with caregivers when one or both parents must absent themselves from home for a few days of even weeks or longer, for whatever reason such as to take care of an ailing grandparent, or on a work assignment, or a vacation, or in the military, may react with feelings of depression that need to be dealt with by telephone calls or a prompt return (when possible) home. Adolescents will of course handle such separations well enough without depressive reactions.

So, when circumstances that cause depression cannot be undone, a prime compensatory action against the reaction of depression can be instituted: talking about it. In the case of mother's being in the hospital, talk about why she had to go there, and reassure as to when she will come back. These are basic requisites to help the child cope with depressive feelings—even with infants under one year of age. Comforting in the face of painful feelings is always a worthwhile effort. Empathic nurturing is always helpful in the face of depression or any painful feeling for that matter, even when the reaction to that empathic nurturing and comforting does not seem to work right away. TLC (tender loving care), which used to be the mantra of professional nursing, has worked its miracles from the beginning of time.

Since one of the common causes of depression in childhood is due to a feeling of having lost mother's or father's love, such as following disruptive behavior, talking about what caused the parent's anger and reassuring that the loss of that love is temporary, if indeed present at all, will be very helpful.

Most important in helping a child cope with feelings of depression is the necessity to allow the child to express and discharge feelings of hostility that are generated by the depression and mobilized by it. The parent has to allow, tolerate, and help the child find acceptable ways of expressing hostility. Allowing the young child to complain, fuss, cry, or verbalize ("Bad mommy!") is essential; older kids should be permitted to verbalize their anger too—along lines detailed in chapter 10.

Again, explaining why the depression-inducing event occurred is important. For the young child for example, "Now mommy is well and doesn't have to go to the hospital anymore," or, "mommy needs to go to work." It is essential for the parent to allow the child to react reasonably to any such explanations.

Such complaining and explanations always need more than one go-round. Each such complaint and explanation contributes to the working through and the lessening of the traumatizing effects of the event that caused the depression.

The earlier such dialogues occur, the better. Again, we want to emphasize that talking to an infant who cannot yet talk is most appropriate, feasible, and helpful. Telling a 10-month-old "I am sorry I upset you," or "I'm sorry that what I did hurt you," has beneficial effects. First, the child will feel your empathy, which is critical for many reasons. Second, the child will feel that what he is experiencing is appropriate, permissible, unavoidable, and understood, and efforts are being made, to make the painful feelings go away.

There is an enormous advantage to both child and parent of establishing the ability and expectation that one can talk together about anything in relationships, good and bad—except where the parent's or the child's privacy needs to be respected. If the ability to talk together begins to be developed from infancy on, talking with the child when he or she is an adolescent—even an adult—will be possible and will take place. Parents, who believe one can't talk with a young child, and that one can't reason with a young child, are wrong. True, one has to take one's cues from the young child's behavior to learn the limits of the child's ability to reason—which only comes with in fact talking to the child.

Helping the child find ways to express and discharge the depression-bound hostility in ways that are acceptable to both the child and the parents is a vital task (see chapter 10).

WHEN TO TURN TO PROFESSIONAL GUIDANCE

When a parent is troubled or getting exasperated by the feeling, "I just don't know what to do to help this kid," it's time to think of consulting someone who is trained to find ways to help parents do so. Being troubled and exasperated with one's own child and finding that nothing the parent has tried works means that the child's reactions and behaviors are happening too often.

As a mental health professional who has studied human development from birth on, both by studying much literature and conferencing on the subject complemented by decades of my own research and clinical work, I owe it to parents to tell them that the earlier in life problems that impede healthy development and adaptation are handled in growth-promoting ways, the easier it is to undo these problems and get healthy development and adaptation back on track. Good mental health, like good physical health begins at the beginning of life because this is when the foundation for health begins to be established. The old beliefs that future heart disease begins in adulthood; that obese children will thin out as they grow on—sure it happens with some—that children do not develop gastric ulcers, and equally, that childhood is the easy time of life are wrong. Notions that blind people to where problems begin in life have led to much misery in the life of many among us.

In short, consultation with mental health professionals when a young child is reacting to the difficulties of life with painful symptoms such as excessive anxiety and depression, excessive irritability and hostility, and other emotional symptoms, can save the child and the parents much further pain, time spent worrying, and money spent for both mental and physical health care. This applies to children and adolescents. While we all agree that "an ounce of prevention is worth a pound of cure"—it often is worth much more—too few among us act according to this wisdom.

So, when is it time to consult a mental health professional for excessive anxiety, and when for clinical depression?

Anxiety: When the child or adolescent's anxiety interferes with his or her well-being at home, persists for too long about going to school or while in school, or going anywhere to do anything reasonably that we might expect from a child or adolescent of his or her age, it is time to consult a professional.

It is also time when symptoms known outright to be due to excessive anxiety persist or occur frequently, such as nightmares, inability to fall sleep or stay asleep before challenges, gastrointestinal aches on Sunday evening or Monday mornings, or any weekday mornings—due to school-linked anxiety, etc. Also, when children with preexisting biological conditions as asthma, diabetes, or allergies for instance, seem to be developing illness "episodes" more frequently than usual, it is likely because stress lowers the threshold for such episodes.

Panic attacks: Panic attacks of themselves make the child or adolescent not only miserable, but also can interfere harshly with a child's or adolescent's well-being, psychological and social development, learning in school, and more. If a child or adolescent has panic attacks more than once a week, professional attention is needed both for evaluation precipitants and determination of best treatment strategies for any given kid. Surely, the intensity and duration of panic attacks are critical dimensions of when to seek consultation.

Depression: We all experience sadness, and even mild depression in the face of painful disappointments—which happens to everyone in one way or another throughout life—or minor losses. In the face of a serious loss, such as a family member, we all tend to mourn. These are normal reactions. They do not require professional consultation. Reasonable attention, talking about the loss, the memories attached to the person, mutual emotional support, and comforting can go a long way to recovery of reasonable well-being.

Other than following a serious loss, such as of a mother, father, or sibling, when evidence of feelings of depression—facial, behavioral, or verbal expressions—persist for more than one or two weeks, professional consultation can be highly advantageous.

Surely, children and adolescents who are subjected to traumatic stress experiences—whatever these may be, whether at home, in school, or in the neighborhood—will be helped by due attention being given to these experiences and their aftermath. Children and adolescents who develop a post-traumatic stress disorder will benefit enormously from therapeutic strategies devised specifically for the given child or adolescent. Some milder forms of such disorders can be handled reasonably well by the child or teenager and their attentive and caring families. But when such conditions persist or are harsh, consultation is really required.

It is highly desirable that attention is finally being given to the post-traumatic-stress disorders associated with military combat service and its dire consequences for many individuals—many of whom are still adolescents—who have not received timely and due mental health attention. We can all appreciate the drastic conditions of being in a war zone, be it in the military or as a civilian, but it too often goes underestimated how many children and teenagers have experienced, to a greater or lesser degree, the traumatization suffered by Richie, and its potential, eventual, destructive consequences (see chapters 2 and 3).

NOTES

1. Psychoanalytic/psychodynamic child development theory.

2. Both Rene Spitz and John Bowlby especially, among others, extensively studied and reported on this question. (1) R. Spitz, Anaclitic depression: an inquiry into the genesis of psychiatric conditions in early childhood. *Psychoanalytic Study Child* (1946) 2:313–342. (2) R. Spitz, *Grief: a Peril in Infancy* [Film] New York University Film Library (1947). (3) R. Spitz, *The First Year of Life* (New York: International Universities Press, 1965). (4) J. Bowlby, Grief and mourning in infancy and early childhood. *Psychoanalytic Study Child* (1960), 15:9–52. (5) J. Bowlby, *Attachment* (New York: Basic Books, 1969).

3. R. Spitz, Hospitalism: an inquiry into the genesis of psychiatric conditions in early childhood. *Psychoanalytic Study of the Child* (1945), 1:53–74.

Chapter 12

Optimizing the Parent-Child Relationship

We have now addressed five most common parent-child interactions where aggression—in both its nondestructive and its hostile, destructive forms—is commonly activated and when, by virtue of what the parent does or does not do, can be lessened or intensified. In these interactions parents have opportunities to substantially help their children cope well, and to determine what kind of human beings they will become (see chapter 7). Our discussions of these child-rearing interactions can provide parents with guidelines on ways to deal with other interactions we have not talked about.

In this chapter, I want to talk about what most mental health professionals believe is among the most important goals parents ought to aim for in their efforts to help their children grow emotionally healthy: to optimize their relationships with their children.

Optimizing your relationship with your child does not mean always being loving, pleasant, reassuring, and praising. There are times to let children fend for themselves, and there are times to be annoyed and angry, to be troubled and worried, to register disapproval, and to scold. Whatever the child's inborn dispositions, strengths, and vulnerabilities, the relationship that parents establish with their child is the most powerful vehicle they have for mediating and influencing their child's emotional development and emotional life.

In forming a positive relationship between parent and child, the parent is loading the love side of the inevitable ambivalence—the balance of love and hate feelings—that occurs in every parent-child relationship. Loading the positive side of the child's ambivalence:

1. enhances love-based compliance rather than fear-based compliance (which often leads to the child's rejecting the parents' efforts to socialize the child);

2. better motivates the development of controls over the child's inevitably generated hostile-destructive feelings;
3. helps secure healthier conscience formation, which will protect against the development of highly troublesome patterns of adaptation; and
4. a positive parent-child relationship is the most powerful tool parents have for helping their child work through and lessen the inevitable hate and hostility the child experiences.

Therefore, whatever the child's psychological-emotional endowment, a sufficiently positive parent-child relationship protects against the development of excessive hostility in the child and optimizes the child's development.

Over the course of a child's life, as much psychological clinical and research has documented, each stage of development brings with it specific challenges. Helping a child master these developmental challenges promotes a positive attachment between parent and child. On the other side of this correlation, a positive attachment facilitates the child's navigating these challenges age-adequately, and promotes the child's healthy development of autonomy, assertiveness (nondestructive aggression), and her or his sense of being a valued, capable, and self-reliant[1] self.

Toward developing a positive parent-child relationship, the parent's loving the child should be conveyed not only in actions, but also in words; the parent's love should be evident. Hand in hand with this, it is essential that the parent respond positively to the child's asking for comfort and reassurance when things get troublesome as happens, for instance, when he experiences anxiety, or limit setting. Also highly important, the parent should establish an emotional and verbal dialogue with the child.

In order to be situation-appropriately responsive to a child, it helps for a parent to understand what the child is experiencing. Therefore, understanding key developmental challenges the child faces—beyond those overtly evident—will enhance the parent's insights into what the child is experiencing and help the parent better calibrate her or his efforts.

In the first section of this chapter, focusing first on the child younger than six years, I first spell out what I know best about *attachment* and touch on its role in the development of the child's autonomy and sense of self (beyond what I have said about these in chapters 7 and 8). I will then look at some influences of the young child's developing *sexuality* on his or her evolving family relationships. Then we will briefly consider major trends in relationships during the elementary-school years and adolescence.

In the next section, I will add a few additional loose thoughts I have found important over the years toward optimizing the parent-child relationship.

And in the final section, I will state the central issue of this book namely, how the quality of the parent-child relatedness correlates positively with the development of the child's aggression profile.

HUMAN ATTACHMENT

Infants are born with instinctive mechanisms and an inner pressure to form an emotional relationship with those who invest emotionally in them.[2] Within moments of birth, human infants react responsively to a caregiver, and within weeks they begin the process of emotionally attaching to those who consistently care for them.

We now know that at birth, by virtue of the gradual development of sensory systems while in the mother's uterus, the infant is already acquainted with his mother's voice, the quality and degree of activity of the mother, and perhaps more. Recent studies have shown that during the third trimester of pregnancy, the fetus is responsive to external stimuli that traverse the mother's abdominal wall, such as sounds, strong lights aimed at the mother's abdomen, and other stimuli. Thus even before birth, infants are already becoming acquainted with elements of the outside world. The newborn responds preferentially to the sound of the mother's voice, and soon distinguishes the odor of her mother's body and breast pad, as compared with those of another.

Much research has documented that infants are born with, in addition to developing sensory systems, ready-to-go systems that compel emotional attachment. These inborn systems make learning by conditioning possible, as well as the patterning of responsiveness, the accumulation of memory, and more. Once born, many a newborn will tend to look at the human face more attentively than other features of his environment. For instance, 12-day-old Bernie, in the course of being fed by his mother, interrupts the feeding and looks at his mother's eyes and forehead. His looking at her is not indifferent; it seems as though he is trying to "take in" the image at which he is staring. I inferred that Bernie was attempting to assimilate the experience he was having, and is linking the feeding process and the gratification it brings with the features of his mother who was feeding him.

Rene Spitz proposes[3] that the face of the caregiver, particularly the eyes, forehead, and hairline, constitutes a configuration that elicits in the infant a response of attentiveness—a powerful configuration to which the infant will attach. Spitz, following the work of Konrad Lorenz on *imprinting,*[4] identified this configuration in the caregiver as a "releasing mechanism" for attachment. At about five to six weeks, most infants will begin to respond to that facial configuration with a smiling response that has the distinctive feature of appearing to be a social smiling response. We believe this response is inborn and is a cardinal factor in setting in motion the infant's emotional attachment to the caregiver, now at a new level of experiencing and organization. We owe our largest debt for understanding this, and much of what will follow, to Dr. Spitz.

Thus, at about five to six weeks, in conjunction with a number of physiological and psychological maturations, the appearance of the social smiling response heralds the beginning of an emotional attachment that is critical for both infant and parent. Who among us can resist responding to the magnificent smile of a six-week-old infant? It arouses in the parent a feeling of being recognized and identified by one's own child. Most parents react to the infant's smile by a global response of love and reciprocity. This, of course, is only the beginning of an infant's signs of what will evolve into love.

At this age, the infant is not yet capable of love (see chapter 4), but this is where it begins. Some mothers are enormously disappointed and distressed when their three-day-old infants are not smiling in response to their demonstrations of affection. Knowing that an infant is not capable of a social smile until about five to six weeks—in some infants, even until three months—will protect many first-time parents from feeling they have an unresponsive infant. Since early responsiveness between parent and infant plays a crucial part in the attachment process, it is important that young parents not be disheartened or feel rejected by the very young infant's not being capable of this more advanced kind of responsiveness (see below for Beatrice Beebe's findings).

Knowing that the social smiling response does not occur until the second month or so of life will also ready the parent and facilitate the response that will complement their infant's earliest social smiles. The parent's response to the infant's social smile is enormously important in enhancing not only the social smile, but also the feeling of being responded to emotionally. This opens and facilitates the pathway of mutual responsiveness, of "the emotional dialogue" between parent and infant.

Fascinating and critical, while the mother's response of smiling adoringly is specific to her infant, Spitz demonstrated that the social smiling response of the six-week-old infant is, in fact, indiscriminate. But, parents are not to worry. The infant is primed to respond to a configuration of the human face with a social smile. Therefore, the smiling response will initially be elicited by any face, even by a diagram of a face drawn on paper. But this indiscriminateness changes rather quickly. It is common that an infant will smile more readily and broadly at his own mother, because by six weeks, he already responds selectively to mother's voice and odor—aspects of the mother the infant recognizes even before he recognizes her face.

One young mother was upset by the fact that her three-month-old smiled at other people. It was her hope that the infant had already identified her as a specific person, as someone the infant could distinguish from all other people in a stable fashion. Although the infant was able to discriminate her mother from others in particular ways—by her voice and caregiving features—she had not yet developed the ability to reliably discriminate her mother emotionally from others.

The process of discriminating specifically who mother is, who father is, and even who brother and sister are, occurs from about the second or third month of life through the fifth, sixth, and seventh month. In other words, from about six weeks through five months of age (in some children, six or seven months of age), the infant more and more recognizes—cognitively and emotionally—the mother as different from others and gradually smiles at her reliably, preferentially. The infant's smiling has now become a specific social smiling response. At about five to seven months, the infant has a somewhat stable feeling of who his prime caregivers are and who the persons are on whom he can rely on for gratifying caregiving. The infant seems to sense who emotionally values him. Most commonly, the infant shows evidence of being first attached to the mother—given that she most tends to the baby–then to the father, and to siblings, and the few people who most frequently appear in his life.

Hand in hand with this increase in specific reactivity, the infant will no longer smile at people whom she does not know. In fact, the five- or six-month-old may even react to people she does not know with a reaction of distress. This stranger response can have a wide range, from sober curiosity in looking at a stranger to acute reactions of distress and stranger anxiety, with turning away from the stranger and clinging to mother. This stranger responsiveness will reach a first peak at about five to eight months of age, tend to subside from 10 to 14 months of age, and peak again due to developmental processes at about 16 through 24 months of age.

The stranger to the infant is not necessarily a stranger to the family. For instance, visiting grandparents whom the infant has not seen for some time may be experienced by a five- or six-month-old as a stranger, and they may elicit an acute panic reaction in the infant. This invariably causes distress to the parents, as well as to the visiting grandparents, who are strangers only by virtue of the infant's not having seen them for some time. Usually, if the grandparents take their time about descending on their grandchild, the infant will soon get used to them, sensing emotionally that these persons are important to her parents, a factor that will facilitate responsiveness and attachment to the grandparents.

Along with the specific social smiling response and the stranger responses, both of which are indicators of the infant's selective attachment to specific persons (usually the parents), comes the reaction of experiencing anxiety and distress on separation from the parents. A separation reaction is well known to all parents of children from the ages of five months to three and more years. Separation reactions and separation anxiety—which is simply a more intense response to separation—are significant indicators that the child is emotionally attaching to his mother and father.

While parents would prefer that their infants not experience anxiety, both separation anxiety and stranger anxiety serve a beneficial purpose for the child's forming emotional relationships. Given the problem stranger anxiety may create later in life, when it becomes a contributor to prejudice, addressing the problem of prejudice, I wrote[5] that " . . . complementary anxieties are activated in the infant that orient the infant *toward* the . . . primary-[caregiver]. *Separation anxiety* means that the infant is attaching to a specific [person]; the threat of losing that [person] elicits this anxiety. *Stranger anxiety* . . . informs us that the infant is beginning to [know] that not every [person] is his/her mother or father. We might furthermore say that *stranger anxiety* serves to contain and direct the infant's inborn . . . attachment tendency *away from any noncaregiving [person], toward the [primary caregivers]*" (26).

Forming an attachment is critical to the preservation of the species, social adaptation, and personality formation. But not all attachments achieve the same result. Spearheaded by Mary Ainsworth,[6] *Attachment Theory* has catalogued attachment types: there are good (secure) attachments; troubled (anxiety-laden) attachments that do not foster in the child a sense of security in the relationship or the world around; and there are unreliable, unpredictable, insufficient (disorganized) attachments that do just that—they disorganize the child's experience of the world around and the people in it. Of course, each type will lead to varying separation and reunion (see next paragraphs) as well as stranger reactions; each will also strongly influence the child's ability to, or difficulty in, relating to others and adapting to his or her social universe. A highly nonsecure attachment may create serious problems in every aspect of the individual's life. An absence of attachment to caregivers will lead to serious emotional problems and antisocial adaptation—adaptation in which human beings are not valued and are treated as things.

Another significant indicator of attachment that complements separation anxiety is the reaction children show when, after having been separated from their parents for a while they are reunited with them. These *reunion reactions* are of two types. One is the simple *positive reunion reaction:* on seeing the mother return, the young child is very happy, reaches out to her, may cling to her briefly, but all in all seems cheerful to see she is back. The second type of reaction is the *negative reunion reaction:* the infant appears to ignore the mother on her return (what attachment theory calls "anxiety-avoidant"), or is clearly angry with her when she returns as we saw with three-year-old

Kenny (see chapter 11). Although the expressed feeling is a negative one, this negative reaction, however, does indicate that an emotional attachment exists. Therefore, in and of itself, even a negative reunion reaction is a positive indicator of attachment to the parent.

And I would add that a negative reunion reaction, like Kenny's for instance, does not of itself mean that the child's attachment to the mother is not secure. Kenny was just mad at her for having been away when he wanted her to be home.

Facilitating Attachment

Indicators of attachment to specific persons, the specific social smiling response, stranger responses, separation reactions, and reunion reactions provide opportunities for parents to facilitate attachment by responding helpfully. Here are a few thoughts on such facilitation.

To the infant's social smiling response: when an infant smiles on seeing the parent and the parent reacts to that smiling response with a reciprocal show of warmth, tenderness, excitement, and pleasure, this enhances the infant's smiling response and his feeling of being responded to and being cared for, and optimizes the child's attachment to the parent. It would be difficult to overemphasize the importance of the parent's and infant's experience of mutual joy and pleasure at this stage—or at any time. This experience enriches immeasurably the further development of the infant and of the parent-child relationship.

Beatrice Beebe[7] reports in video-documented detail the troubling consequences to the infant-mother attachment process, in mothers who experienced post-partum depression. Beebe demonstrates the disequilibrating and distressing effect their infant's social smiling response had on them. As the infant's smile broke out, the depressed mother, seemingly reflexively, gaze-avoided (looked away). The infant's smiling response interrupted, the infant looked dismayed and in turn, gaze-avoided. The mother tried quickly to return her gaze at her infant who had turned away, but when the infant returned the gaze, mother again reflexively looked away. I inferred from this behavior that the depressed mother could not tolerate the emotional state expressed in her infant's powerfully warm smile. Just this miscarried reactivity cast a cloud on the mother-infant interaction and disrupted the priceless process of attachment.

To the child's stranger anxiety response: when the infant experiences a stranger response, how the parent deals with that can enhance attachment to the parent. For example, when grandfather comes in—convinced that he will be received by the infant with open arms—and receives a reaction of distress, fear, and turning away, it is not uncommon for him to react with distress and either push himself onto the infant, attempting to brush aside the stranger response to him, or, offended, pull away. If the grandfather forces himself on the baby, this is going to be experienced by the baby as highly unpleasurable, and will generate hostility, which will not help bring the infant closer to the grandfather.

When the parent of the infant can intervene and convey to grandfather that he needs to take more time in approaching the infant, and then mother attempts to calm and comfort her distressed infant, she will be helping the child cope with his stranger response. Also, this will help to eventually bring the infant closer to grandfather, as well as to the helpful parent. In this way, the parent will be facilitating the child's experience, decreasing the duration and intensity of excessive unpleasure, and lessening the generation of hostility in the infant.

To the young child's separation anxiety reaction: when the infant experiences a separation reaction, the parent's handling of it can enhance the child's attachment to the parent. The mother who responds to her infant's separation reactions with a feeling of understanding and moderate personal distress; tries to comfort her infant; and explains why she has to go, where she has to go, and when she will be back, is making efforts to decrease the intensity of distress the infant is experiencing, and all that follows from it. Although this will likely not stop the separation reaction, the mother's efforts will have registered with the infant. They will contribute to ameliorating the infant's pain and ill-feeling and will heighten the positive quality of their mutual attachment while decreasing the hostility generated in her child. I want to say again that by showing concern and making efforts to comfort—even where she cannot stop the pain—the mother is enhancing the child's attachment to her. It will not be lost on the child that the mother is trying to make the child feel better.

To the child's reunion reactions: Here too, the way the parent reacts to the infant's reunion reaction can further facilitate the infant's attachment to the parent. The mother who reacts with pleasure, affection, and attentiveness to an infant reacting positively in reunion conveys to the infant that he is emotionally valued and loved. This, of course, enhances the infant's positive feelings toward his mother and fosters his attachment to her.

To negative reunion reactions: this reaction poses more of a problem for the parent. How does it feel when you come home after having been away from the baby and are very excited to see him, and he's angry with you, like three-year-old Kenny was (chapter 11)? It hurts. Again, it is important to allow the child to express the feelings of distress he is experiencing. It is helpful to understand the child is angry because he felt acute anxiety at mother's absence. This is a positive indication of attachment. When the parent understands why the child is angry, can allow him or her to express it in acceptable ways and tries to soothe the child, the child's anger will resolve more quickly. The feelings of anger toward the parent will not be as intense and will not last as long, and the feelings of affection will return sooner and be heightened.

The mother or father who reacts to the child's angry reception with, "Well, if you don't want to see me, I don't want to see you" or another rejecting reaction, will lengthen the duration of hostile reactivity and give the attachment a more negative valence. The parent will be interfering with the development of a positive attachment.

While holding in mind this outline of the earliest manifestations of the development of attachment, let's look at another aspect of attachment from another vantage point. However immature the infant's experiencing, we assume that the infant has both: (1) self feelings, perhaps even the beginnings of a sense of self—evolving from his primary narcissism[8]—and, (2) has a primitive awareness of the caregiver—not yet clearly defined, by any means[9]—and is reactive to the interactions between this elemental self and the caregiver. The development of oneself as an individual person goes hand in hand with the development of one's own feelings and awareness of other persons as individuals. It seems to be an internally experienced reciprocity between oneself and one's caregiver. The degree to which we love and respect others goes hand in hand with our respect and love for oneself. Equally, the degree to which we hate and despise others parallels our hating and despising ourselves. In addition, the way others love and respect us makes a large contribution to our loving and respecting ourselves, as the experience of being hated by those we depend on and need contributes to hating and despising ourselves.

Assuming that the development of a sense of self, an awareness of the caregiver, and of interactive processes begin from the first days of life, we can put these in the context of the model of development conceptualized by Dr. Margaret Mahler, which she calls *separation–individuation* theory.

SEPARATION-INDIVIDUATION: BECOMING A SELF RELATED TO OTHERS

Freud's proposal that the newborn comes into the world endowed with "primary narcissism," which I assume is the psychological representative of the biological mandate "living organisms must maintain life."[10] Mahler's Separation–Individuation theory starts from this point, holding that in the earliest weeks of life, the infant's experiences predominantly consists of (1) the perception of his needs, (2) his expressions of these perceived needs, and (3) his experiences of his being gratified. Whatever goes on in his environment is not discerned as being outside of this "self-experience."

Gradually, by about six weeks, mother (the prime caregiver) becomes part of this "self-experience." The infant begins to have increased awareness of that which is him and that which is the caregiver—by virtue of what she does for him. At this time, Mahler proposes, the infant seems to experience self and mother as if surrounded by an enveloping membrane tying the caregiver within the infant's self-experience. During major periods of the infant's waking life, this emotional sense of oneness prevails.

The phase of self-other development during which this experiencing occurs begins at about six weeks of age; Mahler calls it the *normal symbiotic phase.* She used this phrase because she wanted to describe what she inferred from years of work: that the infant seems to experience the mother as a part of the self, especially evident, she thought, during experiences of need and being cared for. She used the term *symbiosis*[11] to describe the character of the child's experience. This normal symbiotic phase peaks at about five to six months of age, and then without a definite termination point, wanes as this state of being evolves into the phases of the development of relatedness that follow.

Prior to five months or so, while on the one hand, much experiencing during periods of wakefulness seems to be in the context of the child's symbiotic relatedness to his mother, we also assume an original and slowly unfolding sense of self, discernible in there being a substantial amount of activity during alert wakefulness that does not involve the caregiver, such as looking at and manipulating things in the environment. I want to note that while I speak of the caregiver as the mother, we can say the same of the caregiving father, and occasionally of a caregiving sibling. I mean those caregivers who invest emotionally in the infant in that very unique, "family" way.

The caregiver who is a substitute for the mother or the father—say the caregiver who comes in when mother goes to work away from home—may invest emotionally in and be valued by the infant. However, this caregiver's investment in the child does not have the emotional weight and quality of the child's own parents.

In the course of our years of work with mothers, one mother convincingly made this point. As she talked about her neighbor's children, whom she found very attractive and toward whom she felt a great deal of affection, she tried to sort out the difference between how she felt about her own children and how she felt about these lovely neighbor children. She felt satisfaction—as we feel when we find a way of expressing something difficult to describe—in having thought that a major difference was that if she felt about her neighbor's children as she did about her own, she would not be able to tolerate the pain of leaving them in the evening.

However much a caregiver substituting for the parents attaches to her ward, however much a teacher invests emotionally in her students, however much a doctor invests emotionally in her patients—that degree of emotional investment cannot (and should not) reach the level, depth, or quality of attachment characteristic of that which parents invest in their children.

To highlight this critical difference in relatedness and attachments, mental health professionals sometimes speak of parents and children as *primary objects,*[12] who form primary attachments to and relationships with one another, in contrast to the secondary and tertiary attachments and relationships we form with people we value who might be our friends, teachers, neighbors, and so forth.

Resuming detailing of separation-individuation theory, at about five to six months of age, the child begins to experience a significant heightening of her awareness of herself and to gradually clarify the distinction between self and the caregiver. For example, five-and-a-half-month-old Susan, while sitting on mother's lap, seemed to pull away from her mother's body, as if to look better at the bustle around her with new interest. She seemed to be awakened from her earlier state of comfortable encapsulation with mother, molded into her on her lap. She seemed much more alert, ready to go, and she looked older. Mahler speaks of this experiencing as *hatching.* Susan seemed as if she was pushing out of her symbiotic oneness with mother.

As this often-seen example suggests, at the midpoint of the first year of life, a second maturational differentiation and heightening of both physiologic and psychological processes occurs. We see increasing locomotion, an ability and interest in exploring, an increased capability in sensory modalities, and an increased capacity in cognitive functioning (as Piaget describes). At this point, the infant thrusts into the process of separation-individuation out of the oneness with mother. This occurs in two major subphases. The first subphase runs from about five to six months on through about 16 months of age. The second subphase runs from 16 months of age to three years. (Mahler subdivided both into yet another subdivision, but this latter subdivision is not essential for this exposition.)

In the beginning, the first subphase is characterized by the infant's pulling away from the mother, just as five-and-a-half-month-old Susan was doing. Next the infant begins to exercise her increasing motor skills and one sees an increasing pressure to explore the environment. I got the impression that the infant wants to learn and understand what the environment is all about and is attempting to gain mastery over it. At the same time, the infant is attempting to gain mastery over her own newly emerging capabilities and skills. A marked thrust toward autonomy, separateness, and individuation becomes evident. Often, at this time, a 12-month-old infant may be so active, busy, and pressed to explore everything (including putting things in her mouth) that many a mother experiences the infant as "getting into everything and causing all kinds of trouble and aggravation." It is regrettable when a mother feels this because she may be failing to see in the child's busyness that the child is driven to learn about the world into which she was born, a world she had never seen before. The child is an explorer, a learner about her new world.

At the height of the thrust toward autonomy, the second subphase of separation-individuation is initiated by the infant's increasing recognition that the mother and she are truly separate individuals. Increasing cognitive (thinking) skills begin to make clear to the 16-to-18-month-old that her relationship to the caregiver is not secured by an enveloping membrane or an emotional oneness. Rather, it consists of being emotionally attached to the caregiver, each a separate individual.

This heightened recognition of the self as separate from the mother initially brings with it an emotional crisis. This crisis is evidenced in behaviors that reveal anxiety and, at times, a benign form of depressive feelings that Mahler calls *lowkeyedness.* We also see behaviors that signal an internal struggle. Mahler emphasizes that this internal struggle is produced by the infant's experiencing conflicting wishes. On the one hand, she wants to remain one with mother, as if in an enveloping membrane. On the other hand, the infant experiences a powerful inner thrust to be an individual separate from that highly valued person, the mother. We can assume that a parallel, although somewhat different, process occurs within the relationship of the infant to the father, and perhaps even with siblings.

Here is an event we saw (see chapter 1) that I believe documents the crisis Mahler talks about; it is evident in the behavior of many a 16-to-24-month-old child.

> When Candy was one year, seven months, and 21 days of age, we witnessed evidence of this crisis. This particular morning, Candy stayed close to her mother from the beginning of our group session. Four other children, whom she knew well, took off their shoes and toddled playfully to our playroom. Candy, who was close to her mother on their sofa busily playing with toys, saw what they were up to and took off her shoes, too, excitedly readying herself to join the others. However, once her shoes were off, her mood sobered and she climbed back onto the sofa with some help from her mother. Five seconds after she had climbed onto her mother's lap, Candy began to cry and twist her body away from mother, giving the impression that she was suddenly experiencing acute pain. Puzzled, her mother sensitively responded to her child's cues by

> putting Candy down. Candy dropped to the floor, crying, twisting, and kicking her legs in a mild tantrum—a reaction most unusual for her. Surprised, her mother tried to comfort Candy by talking and touching. Finally, through mutual accord, mother picked Candy up. But once in her mother's arms, Candy again started to cry and twist herself away. Again, her puzzled mother complied and put Candy down. Mother and daughter twice again enacted this same sequence. It wound down with the sixth hold-me-close communication. Candy's pain and distress—which we inferred arose from her conflicting wishes to be close to, while at the same time, be separate from her mother—were strikingly mirrored in the feelings of confusion her mother showed.[13]

This mother was at first bewildered by the child's behavior, and was much relieved when I explained what we believe was going on in her child. It made sense to her.

Two points are especially important for parents to be aware of, because each presents an opportunity to enhance the positive quality of the parent-child relationship and all that follows from it. The first is that the infant in the first subphase of the separation-individuation phase is powerfully thrust by an inner need to exercise self feelings and self-motivated activities. This remarkable thrust toward autonomy needs to be protected by the parent. This is done by facilitating the one-year-old's opportunities for exploration—such as by baby-proofing the house (see chapter 6)—so that the exercise of emerging skills can be carried out under conditions that are safe and allow for excitement, learning, and mastery. The parent's awareness of the child's powerful thrust to autonomy and effectiveness will facilitate her reacting to her child's inner thrust in growth-prompting ways (see chapter 8 on limit setting).

The second point is that, during the second subphase of the separation-individuation process, the infant will at times experience the awareness of being truly separate from the mother as anxiety producing. This anxiety is usually produced under two conditions. The first is when the infant perceives the self as separate from the mother at a time when this perception leads to an acute feeling of helplessness and of not being ready for that separateness. As I said before, this can bring with it anxiety and the depressive feeling Mahler calls *lowkeyedness.* The second condition that may produce acute anxiety at this time occurs in the context of the experience of, on the one hand wanting to remain one with mother, while on the other hand wanting to be separate from her.

During the second part of the separation-individuation phase, there tends to be a reemergence of or heightening of separation anxiety and stranger responsiveness. We often find the resurgence of these reactions and the clinging they bring are sometimes alarming to mothers. Some mothers feel that the toddler, who two weeks ago freely moved away from her and was an explorer of her universe, has suddenly become an infant again, regressing, needing to cling, experiencing a heightened degree of separation and stranger anxieties. Many mothers construe this to be a loss of gains made earlier. In fact, this is an advance, signaling the infant's move from the first major subphase of separation-individuation into the second.

It is important for the parent to be aware of the fact that this second peak of separation anxiety and stranger anxiety is tied up with the potential stabilizing of a sense of self, of the tolerance of separateness from the caregiver. Both of these, we want to underscore, will be enhanced by the caregiver making herself available for holding, comforting, and reassuring as the child works through this process. In other words, it is important for parents to allow the child's clinging, to give comfort when the infant experiences anxiety. The challenge is significant: the toddler is now attempting to separate, individuate, and consolidate the experience of being a self separate from mother, while, in place of the symbiotic relatedness, the child develops an emotional attachment to her mother of a more mature order.

And in fact, the working through of this challenge progresses gradually during the third year of life. Gradually, the child defines the boundaries of his self and those of others. Here is an example of this phenomenon.

> Thirty month-old Candy, her twin Cindy, and her mother were coming to the project on the bus—their usual mode of travel to our project site. Sitting in one double seat, mother saw Candy rather studiously seem to feel her own knee, then that of her sister, and then that of her mother. Mother, cognizant of the meaningfulness of her children's behaviors, with interest asked, "What are you doing?" Candy said, touching each knee in turn: "I'm Candy, she's Cindy, and you're Joan (mother's name)." Mother said, "I'm not Joan, I'm your mother!" Candy smiled and insisted, "You're Joan."

When mother reported the incident in the project, knowing where the kids were in their development, it was easy to explain that Candy was affirming the separation and individuation of these three, formerly in Candy's experience, enmeshed into one threesome, into now separate persons, intimately tied by a powerful secure emotional bond. I inferred that in Candy's eye and mind, she was now the self-called Candy, who has a sister Cindy, and a mother named Joan.

What we have talked about so far pertains to the development of the relationship between child and parent during the first three or so years of life. The major thrust of that development occurs in twosome (dyadic) relatedness of infant and parent. This is so even with twins like Candy and Cindy. However, while things are more complicated with twins and other multiple birth siblings, dyadic relatedness prevails.

But parents know that during these first years of life, many infants at times experience anger, even hostility toward primary caregivers, when, wanting the parent's attention, mother or father pays attention to another person, most commonly a sibling. This kind of interaction is more complex than dyadic; it is now a threesome, a triadic interaction.

These early forms of triadic relatedness, as self-sibling-mother bring with them conflicts of rivalry. These too, like so much in the early years—and later—need to be dealt with emphatically, with reassurance, especially with a clear recognition that of all siblings have equal rights to a relationship with the parent, with assurance that any one sibling is not more important to the parent than the others. Ultimately, each child will experience this as reassuring and protective. Although each child would like to be the only child, the experience of being preferred over another child commonly brings with it the threat that someday, when I am bad, I will no longer be the preferred child and will be demoted to being the less-cared-for child of the family. Equality among siblings in the eyes of the parents is desirable and needs to be protected.

Psychoanalytic clinicians and child developmentalists have long established that at about two and a half years of age, a development of substantial consequence to the child emerges; it adds a new dimension to the relationship between child and parents. It is the emergence of infantile sexuality.

THE IMPACT OF INFANTILE SEXUALITY ON CHILD-PARENT RELATEDNESS

Many parents, worried about behaviors they see in their young children, claim that these behaviors surely can't mean what they think it might. But, parents who can accept their children's behaviors for what it looks like will see behaviors that pertain to their children's emerging sexuality. Although infants younger than two years of age seem aware of and touch their own genitals from time to time, from about two-and-a-half years, the increased frequency and persistence with which they do so is quite striking.[14] Parents will, in other words, note an increase in persistent self-touching, in what we consider "infantile masturbation." They will also notice a new or increased interest in, and tender attention to, babies, especially so in little girls. Many a little girl will then begin to ask questions about babies. Children will begin to ask all kinds of questions about genitals—their own and those of others, especially of siblings and parents. Parents will note that when children two-and-a-half-, three-, and four-year-olds play games, they often play "house."

Another more complex type of behavior can be also observed: quite often, a three-to-four-year-old girl's relationship with her mother becomes more conflicted and troublesome. In the project described in chapter 1, a mother of several children, who up to now had a very warm relationship with her nearly three-year-old daughter, found things were becoming quite difficult between them. One day, when her daughter was about three-and-a-half-years-old, the exasperated mother jokingly asked, "Anybody want her for a year?" Another little girl, just under four years of age, who also had a good relationship with her mother, dumped her mother's perfumes and powders in the toilet on several occasions. One time she did so after she had put some of each on herself.

The first little girl when she was almost four years old, told her mother that she wanted to go on a camping trip alone with her father this weekend and nobody else was allowed to come. The second little girl at nearly four years of age, according to father's actual words, "fluttered her eyelashes and asked me to take her dancing and to the movies." A similar, parallel phenomenon occurs in the little boy with relation to his mother and father. One three-year-old boy complained to his mother that he did not want his father to come home for dinner that night.

What causes these behaviors? One of Freud's insufficiently recognized hypotheses about the sexual drive is pertinent to what I am addressing in the text that follows. I have found elucidating and useful his hypothesis that the libido (what has become known as "the sexual drive") has two currents. These are (1) *an affectional current* and (2) a *sensual (or specifically sexual) current.* Amplifying on what Freud proposes, I hold[15] that the affectional current is the first to emerge in the early weeks of life. It is the fundamental aspect of the libido[16] that fuels attachment. This current of the libido is most gratified in good (secure) attachments. In troubled attachments it is insufficiently gratified. Speaking teleologically, this current of love is what binds people together; it is linked to empathy and altruism.

The second current of the libido is the sensual current, or specifically the sexual current. Its function is better understood and unequivocal: it serves the preservation of the species. The behaviors of two-and-a-half-, three-, and four-year-olds I just described are propelled by and are the earliest discernible evidence of a psychobiological maturation in the sexual current of the libido. This current of the drive makes its first behavioral appearance about the third year of life and leads to what we have specifically identified as infantile sexuality. The dramatic development these examples illustrate in a child's relationship to his or her parents have been variably conceptualized as the "Oedipus complex" for boys and the "Electra complex"[17] and other identifiers for girls.

It is important to note that the attachment they have attained prior to the emergence of their sexual complexes in both boys and girls remains the same. But this attachment now becomes more complex with the additional molding that comes with the child's specific sexual development.

These sexual development complexes unfold like this. At about two-and-a-half years of age, a parent first notes her child's increased interest in his or her own genitals. This includes their manipulation through the child's using his or her hand or some indirect means. With it, a parent also begins to hear questions about genitals: "Does so and so have a penis?" or "Where is so and so's penis?" One little girl insistently demanded that her mother show her, mother's penis. These third year of life genital feelings seem to not be attached to anyone in particular—a child might like to be bounced on mother's or father's foot—or they sometimes use hard objects, such as toys. These first feelings do not seem to be directed preferentially toward one parent or the other.

Then, at about three years of age, the child's sexual feelings tend to become more selective. In little boys, they tend to be preferentially directed toward their mothers. In little girls, dominantly, but not exclusively, they tend to be directed toward their fathers. I repeat that although the prior attachments to mother and father remain much the same, some degree of modification now begins to occur. As we mentioned before, one little girl who had a very warm relationship with her mother prior to three years of age now began to experience a good deal of difficulty with her.

One might ask, why does the child turn his or her sexual feelings toward his or her own mother or father? Why not to just any other male or female? Would it not be even better if these feelings, from the outset, were attached to someone other than one's parents, to protect against incest?

Yet, the child seems quite determinedly selective: for the boy, it tends to be his mother, and for the girl, her father. But given that the libido has two currents, an affectional and a sensual, and the affectional feelings are attached to the parents, wouldn't the sensual feelings the child is newly experiencing tend to follow the path forged by the affectionate current? By this age, affectional feelings are already more or less stabilized in the child's relationships to her parents. This, along with the seemingly dominant inherent tendency of sexual feelings to be heterosexual, is why the little girl selectively turns to her father with her sexual feelings, rather than to the postman, and the little boy turns to his mother rather than his pretty neighbor. However, because the sexual drive is so powerful, even at this age, there is some spillover onto other persons.

It is when the sensual feelings become specifically directed toward the parent of the other sex that we find a little girl fluttering her eyelashes at her father and asking him to take her dancing and to the movies. Or she might say that she would like to go on a camping trip alone with her father. The little boy would like father not to come home for dinner so that he would not have to share his mother with his father.

Of course, wishes such as these must and usually are reasonably frustrated. In fact, it is helpful that they be frustrated. But it does not take much for the child to recognize that the gratification she yearns for and does not get from her father, someone else does get; although father does not take his lovely daughter dancing and to the movies, he does take her mother. And the little boy, of course, sees the same as well.

As a result, given the intensity of the sexual feelings young children experience—and they do—intense feelings of jealousy erupt. The first little girl pretended that she was shooting her mother dead. The little boy wished that his father would not come home for dinner and pouted because father did. This creates a significant conflict within the child: the little girl wants to shoot the mother she loves; the little boy wishes that the father he loves would not come home. We all know how feelings of jealousy bring enormous pain. This then generates hostility and hate toward the loved parent of the same sex. It creates a substantially difficult and threatening conflict within the child, a conflict due to the child's feelings of ambivalence. Since the rival is one of the prime persons the child loves, and since the feelings of hostility and hate tend to be quite intense, the child feels a great deal of anxiety. Also, these circumstances arouse the threat of punishment of largest consequence. All in all, this creates an internal state—as well as an external situation—that demands the child's attention and large coping efforts.

The child cannot easily tolerate hating the parent whose love he or she wants to hold on to. In reaction to this conflict, he or she begins to feel acute guilt. This guilt, generated by the little boy's hating and wanting to destroy his beloved father further organizes in the child his developing conscience; in fact, this inner conflict is a powerful motivator of conscience formation. And similarly this occurs in the little girl for hating and wanting to destroy her beloved mother. This seems to happen to a child even when the parent he or she rivals is not reliably in the home. Some early life notion of right and wrong seems to play a part in the child's reaction to his or her transgressive wishes.

Problematic as all this is, some very important positive developments are set in motion. Given that the resolution of these wishes and fantasies is not achieved overnight, efforts are made by preschool and school-age children for an unpredictable period of time, during which these developments unfold. In fact, these wishes and fantasies often return as the young teenager undergoes dramatic physical and psychological maturational changes that lead to the upsurge of sexuality in adolescence.

Among the major developments that occur, although it does not occur right away, is that the little boy comes to terms with his conflicted wishes by trying to give up the wish to marry his mommy, and the little girl gives up her wish to marry her daddy. When whatever is repressed of these fantasies resurge in adolescence (see below), both boys and girls will have to do more work to bring closure to the then teenager's repressed Oedipal and Electra complex wishes and fantasies.

Another development that follows from this conflict is that the child takes on the task of taming and controlling the hostile feelings that have been generated within her or him toward the loved parent. Given the intensity of the feelings experienced, the child increases her or his capability to cope constructively with and master feelings of hostility generated within her or him, not only by this conflict, but also by other life events. More of this psychic work may need to be done in adolescence, where the residual repressed wishes and fantasies push for expression.

Still another development follows: the child intensifies her or his identifications with—and wants to be like—the parent of the same sex. And yet other highly salutary developments follow during the youthful growing years as well, such as, a heightening of efforts to sublimate, do something creative—educational, artistic, or in any skills development—rather than act on some of this troublesome feelings and wishes.

One more highly important phenomenon follows from this conflict: the transgressive wishes that cannot be fully given up as well as the feelings of rivalry and hate for the same sex parent that cannot be resolved by the young child by the time she is five or so years of age, these will become repressed. They are pushed into the child's unconscious part of the mind where, because they are not resolved, do not just vanish, they remain active. It will especially be in early adolescence that, under the influence of the large upsurge of sexual feelings and fantasies that come with the transformative maturation of the young teen's body, these repressed wishes and fantasies, often in some disguised form, may reemerge. This may apply to just the sexual feelings, or to both the sexual feelings and the feelings of rivalry. Obviously, these would bring about some further changes in the parent-child relationship.

As I noted before, the Oedipus complex seems to also occur in boys where, for whatever reason, there is no father at home. The same can be said for the girl—although it is highly uncommon for a mother to not be in the home. Just how a child reared in a one-parent family goes through this process is not firmly established. A number of factors probably play a part. Where there is no father at home due to a separation or divorce, the child will often feel responsible for that separation because of his Oedipal or Electral wishes. Or, quite often, the child discovers that mother does have a man in her life. The child also knows that his father was there at one time, however briefly, and also tends to experience his sexual wishes as transgressive. Also, a major contributor to the child's experiencing prohibitions against the gratification of his sexual wishes comes from the parent's reactions to their expression, verbal or behavioral. Responsible parents do, of course, prohibit sexual activity with them and tend to reject more or less gently their children's amorous declarations of intent.

We must also add the likelihood that three- and four-year-old children's increasing cognitive capabilities may contribute to their feeling conflicted about their wishes and desires. These capabilities lead them to take in what they see and hear, to think at an increasingly sophisticated level, and to fantasize richly, all of which may make them cognizant of problematic consequences to their wishes.

All in all, the unfolding of the Oedipus and Electra complexes modifies dramatically the child's relationships to his or her mother and father and creates in the normal child a large, internal emotional conflict. But as I said before, at the same time, it brings with it enormously salutary emotional and personality developments within the child including especially higher level organization of a conscience, further identification with the rivaled parent, heightens controls over transgressive wishes and hostile feelings, and more.

LATER TRENDS IN THE EVOLVING OF RELATIONSHIPS IN CHILDHOOD

Let us say a few words about trends in the evolving of relationships that occur during the child's elementary-school years and adolescence.

Current social trends bring with them large modifications in psychic life, such as sending children to school earlier and placing them in day-care centers even from the first months of life on. Such trends unavoidably influence the character and the quality of relationships, sometimes for the better and sometimes not. Clearly, there are individual variations as to what families do and as to how children and their parents cope with what they do.

Whatever they do, relationships change significantly during the elementary-school years. The prime tasks of emotional development during the first five to six years of life have centered within the nuclear family. First, during the first three years, is the establishment of the self in relatedness with the parents—as spelled out by separation-individuation theory. And second, from about two-and-a-half to six years of age, is the emergence and partial resolution of the Oedipus and Electra complex. Hand in hand with other factors, the resolution of these complexes pushes the child into relationships outside the nuclear family.

There are gradations of relatedness, where those children experience with their parents and siblings have led to the formation of primary relationships; and now adding to these—although these days many younger children already have done so—elementary-school-age children also form relationships with other adults and peers that may usefully be considered *secondary relationships*. This grading of relationships is dependent on the degree and quality of emotional attachment between a child and the other person. Bearing in mind this difference in both the character and the quality of relatedness, consider the following. The extent to which peers and other adults become important to a child less than five years of age depends on the quality of relationships with primary persons, and the degree to which the child's needs are met, as well as the quality of relationships outside the home with persons with whom the child forms secondary relationships. Children, of course, vary in their experiences in both sectors of relatedness, inside the home and outside the home. We are using a model that is simpler than actual life when we assert that primary relationships and the prime tasks of development during the first five years of life reside in and most optimally are dealt with within the nuclear family. But we do so because we believe it to be basically true. Within the framework of this model, secondary relationships can be strongly enriching, and may in fact play a vital salutary part, especially where primary relationships are not secure.

No doubt the above-mentioned social trends impact on the character and quality of children's relationships. Nonetheless, the experience and partial resolution of the Oedipus and Electra complexes pushes the five-to-six-year-old child into relationships outside the nuclear family. During the elementary-school years, persons outside the home, both adults (particularly teachers) and especially peers, become progressively more important to the child. During this period, siblings with whom children have primary relationships are the great bridging relationships between the family and the outside world. A child who has a sibling one or two years older commonly finds it easier to enter the world of school and the neighborhood. This occurs, both, when the older sibling is an active facilitator for the younger one, and when the younger one sees his or her brother or sister manage and even do well, which usually gives the younger one the feeling, "I can do it too." In fact, some younger ones are eager to follow their older sibling's footsteps.

Peer relationships and relationships with teachers bring both gratifications and frustrations. Playing with one's friends is not always fun. Parents at times make the mistake of thinking that the child who was outside playing with her friends was having a great time. When the child comes home, it is now time to set the table or do homework. The idea is: "You were out having fun; it is now time to get down to work." The problem is that being out playing with friends may be painfully frustrating, disappointing, indeed, at times humiliating and infuriating. Not uncommonly, one's friends want to do what they want to do, not what the child wants to do. They may, in fact, abuse him or her in the course of their own efforts to master their difficulties and the injuries to which they have been subjected at home, in school, or elsewhere.

During the elementary-school years, however, the shift to persons outside the home is limited. Peers cannot yet serve the protective and caring functions parents serve; therefore, they cannot be leaned on securely and reliably. Indeed, parents continue to be vitally central in the elementary-school-age child's life and are turned to for continuing support in development and mastery of life's increasingly larger demands.

The next phase of development brings with it a dramatic shift in relationships. Those remarkable bodily changes that begin the transformation of the child into the adult-to-be centrally define adolescence. Adolescence brings with it the challenging and exciting upsurge of adolescent sexuality and of aggression. This growth of the physical and psychical self brings with it an increase in importance of peers, an importance that of itself is transformative. Both, the transformations of the physical and psychical self and the new importance of peers, lead to a further evolving of the self with a progressive structuring of the adolescent's identity. In addition, large strides in cognitive (mental) skills and the heightening demands made by school, lead to dramatic intellectual development. All these phenomena, the bodily changes (especially those that are hormonally driven), the increasing importance of peers, and the dramatic heightening of intellectual functioning, lead the adolescent to behaviors that evoke his or her parents' efforts to mediate them, which is often experienced by the teenager as annoying if not infuriating. All these enormous changes and challenges contribute to the mood swings so typical of adolescents.

Highly challenging for both parents and their adolescents is the major shift in relationships that occurs during this developmental period: from the parents' being the central persons of attachment in the younger child's life, and while remaining strongly emotionally tied to them, the adolescent gradually places peers at the center of her or his life. This shift in relationships, which takes about a decade in its course, is a task that should be well underway by late adolescence and should be concluded during young adulthood. It is crucial for parents to know when to allow and when not to allow, and where needed, to guide and support the teenager's efforts to make this important shift in relationships.

All parents know that the child's traversing this passage into adulthood is achieved with a good deal of difficulty, which indeed at times, leads to highly conflicted relatedness between the adolescent and her or his parents.

This difficulty is particularly evidenced in the adolescent's behavioral and mood swings in the need to be very close to the parents at one time and then at another time, fending for and coping with the realistic need for separateness and individuality and wanting nothing to do with parents. This leads the adolescent to at times be proud of her or his parents and at another time be highly embarrassed by them. Sometimes, teenagers go so far as to need to diminish the stature of, and at times even depreciate the parents, as well as at times needing to reject some of the parents' beliefs and attitudes, and more. Thus the quality of relatedness between parents and adolescents during this decade may vary widely over time.

Of course, the overall relationships among adolescents and their parents vary, depending on the quality of their relationships as these have evolved from early childhood on. And in addition, the experiences the adolescent has outside the home are equally critical to the adolescent's safe passage through this challenging decade of life.

FURTHER THOUGHTS ON OPTIMIZING THE PARENT-CHILD RELATIONSHIP

From Birth On, Children Feel Pain and, Good or Bad, They Remember What They Experience

The assumption that infants do not feel and that they cannot remember has now firmly been proven wrong. Years of research and clinical work in neuroscience, psychology, and psychoanalysis inform us that infants are sensitive to their experiences, and are affected by them and remember them.

Susan Coates[18] recently reported on just this, pointing first to the history of the use of anesthesia going back to 150 years ago, when "Dr. Henry Bigelow of Boston [said in 1848 that] anesthetics were unnecessary for infants because they lacked the 'remembrance of suffering'" (1–2). Even for heart surgery, children younger than 18 months received no anesthesia. Finally, some 30 years ago, Coates adds, a number of medical experts got the medical establishment to recognize that newborns do experience pain (2). Adding more recent findings in neuroscience and psychology that document the fact that infants feel pain and remember it, Coates describes an extremely bright four-year-old whom she treated who had been traumatized at 10 months:

> She "had been stabbed in the stomach by a deranged psychiatric patient" and survived by heroic and prompt action. Well cared for, medically and at home, she seemed a quite well-adjusted toddler. "When she was about

> three years old, Betsy was in the kitchen leaning against a sink that was pressing on her scar and said, 'Dad my line hurts.' Her dad said, 'You mean your special boo boo?' using her word for her scar and Betsy said, 'No Daddy,' and then took her hand and made a violent slashing gesture and said 'It was a very bad day.' She clearly had a somatic memory of this trauma" (5–6).

Coates writes, "both pediatricians and psychiatrists (had over time told her acutely concerned parents) there was no way she could remember what happened to her and advised them to never talk about it" (11). Time passed. Wanting help, the parents got in touch with Coates. She writes, "Now, as she reached the age of four-and-a-half, they wanted my help to figure out how to talk with her about the stabbing in a manner that would not retraumatize her" (11). After a period of working with Betsy and her parents, the parents succeeded in talking with her about it and Betsy seemed relieved to know. Her wish to know the details of what happened and how she was helped are noteworthy. She wanted many repetitions of the story and played some aspects of it out in therapy with Coates. According to Coates, "Placing a trauma into a cohesive narrative is therapeutic in and of itself. . . . It is . . . important . . . [for] the child to be able to reprocess the traumatic experience in [her] family setting for as long as [she] needs to" (16).

Even many years later, in intensive psychotherapies, severe trauma in infancy can be reconstructed from pain-laden experiences these patients report in fantasies and in verbalizations while in treatment. These affect-laden fantasies and verbalizations experienced within the relationship to the analyst—what we call transference—compel us to infer that these fantasies and verbalizations represent a reliving of what they experienced in early childhood.[19] But the pain that is actually reexperienced in the treatment setting, unrepressed by the process of psychoanalytic association, is strikingly convincing that what is reexperienced in treatment, happened; fantasies of that order do not come from thin air. Infants feel and they do remember.

Given these research and clinical findings, parents need to understand that it is much safer to assume that how we impact on our children is going to influence them from the first days of life on, indeed even while still in the uterus.

But, I also want to underline that traumatic events will not unavoidably cause the child pain forever—if, in the course of growing up, opportunities and experiences occur that can lead to the mitigation of the trauma, and allow for the repair of the harm the given trauma has caused. Parents should never despair about trying to undo, repair, and make up for mistakes they feel they have made that may have led to traumatic experiencing in their child. This applies even for parents whose children are already grown up.[20]

So, patterns of interaction between infant and parent become established over time, but they do start at the beginning.

Trust Your Feelings—But Have the Courage to Wonder: Am I Right?

This sounds contradictory. Trust yourself, but keep an open mind about what you feel. I stand on that. Hand in hand with understanding one's child, it is critical that parents trust their own perceptions and feelings as a guide to effectively dealing with their child's feelings, including their aggression, nondestructive and hostile destructive. But it is wise to check back on oneself to see if one was right, and duly took the child's feelings and rights into consideration. Did I say "the child's rights?" Yes, because by giving the child rights you empower him and make him responsible for his actions.

It is well established in the mental health field that in order to develop optimally, all humans need to be involved in relationships that are characterized by a positive emotional investment in us, by open and reasonably direct, and honest communication about emotional experiences, and by a sufficient degree of responsiveness by those close to us, to our needs for emotional involvement as well as for autonomy and individuality. When parents are able to form such relationships with their children, development is most likely, almost guaranteed, to proceed as optimally as the child's inborn givens will allow.

We have to recognize the fact that even when the child's development proceeds optimally, development makes large demands on the child. For one thing, development and change bring not only the excitement and pleasure of being able to do new things, but also anxiety over what is new, strange, and uncertain. Among the many difficulties that normally occur, development brings sadness over inevitable losses brought about by growing up—"Mother nurses my baby brother, but not me anymore"—anger over hurts, anxiety, and sometimes even guilt over becoming more and more self-reliant and separate from those we love. In other words, strong and disturbing feelings such as anger, anxiety, sadness, and guilt result not only when there are external problems or interferences. And these feelings occur when development is proceeding well in good relationships. Fortunately however, when development is proceeding optimally, there are long stretches of time when the predominant feeling a child or an adolescent has is one of delight and well-being, accompanied by interest, curiosity, and energy for autonomous initiative, exploration, and work, as well as for investment in important relationships.

Development does not occur in a straight line. It has many ups and downs. Also, development usually proceeds in small steps. The developmental progress may go unnoticed except at milestones like the baby's first smiles, first steps, first words, kindergarten, first grade, or high-school graduation. Adding to the stresses that development brings, we find that the inner pressure to develop and to master is such that once a child or adolescent achieves mastery and competence in one area, she or he seldom pauses to savor her or his accomplishments. Kids—and adults for that matter—almost immediately begin working on another new developmental task or return to an old, recurrent, still insufficiently mastered one.

Growth is accompanied by regression, and even by temporary disorganization. This is so when basic aspects of a child's organization are changing and developing positively toward maturation, but have not yet stabilized at the new level of functioning. At these crossroads of development, we may see regression or disorganization against a background of small, but significant, signs of growth and a basically positive mood. For example, a child who is beginning to see herself more as a separate individual, and feels strong and delighted by it, may temporarily evidence brief periods of anxiety and cling to mother. The parent's being available to help the child deal with the anxiety and, at the same time acknowledge the child's developing sense of individuality, helps to stabilize the child's new capabilities. The child will sense not only the parent's emotional availability, but also the parent's recognition and approval of her or his growth and the parent's confidence and predictable support in times of uncertainty. More than likely, the child will begin to internalize her or his parent's helpfulness and at some point, by identification with the parent's helpfulness become able to be self-reliant. A good example of this is that when a parent is able to calm and comfort a child, the child will, by identification with his mother become able to calm and comfort himself when needed.

A Crisis Is an Opportunity

I learned somewhere that the Chinese symbol for *crisis* is the same as that for *opportunity*. In the ups and downs of normal development, growing up at times occurs in a pattern of three steps forward, one step back. Despite the burden it places on us as parents, when our kids feel anxious, depressed, or experience pain of any kind, maintaining a positive attitude in our efforts to help them is growth-promoting. Complaining about the child's yet again experiencing such an episode, humiliating the child, shaming him into "Be a big boy!" undermines the child's self-esteem and his potential for growth. And if the child, feeling shame, tries to comply with the parent's admonition, he may play-act that he is a "big boy" with at times costly consequences—learning to deny what he feels, becoming intolerant of experiencing pain in himself and in others, and more. In addition, feeling hurt by the parent's insult, his hostility toward the parent, which he will struggle to suppress, will mount. And he'll learn, "Don't expect your mom or dad to help you."

As a clinician, I think that, burdensome as it may be in our very busy lives, when one's child experiences trouble of any kind, it is another opportunity for us parents to help the child continue to learn to cope with everyday's unavoidable pains, to solve problems and adapt as best as the child can to the demands of life. There are many instances when caring for a challenged child and responding to her needs provide an important developmental opportunity for mastery and growth—for both child and parents. Who would be more devoted to help the child well than the child's own parents?

It's OK To be Angry, Even Very Angry with One's Child or Adolescent

Being emotionally available and attentive, a parent may find herself having very powerful troubling feelings toward her or his child or adolescent, and yet the parent may not be able to reign in these feelings and respond helpfully. Parents are at times shocked at the feelings their children may elicit in them. This is especially so when parents experience intense feelings of anger, surely when they feel rage, and even momentary hate, and then guilt. No parent likes to feel angry, and surely not rage or hate toward her or his child. In unfortunate circumstances, some parents will lash out irrationally at their child; this is risky with young kids and adolescents. Or, intensely conflicted by having these feelings, a parent may feel overwhelmed, immobilized and give up.

In addition to potentially causing harm, the parent will not be effective in dealing with the child. This is true not only because the parent's feeling overwhelmed may be immobilizing, but also because the parent's emotional openness, crucial to understanding the child's experiencing will be incapacitated. The parent's emotional openness represents a basic point of contact with the child. It is the parent's most important source of information about the child's inner experience at a moment of strain or crisis, and the best guide to a helpful parenting intervention.

Whether or not the parent has exploded, a time-out is required for both parent and child or adolescent. And then the event has to be revisited—without too much delay. How long either child or adolescent or parent stays so angry that he or she is inaccessible to communication except by yelling and continuing in the rage mode—will determine when one can get back to what happened and talk about it. It is best for parents to encourage the child or adolescent to be accessible for going over the painful interaction between them.

If such events are infrequent, the parent's starting with a sincere "I'm really sorry this happened" can have remarkable reconciliatory power. If they occur frequently, apologies will hardly undo the hurt experienced and the rage generated in the child or adolescent. Note that saying "I'm really sorry this happened between us" or something of this kind, does not say it's the child or adolescent's fault or the parents, but that "it happened between us."

Given that the parent is the adult and more mature, the parent should take the initiative to repair, not the child. If the child does, the parent needs to wonder if it's out of fear of loss of the parent's love, or if it's out of generosity and goodness on the part of the child—which should be enormously appreciated. Regrettably, some parents think that it's weak, or not right, for the parent to initiate the reconciliation and repair. It is not. In fact, it takes maturity and strength of character to initiate reconciliation by a sincere apology. In addition, it provides the child or adolescent with a model for how to deal with conflicts in love relationships.

What started the painful interaction needs to be brought out. The child or adolescent needs to feel that he is allowed to say what he believes happened, and parents need to be in a state of wanting to know and understand what led to this kind of event. Passing judgment and criticism do not win in these talks; taking responsibility for one's actions that are detrimental to oneself or another, do much better. Clearly, one wants to prevent such blow-outs from repeating themselves too frequently.

It is also well to bear in mind that an important lesson may be learned during these unpleasant events. Again, this is usually occurs outside of awareness. The child will learn: can my father and my mother feel angry, even very angry, without being overwhelmed, without having a tantrum, without becoming destructive, without having to ignore how they are feeling? What might the kid learn if mother or father just goes haywire? But what if the parent is able to deal with such difficult feelings by controlling them and not causing damage? In this case, the child gains useful experience in managing anger and is likely to internalize this event, to identify with her or his parent, and learn to manage her or his own anger and hostility better.

Does the Parent Always Have to Have It Right, Always Be There?

There are going to be times when parents will not be able to be physically or emotionally available to their children. When one cannot at a given time be emotionally available to one's child, one ought to make oneself emotionally available as soon as one can. If a parent is busy at work and can't be disturbed by a telephone call from an anxious child, it can be made clear that the parent will call as soon as possible.

For example, a father who was grieving the loss of his own father was too turned inward to respond to his four-year-old son, Tommy, who just fell and hurt his knee. Tommy, seeing his father withdrawn, sulks, but says nothing. One-half hour later, as if coming out of a cloud, father awakens to what had happened. He takes occasion then, when he and Tommy are together, to tell him, "You know, I saw that you fell. I'm sorry. I was thinking about grandpa and feeling very sad. Are you okay?" Tommy points to his knee without saying a word. Father says: "Let me see it." Tommy seems to resist for an instant, but he comes to his father, pats him on the shoulder, and says, "It's okay, Daddy." Indeed, he comforted his father.

In instances such as these, acknowledging a lapse of emotional availability can be reparative in and of itself.

Similarly, one does not have to always be responsive to a child at the moment of need. Of course, "as soon as possible" has its limits: if possible it should not go longer than a few hours. But there are conditions when a young child will be able to wait for longer than that. For instance, if mother is sick and unavailable for several days, the young child will be able to integrate the fact that the mother is sick and cannot be responsive to the child's needs until she feels better. But if the young child can see that there is nothing particularly wrong with the parent and the parent is not there, the child is likely to feel hurt and feel that the parent is not sufficiently accessible.

"My Mother Tells Me I'm Holding My Baby Too Much"

Mothers have told me that they have been told, sometimes by their own mothers, that if they "hold their infants too much," the infant will become too dependent. Generally, that is not so. Although it is true that parents may hold their infants too much, this usually occurs when a parent is not reading the infant's expressed wishes and needs well. For instance, a mother who insists that her infant stay on her lap when the infant is giving clear evidence of wanting to slide off her lap, this mother is imposing her wish for closeness without being aware of the infant's wish for separateness.

A child's expressed wishes are discernable from neonatal life on. Gestural language is most often very clear well before the child can speak. For instance, we all know that the need for closeness is usually expressed in young children by the outstretching of arms toward the parent, by clinging to the mother's leg, by pulling toward or onto the mother. On the other hand, the child's wish to move away from the mother is usually expressed by turning away from the mother, squirming to get off the mother's lap, or pulling away from the mother. It is in fact important to respond to both, the child's need to be close as well as the need to be separate.

Therefore, it is inaccurate to say that the mother's holding her young child in response to her child's expressed need to be held will lead the infant to become too dependent. In fact, when young children are held when they ask for it, they are less likely to continue to feel the need to be held. Therefore they are less likely to become overly dependent and clinging than the child whose need to be held is too often frustrated. Such frustrated needs for emotional and physical closeness continue to clamor for gratification and foster a greater degree of neediness. Furthermore, every mother knows that toddlers do not tend to stay on their mother's laps too long when they feel secure.

The Golden Rule in Parenting

Another cardinal guideline every parent has at her or his disposal is to abide by the golden rule: "Do unto others as you would have others do unto you." One has to be honest with this exercise: is the way you're thinking "This is what I would want," really what you would want were you in fact a child or adolescent, or are you rationalizing as a mother or father that this is what you really wish the child would want? Sure you're right that there are times when what you know is best for the child is not what the child will want. Then, tell the child, what you want the child or adolescent to do. You will not always be wrong.

It's important to bear in mind what journalist Elizabeth Cooney wrote concerning Neurologist Frances Jensen teachings about the adolescent brain—that its development is complex, and it is not yet fully achieved in adolescence. While teens do deserve our admiration for their vast cognitive growth, their frontal lobes, that part of the brain that, as best as we know to date, governs " . . . insight, judgment, inhibition, self-awareness, cause and effect, acknowledgment of cause and effect"[21] is not yet sufficiently developed. Despite their protests, adolescents at times absolutely need to be told to abide by our guidelines, mores and wishes and then, no bargaining. And as I said in chapter 8, parents ought not to despair if their adolescents challenge them. Eighty percent compliance is an A+ in parenting, I said; 60 percent is probably average. And where the relationship is troubled from early childhood on, parents' wishes will not go far.

In rearing children, being guided by the golden rule can have remarkable benefits for both child and parent.

PARENT-CHILD RELATEDNESS AND THE CHILD'S AGGRESSION PROFILE

In considering how to help our children cope with their aggression in constructive ways, I have emphasized the importance of forming a positive, secure, emotional attachment between child and parents (see chapters 2 and 3). As my chapter 1 study documents, parenting in growth-promoting ways enhances the development of healthy nondestructive aggressiveness (such as assertiveness) and prevents or reduces the development of excessive hostility in children.

As I close this book, I look back to 1970 when my colleagues and I started the project I report on in chapter 1, a project for which, as the principal investigator and director, I take all responsiblity. Having developed what we (the project designers) felt were quite good protocols to measure our observations, my colleagues and I set out to study whatever we might discern to be or to not be correlations between qualitative aspects of the mother-child relationship (we did not have regular access to the fathers) and the development of specified adaptive functions, what we consider technically to be "ego functions," in their children. But forces operative in me of which I was not then conscious,[22] derailed my plans and compelled my attention to the development of aggression in childhood.[23]

In our 19-year follow-up study the data revealed a positive correlation between, on one hand, the positive, secure quality of the relationships between the project mothers and their children, and on the other, the children's aggression profiles. I ascribed the positive, secure attachment of the children with their mothers to the mothers' remarkably improved parenting skills into what I have come to call "growth-promoting parenting" (see tables in chapter 1).

I now recognize that my original hypothesis was tested—but not vis a vis specific ego-adaptive functions.

Rather, I say again, the correlation was between the quality of parenting the children got that secured good relationships between them[24] and their mothers and the children's aggression profiles.

NOTES

1. In *Dependence in Man—A Psychoanalytic Study* (H. Parens & L. J. Saul published by International Universities Press, NY, [1971]), I said that the counterpart of "dependence" in humans is not "independence" but rather, "self-reliance." My reasoning in the context of human dependence is that humans are not truly independent beings; while we may do some things on our own, I say "self-reliantly," we are never in need of no one.

2. I speak of "what I know . . ." because attachment is a domain of human experience that has been studied by different disciplines that concern themselves with mental health development. My orientation to understanding attachment is based primarily on what we know in *Ego Psychology* (a theoretical orientation in psychoanalysis), which derives especially from the work of Sigmund Freud, Rene Spitz, Erik H. Erikson, Margaret S. Mahler, Louis Sander, Daniel Stern, and others, as well as on my own research and clinical work. I have some grasp of but am not as well informed

as are others on the attachment theory of John Bowlby, Mary Ainsworth, and many others. Bowlby, himself a psychoanalyst, developed his own "school" in the late 1950s—which has come to be known as *"Attachment Theory"*, in reaction to interpersonal conflicts that arose between him and (oppressive) psychoanalytic authorities of the day. As I see it, the work done by "ego psychologists" and "attachment theorists" is highly compatible despite disagreements on certain noncritical points of theory that do not invalidate the models developed in each school of thought. The crossover of students from each discipline into the other has increased progressively since the storms of the 1960s have passed with the passing of their instigators.

3. While Spitz's research findings on attachment date back to the early 1940s (published from 1945 on) he recapitulates his later aggregated theory of the infant's progressive emotional attachment in his *The First Year of Life* published in 1965 by International Universities Press, NY, NY.

4. K. Lorenz, Comparative behaviorology. In *Discussions on Child Development*, Eds. J. M. Tanner and B. Inhelder, (New York: International Universities Press, 1953) Vol. 1:108–117.

5. In "Toward understanding prejudice—benign and malignant" (chapter 2, in: *The Future of Prejudice—Psychoanalysis and the Prevention of Prejudice,* Eds. H. Parens, A. Mahfouz, S. W. Twemlow, & D. E. Scharff, (Rowman & Littlefield Publishers, Inc., [2007]), 26.

6. A close colleague of John Bowlby, Mary Ainsworth (M. D. S. Ainsworth, M. C. Blehar, E. Waters, & S. Wall, *Patterns of Attachment: A Psychological Study of the Strange Situation* (Lawrence Erlbaum: Hillsdale, NJ, [1978]). operationalized Bowlby's theory of attachment into discernible categories, which led to highly productive research that has contributed enormously to both treatment and prevention in mental health.

7. Beatrice Beebe presented her study "Maternal Depression at 6 Weeks Postpartum and Mother-Infant 4-month Self- and Interactive Regulation" to the Vulnerable Child Discussion Group, Chair, T. Cohen, at the Meetings of the American Psychoanalytic Association, January 22, 2004.

8. Freud, "On narcissism: An introduction" (1914) in the *Standard* edition of Freud's writing, volume 14:69–102..

9. I defined and discussed this question in H. Parens, . A Contribution of Separation-Individuation to the Development of Psychic Structure. In: *Separation-Individuation: Essays in Honor of Margaret S. Mahler,* Eds. J. B. McDevitt & C. F. Settlage, (New York: International Universities Press, 1971) 100–112

10. Separation-Individuation theory was detailed in M. S. Mahler, F. Pine, & A. Bergman, *The Psychological Birth of the Human Infant* (New York: Basic Books, 1975).

11. Mahler's use of this term is a bit regrettable because she did not intend it to describe what the mother experiences. In biology "symbiosis" describes two individual organisms that live in a tight relationship that benefits each reciprocally. It describes the relationship of both organisms. This is in contrast with "parasitic," which means one organism living upon another at the expense of the other; the parasite may even destroy the other. Mahler was not speaking of the experience of both the child and the mother, but only that of the child.

12. "Object" in psychology means "person" or "other."

13. H. Parens, *The Development of Aggression in Early Childhood* (New York: Jason Aronson, 1979), 227.

14. Much child analytic literature has reported on this. While it was not the focus of the principal study reported in this book (chapter 1), the behaviors I detail here were observed, gathered, and reported in H. Parens, L. Pollock, J. Stern, & S. Kramer, On the Girl's Entry into the Oedipus Complex. *J. Amer. Psychoanalytic Assn.,* (1976) 24(5): 79–107.

15. In H. Parens & L. J. Saul, *Dependence in Man—A Psychoanalytic Study.* (New York: International Universities Press, 1971). See pages 54–69 where I report on Freud's writings on this component hypothesis of the sexual drive.

16. In 1970, after I had finished my draft of what L. J. Saul and I would publish as *Dependence in Man* (see above note), I wrote to Harry Harlow whose renowned work on Macaque infant monkeys' attachment dynamics he had studied was pertinent to what Saul and I were writing about human infants. I wanted Harlow's confirmation that I had not misrepresented his findings and that what he hypothesized from them. He replied that I had duly represented his work, but playfully he wrote, "But please tell me Dr. Parens, what is libido?" Of course, I couldn't and then, I didn't dare answer his question. I would say this of it: libido, as I see it, is that force or inner pressure that arises from our soma (our physical body) that pushes us to need and value (i.e., love others). I proposed then that it compels attachment. Freud said that libido has two currents: one is *affectionate* and the other is *sexual* (in its narrow sense). This makes a great deal of sense to me. Clinically, it is a very useful distinction to make; it explains what is otherwise difficult to explain. Some parents are afraid to hug their children—because they have come to believe that touching your child lovingly is driven by some sexual perversion in them. Many men are afraid to hug their sons because their fear it may be perceived or that it is a manifestation of homosexuality. The unclarity people have about love and sex leads to no end of problems.

17. A number of analytic scholars and researchers have pressed for a model of development specific for the girl, asserting, rightly I think, that the model for the boy, the Oedipus complex is not competent to define the girl's development. Rachel Parens has offered such a model, the Electra complex; other models have also been put forward.

18. Susan Coates presented her article "Can babies remember trauma? Pre-symbolic forms of representation in infants who have been traumatized." at the Association of Psychoanalytic Medicine in New York on March 2, 2010. During the past 20 years, neuroscience has documented that affective experience is recorded in the amygdala and hippocampus from birth on (J. E. Ledoux, . *The Emotional Brain.* New York: Simon and Schuster, 1996). Also, Kagan & Herschkowitz [2005] *A Young Mind in a Growing Child* (2005), as well as Koehler, "On the development of the autobiographical self" (2005).

19. In the course of years of clinical psychoanalytic work, with a handful of severely traumatized patients' agonizing cooperation, I have reconstructed (i.e., retrieved from repressed pre-verbal memory) extremely painful very early life experiences that have had lifelong, emotionally very costly, consequences. Two factors seem to account for

the patients' difficulty in remembering what is inscribed in their midbrain: (1) that neural connections between the midbrain and the frontal cortex (the cognitive center of the brain) are not yet laid down at birth; they develop only from two years of age on through seven (see this book, chapter 7); and (2) that primary psychic defensive mechanisms mask the remembrance of the pain experienced—as I have learned from my patients, by what might be a primary form of dissociation ("It's not happening to me!"), and by "spore formation" (walling oneself off to not experience the environment of pain).

20. See D. Sifford's *Father and Son* (1982) published by Bridgebooks, Philadelphia, for an example of a father working with his grown son who succeeded in diminishing and moving toward resolving his son's traumatic experiencing of his parents' divorce, which had created a major disturbance in the son's relationship to his father.

21. Cooney wrote this article for the *Globe*, which via the Internet was distributed to its members by the Regional Council of Child and Adolescent Psychiatry of the Greater Philadelphia Region. Cooney can be reached at ecooney@globe.com..

22. In fact, I became aware of what had then driven my unexpected and unyielding interest in the development of aggression in the children as I was writing my Holocaust memoirs, *Renewal of Life—Healing from the Holocaust* (H. Parens, Rockville, MD: Schreiber Publishing, 2004), which took place 30 years later. The reader may be skeptical about the veracity of my remark, but the fact is that I discovered in writing my memoirs that much of my life's work has been driven by what happened to me and my family as I began my teen years during the Holocaust.

23. I first reported on this study in 1973 (H. Parens, *The Development of Aggression in Early Childhood,* Lanham, MD: Jason Aronson, 2008) and have done so extensively since.

Index

About the Author

HENRI PARENS, MD, FACPsa is professor of psychiatry at Thomas Jefferson University Medical College and a training and supervising analyst (adult and child) at the Psychoanalytic Center of Philadelphia. He is in private practice in psychiatry and psychoanalysis.

He is the author of over 200 scientific and lay publications and multimedia programs, including 17 books, 8 of which he authored:

Dependence in Man (H. Parens & L. Saul, 1971),

The Development of Aggression in Early Childhood (H. Parens, 1979[2008]),

Aggression in Our Children: Coping with It Constructively (H. Parens, E. Scattergood, S. Duff, & W. Singletary, 1987; also in German [1994] and Russian [1997] editions),

A four-volume set of *Parenting for Emotional Growth:* (1) *The Textbook,* (2) *A Curriculum for Students in Grades K Thru 12,* (3) *The Workshops Series* (H. Parens, E. Scattergood, A. Duff, & W. Singletary (1995), and (4) *Helping Children Cope with Trauma Workshops* (H. Parens & C. Rose-Itkoff, 1997); and

Renewal of Life—Healing from the Holocaust (2004; also in German [2007] and French [2010] editions).

Nine co-edited books, including

Prevention in Mental Health (with S. Kramer, 1993),

The Future of Prejudice: Psychoanalysis and the Prevention of Prejudice (Eds., H. Parens, A. Mahfouz, S. Twemlow, & D. Scharff, [2007]).

The Unbroken Soul: Tragedy, Trauma, and Human Resilience. (Eds., H. Parens, H. Blum, S. Akhtar, [2008]).

Six scientific films (1974–1981);
One documentary, *The Urgent Need for Universal Parenting Education* (2008)*;* and
One CD, *Parenting for Emotional Growth* (containing the four books that constitute this work [2010]).
Thirty-nine one-half-hour television programs, a series for CBS entitled, *Parenting: Love and Much More* (1979).

Recipient of more than 20 honors and awards, including *Miriam Brown World of the Child Award* (1993); *Life Time Achievement Award,* Philadelphia Psychiatric Association (1999); Pennsylvania Psychiatric Society's *Presidential Award* (2004); *Dean's Citation for Significant Contributions to the Advancement of Education at Jefferson Medical College* (2004); and the *Arnold Lucius Gesell Preis*—Maximilians Universitaet, Munich, Germany (2008).

Dr. Parens is a Holocaust survivor.